T0312099

# Microeconomics of Market Failures

# Microeconomics of Market Failures

Bernard Salanié

The MIT Press
Cambridge, Massachusetts
London, England

This book was set in Palatino by Best-set Typesetter Ltd., Hong Kong.

Library of Congress Cataloging-in-Publication Data

Salanié, Bernard.
    [Microéconomie. English]
    Microeconomics of market failures / Bernard Salanié.
        p.   cm.
    Includes bibliographical references and index.

    ISBN 978-0-262-19443-3 (hc. : alk. paper)—978-0-262-52856-6 (pb.)
    1. Equilibrium (Economics).   2. Efficient market theory.   3. Welfare economics.
4. Industrial organization (Economic theory).   I. Title.

HB145 .S255   2000
338.5—dc21                                                                    00-038670

The MIT Press is pleased to keep this title available in print by manufacturing single copies, on demand, via digital printing technology.

# Contents

# Preface

As the title indicates, this book is organized around the unifying theme of market failures in microeconomic theory. As such, I hope that it may be useful to both advanced undergraduate and graduate students. The book originates in a course I taught at the Ecole Nationale de la Statistique et de l'Administration Economique in Paris and which was published by Economica in 1998 as *Microéconomie: Les défaillances du marché*. This course owed much to my predecessors, and in particular (in chronological order) to Jean-Jacques Laffont, Jean Tirole, Roger Guesnerie, Pierre-André Chiappori, Jean-Charles Rochet, and Patrick Rey. I thank Isabelle Braun-Lemaire, Elyes Jouini, Pierre-François Koehl, Jean Lainé, Guy Laroque, Laurent Linnemer, Tom Palfrey, Anne Perrot, Jérôme Philippe, and Patrick Rey for their comments on several versions of the original French manuscript. I stand, of course, responsible for all errors and imperfections.

# The Microeconomics of
# Market Failures

# 1        Introduction

This book has four parts. It treats, respectively, collective choice, welfare economics, industrial organization, and incomplete markets. As the title indicates, the unifying theme, which justifies the grouping of these four parts, is constituted by market failures. These are circumstances where market equilibrium is not optimal. The first fundamental welfare theorem tells us that such situations can only be produced if at least one of the standard hypotheses of the theory of general equilibrium is violated. Therefore throughout this book the objectives will be to examine diverse deviations from these hypotheses, learning of their consequences, especially where optimum conditions of equilibrium are concerned, and studying what economic policy measures can help remedy them.

## 1.1 The Fundamental Theorems

The object of this section is to briefly remind the reader of the two fundamental theorems of welfare economics. To this end, consider the primitives of an economy:

• $L$ goods indexed by $l = 1, \ldots, L$ and an initial dotation of the economy represented by a vector $\omega \in \mathrm{IR}^L$

• $I$ consumers indexed by $i = 1, \ldots, I$; consumer $i$ is endowed with a convex consumption set $X_i$ included in $\mathrm{IR}^L$ and a preorder of preferences[1] $\succeq_i$ defined on $X_i$ (or, under very general hypotheses, with a utility function $U_i$)

---

1. Throughout this book, transitive and complete binary relations will be called "pre-orders."

• $J$ producers indexed by $j = 1, \ldots, J$; producer $j$ is represented by a production set $Y_j \subset \text{IR}^L$ or, under very general hypotheses, a production function $F_j$ such that

$$y_j \in Y_j \Leftrightarrow F_j(y_j) \leq 0$$

### 1.1.1   The Pareto Optimum

By definition, a Pareto optimum of such an economy is an allocation. That is, the Pareto optimum is a set of consumption and production plans $((x_i)_{i=1,\ldots,I}, (y_j)_{j=1,\ldots,J}))$,

• that is feasible—such that every consumer chooses from within his or her own consumption set, every producer respects his or her production set, and the sum of the consumptions does not exceed the resources of the postproduction economy

$$\begin{cases} \forall i = 1,\ldots,I, \quad x_i \in X_i \\ \forall j = 1,\ldots,J, \quad y_j \in Y_i \\ \sum_{i=1}^{I} x_i \leq \omega + \sum_{j=1}^{J} y_j \end{cases}$$

• that is efficient—in the sense that there is no other feasible allocation

$$\left((x_i')_{i=1,\ldots,I}, (y_i')_{j=1,\ldots,J}\right)$$

such that for every consumer, $U_i(x_i') \geq U_i(x_i)$, and that at least one of these inequalities be strict.[2]

### 1.1.2   General Equilibrium

Now assume that the initial resources $\omega$ and firms' property rights are spread among the consumers, every consumer $i$ receiving a dotation $\omega_i$ and shares $(\theta_{ij})_{j=1,\ldots,J}$ of the $J$ firms, with

$$\begin{cases} \sum_{i=1}^{I} \omega_i = \omega \\ \forall j = 1,\ldots,J, \quad \sum_{i=1}^{I} \theta_{ij} = 1 \end{cases}$$

In such a private property economy, the hypothesis of pure and perfect competition is represented by the following behavior when met with a price $p$:

---

2. It should be noted that if the $U_i$ are strictly increasing, efficiency will again prohibit that for the consumer, $U_i(x_i') > U_i(x_i)$.

- The producer $j$ maximizes his profit and chooses

$$y_j(p) \in \arg\max_{y_j \in Y_j} p \cdot y_j$$

- The consumer maximizes his utility under budgetary constraints and chooses

$$x_i(p) \in \begin{cases} \arg\max U_i(x_i) \\ x_i \in X_i \\ p \cdot x_i \leq p \cdot \omega_i + \sum_{j=1}^{J} \theta_{ij} p \cdot y_i(p) \end{cases}$$

These rival supplies and demands so defined, a *competitive general equilibrium of private property* is composed of a price system $p^*$ and of an allocation $((x_i^*)_{i=1,...,I}, (y_j^*)_{j=1,...,J})$ such that

$$\begin{cases} \forall i, x_i^* = x_i(p^*) \\ \forall j, y_j^* = y_j(p^*) \\ \sum_{i=1}^{I} x_i^* \leq \sum_{i=1}^{I} \omega_i + \sum_{j=1}^{J} y_j^* \end{cases}$$

### 1.1.3 The Two Fundamental Welfare Theorems

Armed with these definitions, we can now recall the two fundamental welfare theorems:

THEOREM 1.1 (FIRST FUNDAMENTAL WELFARE THEOREM) If the utility functions $U_i$ are strictly increasing, any equilibrium is efficient: if

$$(p^*, (x_i^*)_{i=1,...,I}, (y_j^*)_{j=1,...,J})$$

is a competitive equilibrium, then the allocation $((x_i^*)_{i=1,...,I}, (y_j^*)_{j=1,...,J})$ is a Pareto optimum.

*Proof*  The proof is very simple and proceeds ad absurdum. If $(x^*, y^*)$ is not a Pareto optimum, then there is a feasible allocation $(x, y)$ such that

$$\forall i = 1,...,I, \quad U_i(x_i) > U_i(x_i^*)$$

But since $x_i^*$ was the preferred basket of consumption of $i$ in its budget set for the prices $p^*$, it can be deduced that $x_i$ cannot belong to this set, by which

$$\forall i = 1,...,I, \quad p^* \cdot \omega_i > p^* \cdot \omega_i + \sum_j \theta_{ij} p^* \cdot y_j^*$$

So adding all the consumers yields

$$p^* \cdot \sum_i x_i > p^* \cdot \left( \omega + \sum_j y_j^* \right)$$

But for every producer $j$, $y_j^*$ maximizes the profit at prices $p^*$, and we then have

$$p^* \cdot y_j^* \geq p^* \cdot y_j$$

It can be deduced from these two inequalities

$$p^* \cdot \sum_i x_i > p^* \cdot \left( \omega + \sum_j y_j \right)$$

which, since the prices are positive, contradicts the hypothesis that $(x, y)$ is feasible.                                                                    □

THEOREM 1.2   (SECOND FUNDAMENTAL WELFARE THEOREM)   If

• utility functions $U_i$ are continuous, increasing, and concave (i.e., preorders $\succeq_i$ are convex)

• consumption sets $X_i$ are closed and convex

• production sets $Y_j$ are closed and convex

then every interior optimum can be decentralized in equilibrium: if the allocation

$$\left( (x_i^*)_{i=1,\dots,I}, (y_j^*)_{j=1,\dots,J} \right)$$

is a Pareto optimum such that $x_i^*$ is interior to $X_i$ for every $i$, there is a distribution of the economy's initial resources

$$\left( (\omega_i)_{i=1,\dots,I}, (\theta_{ij})_{\substack{i=1,\dots,I \\ j=1,\dots,J}} \right)$$

and a price system $p^*$ such that the price-allocation pair

$$(p^*, (x_i^*)_{i=1,\dots,I}, (y_j^*)_{j=1,\dots,J})$$

is a competitive equilibrium for the economy of private property so defined.

*Proof*   Define the sets

$$C_i = \{ x_i' \mid U_i(x_i') > U_i(x_i') \}$$

along with $Z = \Sigma_{i=1}^I C_i$ and $W = \omega + \Sigma_{j=1}^J Y_j$. $Z$ is in fact the set of aggregate demands born of preferred individual consumptions via the Pareto optimum, and $W$ is the set of available postproduction resources. Under the hypotheses of the theorem, $Z$ and $W$ are convex. Moreover they cannot have any point of intersection; otherwise, $((x_i^*),$ $(y_j^*))$ would not be a Pareto optimum. By the convex separation theorem, there exists a vector $p$ such that $p \cdot z > p \cdot w$ for every $z \in Z$ and $w \in W$.

What this amounts to is that for every allocation $((x_i), (y_j))$ such that $U_i(x_i) > U_i(x_i^*)$ for every $i$ and $y_j \in Y_j$ for every $j$, we have

$$p \cdot \sum_i x_i > p \cdot \omega + p \cdot \sum_j y_j$$

or even, since $\Sigma_i x_i^* = \omega + \Sigma_j y_j^*$,

$$p \cdot \sum_i (x_i - x_i^*) > p \cdot \sum_j (y_j - y_j^*)$$

Take all the $x_i$ close to $x_i^*$. Then in the limit we get

$$p \cdot \sum_j (y_j - y_j^*) \le 0$$

that is, the production plans $y_j^*$ maximize the profit to prices $p$. Now let us equate all the $y_j$ to the $y_j^*$ and make all the $x_k$ close to $x_k^*$ for $k \ne i$. Then we get

$$U_i(x_i) > U_i(x_i^*) \Rightarrow p \cdot x_i \ge p \cdot x_i^*$$

Suppose that $U_i(x_i) > U_i(x_i^*)$ and that $p \cdot x_i = p \cdot x_i^*$. Choose $x_i'$ such that $p \cdot x_i' < p \cdot x_i$. Then for every strict convex combination $x_i''$ of $x_i'$ and $x_i$, we have $p \cdot x_i'' < p \cdot x_i^*$. But one combination can be selected such that $U_i(x_i'')$ $> U_i(x_i^*)$, and this is contradictory. We can conclude then that

$$U_i(x_i) > U_i(x_i^*) \Rightarrow p \cdot x_i > p \cdot x_i^*$$

which implies that $x_i^*$ maximizes consumer utility $i$ under the budgetary constraint $p \cdot x_i = p \cdot x_i^*$. $\qquad\square$

The convexity hypotheses are crucial here. They allow one to move easily from differential conditions of optimality to global optimality. To better understand this, consider the example of an exchange economy ($J = 0$) with two consumers and two goods ($I = L = 2$). One could use an Edgeworth box. Since preferences are convex, the two sets $\{U_1(x_1) \ge U_1(x_1^*)\}$ and $\{U_2(x_2) \ge U_2(x_2^*)\}$ are convex and have the point $(x_1^*, x_2^*)$ in common. One could separate them by passing a line through that point. The slope of this line gives us the ratio of prices $p^*$. If one chooses any distribution of initial resources $(\omega_1, \omega_2)$ on that line, then $(x_1^*, x_2^*)$ is indeed an equilibrium sustained by the price vector $p^*$, as shown in figure 1.1.

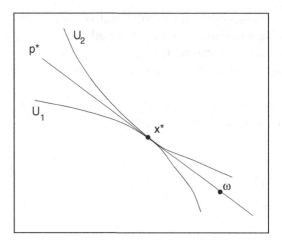

**Figure 1.1**
Second welfare theorem

## 1.2   Return to the Hypotheses

The "philosophical" importance of these two theorems cannot be exaggerated. First they suggest that the market is an efficient organization (first theorem). This was a perception of Adam Smith which he stated in his famous metaphor of the invisible hand. The entire passage from *The Wealth of Nations* (bk. IV, ch. 2) deserves repeating here (the italics are mine):

As every individual, therefore, endeavors as much as he can both to employ his capital in the support of domestic industry, and so to direct that industry that its produce may be of the greatest value, every individual labors to make the annual revenue of the society as great as he can. He generally indeed, neither intends to promote the public interest, nor knows how much he is promoting it. By preferring the support of domestic industry to that of foreign industry, he intends only his own security; and by directing that industry in such a manner as its produce may be of the greatest value, *he intends only his own gain, and he is in this, as in many other cases, led by an invisible hand to promote an end which was no part of his intention.* Nor is it always the worse for the society that it was no part of it. By pursuing his own interest he frequently promotes that of the society more effectively than when he really intends to promote it. I have never known much good done by those who affected to trade for the public good. It is an affectation, indeed, not very common among merchants, and very few words need be employed in dissuading them from it.

What is more surprising, the results also show that the market permits the attainment of any efficient allocation (second theorem). So even those among us who find revenue distribution to be uneven can turn to the market to realize an optimum once the desired redistribution has been carried out. In principle, this is the position adopted by the proponents of "market socialism," and among them Léon Walras himself can be counted.

Clearly, the hypotheses behind these two theorems merit examination. First, let us note that they assume the existence of a complete set of markets. This hypothesis is particularly strong when we take into account intertemporality and uncertainty: it then seems unlikely that we can have a complete set of futures and contingent markets, and in particular, in the presence of asymmetries of information or transaction costs. However, the consequences of market incompleteness are presented in the fourth part of the course. For now, we simply note that the first theorem no longer applies (generically) in such an economy.

Second, three failures concern what is called *welfare economics*:[3]

• In certain cases the use of goods by one consumer does not preclude their being consumed by others. One speaks then of a public good (see chapter 5) and aforementioned expressions, such as the sum $\Sigma_i x_i$, no longer have meaning.

• Up to this point we have implicitly assumed that the utility of the consumer $i$ depends only on his or her own consumption $x_i$, and that the profit of the producer $j$ depended only on a production plan $y_j$. Such is no longer the case in the face of external effects like pollution. This will be the object of chapter 6.

• The hypothesis of the convexity of production sets $Y_j$ which subtends the second theorem is particularly strong because it prohibits all form of increasing yields in production. The convexity of preferences can equally pose problems in certain cases. We will see the consequences of nonconvexities in chapter 7.

Finally, third, we focus on the hypothesis of pure and perfect competition which permits the definition of rival supplies and demands: here lies the domain of industrial organization.

The phenomenon of macroeconomic fluctuations, accompanied by unemployment and inflation, can be considered a market failure, but macroeconomic aspects of markets will not be discussed in this book. We will limit ourselves to the microeconomics. Nor will informational

---

3. The term *public economics* is reserved for the economics of the public sector (fiscal policy, public firms' pricing, etc.).

aspects be covered (on this I take the liberty of referring the reader to Salanié 1997). Nevertheless, in some form these issues will appear at various junctures in the book. Finally, the book will not treat models where there is an infinite number of goods or agents, for example, models with overlapping generations.[4]

## 1.3   The Government's Role

We will see again and again in this book that market failures can, in theory, be moderated by adequate governmental intervention. Some students may be quick to deduce from this that in situations of market failure the government *should* intervene. This conclusion is a bit hasty, as the classical economists had already found out:

It does not follow that whenever *laissez faire* falls short, government intervention is expedient; since the inevitable drawbacks of the latter may, in any particular case, be worse than the short-comings of private enterprise.[5]

The government has an undeniable advantage on the market: it has at its disposal the monopoly of legitimate constraint and, in particular, the power of taxation. It does not follow that the government possesses unlimited power. The government is especially obligated to take into account private agents' responses to its decisions. Often cited in this regard are the taxes on doors and windows that existed in various European countries a few centuries ago. The unexpected effect was considerably darkened houses. Economic history (even more recent) is full of examples where the government has very badly foreseen the reactions of private agents. The limited information in its possession is largely responsible. One consequence of this is the government's inability to enact the lump sum transfers necessary to decentralize the optimum in the sense of the second theorem.[6] Therefore the government will have recourse only to direct or indirect taxes which modify the prices perceived by agents and which then create distortions in the

---

4. In overlapping generations models the value of the total resources can be infinite, so it is easy to see that the proof of the first fundamental welfare theorem is no longer valid. I refer the reader to the fairly technical survey by Geanakoplos-Polemarchakis (1991).

5. Henry Sidgwick, *Principles of Political Economy* (1887).

6. The characteristic of a lump-sum transfer is that the agent concerned cannot change its value by altering his behavior. In the course of history there have been several attempts to make use of such transfers. The old poll tax which affected men on the basis of their social level, corresponded to this description in that that social class was determined initially by birth. More recently one can cite the aborted introduction of the *poll tax* in the United Kingdom.

economy. These distortions are at times desirable in order to correct others (as in the case of externalities); at other times, for instance, to finance a public good, they are a necessary evil.

As is generally the case in microeconomics, this book will content itself with describing the government as a "benevolent planner" that takes into account the preferences of agents for determining the social optimum and then attempts to make use of it. The reader must realize the narrowness of this point of view. It neglects all the complexity of the political process, in which the agents act through their representatives and with the aid of various lobby groups, and where the administrations themselves have a certain interpretive latitude in acting on completed decisions. Ideally an analysis of measures that the government can take to correct the effect of a market failure should take these factors into account.[7]

## Bibliographical Note

I will cite useful works and articles within the chapters themselves. A general reference for welfare economics is Laffont (1988). The reader may also profit from consulting Stiglitz (1988), which is less advanced but contains numerous interesting discussions, and Henry (1989). In regard to the industrial organization course, the reference work is Tirole (1988), for the more ambitious student. I am greatly indebted to the works of Laffont and Tirole, as the reader will perceive as the chapters progress.

This book contains but elementary mathematics and requires only the basics usually taught in introductory microeconomics courses (e.g., Varian 1992, Kreps 1990, or the first part of Mas Colell–Whinston–Green 1995).

The Ecole Nationale de la Statistique et de l'Administration Economique course which engendered this book calls for only eight class sessions of two hours each. These are several parts of the book that I do not teach in my own course for lack of time, in particular, chapters 3, 8, and 13. Nevertheless, I think that a good student should read the entire text.

Beginning on the principle that we can learn much from the errors of those who have gone before, I have strived to give some historical information on the theory's development. Thus I hope to make

---

7. Readers interested in these aspects should consult Wilson (1989) and Dixit (1996).

it better understood to the reader that economics is not a finished science for which this text will reveal the Commandments, but that it is in constant evolution, which makes studying it all the more interesting.

Since this book is a manual, I did not seek to give an exhaustive bibliography. Certain chapters have very short bibliographies because the principles discussed have long been known or because one of the references gives a longer bibliography of its own; this is particularly the case in part III. Conversely, at times I give many more references, for example, in part I where some of the results presented are fairly recent.

## Bibliography

Dixit, A. 1996. *The Making of Economic Policy*. Cambridge: MIT Press.

Geanakoplos, J., and H. Polemarchakis. 1991. Overlapping generations. In W. Hildenbrand and H. Sonnenschein, eds., *Handbook of Mathematical Economics*, vol. 4. Amsterdam: North-Holland.

Henry, C. 1989. *Microeconomics for Public Policy: Helping the Invisible Hand*. Oxford: Clarendon Press.

Kreps, D. 1990. *A Course in Microeconomic Theory*. Oxford: Harvester Wheatsheaf.

Laffont, J.-J. 1988. *Fundamentals of Public Economics* Cambridge: MIT Press.

Mas Colell, A., M. Whinston, and J. Green. 1995. *Microeconomic Theory*. Oxford: Oxford University Press.

Salanié, B. 1997. *The Economics of Contracts: A Primer*. Cambridge: MIT Press.

Stiglitz, J. 1988. *Economics of the Public Sector*. New York: Norton.

Tirole, J. 1988. *The Theory of Industrial Organization*. Cambridge: MIT Press.

Varian, H. 1995. *Microeconomic Analysis*. New York: Norton.

Wilson, J. 1989. *Bureaucracy*. New York: Basic Books.

# I                          Collective Choice

The existence of market failures clears the way for government interventions that are destined to correct it. But according to what objectives
does the government act? Each consumer-voter has preferences, and it
is rare that a government decision has societal unanimity. I present the
problem of the aggregation of preferences in its most general form in
chapter 2. Chapter 3 is dedicated to cost-benefit analysis, a more
applied domain where the object is to evaluate the social significance
of a given government decision. Finally, in chapter 4 I analyze the consequences stemming from the fact that the information the government
has at its disposal is limited.

# 2        The Aggregation of
          Preferences

This chapter attempts to answer the question: Given a limited set of possibilities, how does society make the "right" decision? Every economist brought up in the neoclassical tradition will think first of a Pareto optimum. Indeed the criterion of Paretian efficiency has the great advantage of being practically irrefutable. Every Pareto-dominated allocation entails a waste of resources, and society should distance itself from them as a whole. The Pareto principle consists precisely in preferring allocation $A$ to allocation $B$ if $A$ dominates $B$ in the Pareto sense. Unfortunately, this criterion constitutes but a very partial order: when there are $n$ consumers in the economy, the set of Pareto optima is (generically) a manifold of dimension $n - 1$. A position considered orthodox in economics (and developed in particular by Robbins 1932) has long been to remain at the Pareto optimum, since any other choice criteria risks the intervention of comparisons between persons of fragile status. As Robbins (1938) wrote,

Every mind is inscrutable to every other mind and no common denominator of feelings is possible.

Such a rigid methodological choice made economists' prescriptions unconvincing. In the words of Harrod (1938),

If the incomparability of utility to different individuals is strictly pressed, not only are the prescriptions of the welfare school ruled out, but all prescriptions whatever. The economist as an adviser is completely stultified, and unless his speculations be regarded as of paramount aesthetic nature, he had better be suppressed completely.

At the end of the 1930s, the Pareto principle was therefore often completed by the "compensation principle." This was also called the Hicks-Kaldor criterion, and it led to what was called the *new welfare economics*.

The compensation principle states that $A$ must be preferred to $B$ if in leaving $A$ and in effecting lump-sum transfers, one can attain an allocation $C$ that dominates $B$ in the Pareto sense. The compensation principle still defines only a very partial order,[1] and it is far more debatable than the Pareto principle. In effect, we saw in chapter 1, lump-sum transfers are not easily put into practice. Consider, for example, the opening of borders in a small economy. It is possible that it be harmful to a certain group of producers, but in general, liberalization of exchanges is more profitable for consumers than it is detrimental to producers, so it is recommended by the compensation principle. This is but meager consolation for the producers if the corresponding transfers are never enacted, and so on.[2]

On the other hand, neither the compensation principle nor Pareto optimality comprises the notion of equity. For example, an allocation where one consumer assumes all of the economy's resources are always a Pareto optimum. One solution suggested by Foley (1967) for an exchange economy entails allocations $(x_1, \ldots, x_n)$ that verify

$$\forall i, j, \quad U_i(x_i) \geq U_i(x_j)$$

so that no consumer covets another's allocation. Such an allocation is said to be a no-envy allocation. This concept incorporates a certain idea of justice but does not in fact imply optimality. For that it is necessary to limit oneself to "fair" allocations, that are at once no-envy and Pareto-optimal (Varian 1974).

It is easy to see that Walras equilibria obtained from the egalitarian allocation[3] are fair allocations. We let $(p, x_1, \ldots, x_n)$ be such an equilibrium and consider two consumers $i$ and $j$. If the preferences are not satiated, we have

$$p \cdot x_i = p \cdot x_j = p \cdot \frac{\sum_{i=1}^{n} \omega_i}{n}$$

so $x_j$ is a possible choice for $I$. We must therefore have $U_i(x_i) \geq U_i(x_j)$, and the equilibrium is no-envy. The first welfare theorem implies that it is equally Pareto-optimal and therefore fair.

---

1. When utilities are nontransferable, that is, when there is no good whose marginal utility is constant, the compensation principle does not even define an order: it is quite possible that $A$ be preferred to $B$ *and* $B$ preferred to $A$.
2. The history of *new welfare economics* and of its relative failure is reported by Chipman-Moore (1978).
3. Where the initial allowance of each consumer is $\sum_{i=1}^{n} \omega_i / n$.

Do other fair allocations exist? Champsaur-Laroque (1981) showed that the answer to that question is disappointing: if there is a continuum of consumers, the only fair allocations are the Walras equilibria obtained from the egalitarian allocation. Moreover the idea of no-envy allocation does not allow for definition of an order (when does one allocation generate "less envy" than another?), and it does not lend itself well to generalizations in the case of production economies. We do not have here simply a matter of technical difficulty. Suppose that John enjoys greater productivity than Peter. Is it unfair that John have an allocation that Peter finds preferable to his own? If it is not, then the no-envy criterion becomes less attractive. However, most moral philosophers argue that innate differences in productivities are morally arbitrary and should not determine ethical judgments. If we think that most differences in productivities are innate, then no-envy remains an appealing property.[4]

Can we go further? This question actually can be broken down into two subproblems:

1. Define a collective preference. This is the problem of the *aggregation of preferences*.

2. Collect the information necessary in order to put the optimum of this collective preference to use. This is the problem of *implementation*.

To illustrate, let us take two examples. The first applies to distinguishing a particular Pareto optimum from among all Pareto optima of an economy. One way to proceed consists in defining a functional $W(U_1, \ldots, U_n)$, called the Bergson-Samuelson functional, and maximizing it over the set of possibilities. This supposes first of all that one knows how to define the functional $W$ (aggregation of preferences),[5] and also that one has obtained the necessary information—the utility functions, which are private a priori (implementation).

The second example is that of an election where $m$ candidates compete for an office. If $m = 2$, it is easy to see that the simple majority vote, which consists in electing $a$ over $b$ if the number of voters who

---

4. Production economies present a more technical difficulty: Pazner-Schmeidler (1974) showed that contrary to the case of exchange economies, fair allocations may fail to exist. However, Piketty (1994) showed that if more productive agents also face a lower disutility of labour, then fair allocations do exist.

5. We will see in this chapter that very few of the Bergson-Samuelson functionals satisfy minimal conditions.

prefer $a$ to $b$ is higher than the number of those who prefer $b$ to $a$, is a process that has good characteristics: it leads no voter to manipulate his vote. One can hardly do better if (as is always the case in an election) one cannot make use of more precise information on voters' preferences. Things become complicated when $m > 2$. One might think of extending the simple majority vote in categorizing all the candidates according to their performances in tournaments where they compete in pairs. Then $a$ would be ranked above $b$ if the number of voters who prefer $a$ to $b$ is higher than the number of those who prefer $b$ to $a$. Unfortunately, this process often ends in the famous Condorcet paradox (1785): as the reader will easily see, it is very possible for this process to lead to a situation where $a$ is preferred to $b$, who is preferred to $c$, while $c$ is himself preferred to $a$. The resulting order is therefore not an order, since it is intransitive, which makes finding the socially optimal choice impossible. This phenomenon is not at all pathological. Suppose, for example, that there are 3 candidates and 21 voters. Eight voters prefer, in order, $a > b > c$, seven prefer $b > c > a$, and six $c > a > b$. The reader will verify that these preferences result in Condorcet's paradox.[6]

The simple majority vote is not the only procedure that entails difficulties when there are more than two candidates. Consider, for example, the classification procedure suggested by Borda (1781). According to Borda, each voter can assign one point to his favorite candidate, two to his second favorite, and so on, and then the candidates are ranked in order from the most points collected to the least. Note that this is the exact method practiced in numerous sports competitions, for example, in Formula One racing.[7] The disadvantage to the Borda method is the possibility that the relative ranking of $a$ and of $b$ will depend on the ranking of $c$ in relation to them. Thus, if Schumacher has three points more than Hill before the last Grand Prix of the season, their final order will depend on whether or not Berger or Alesi succeeds in defeating one of them. In regard to elections, any third candidate that pulls out of the election can affect the social classification of

---

6. It can be shown that if there were a perfect shuffle of the voters' candidate preferences then the probability of an electoral paradox is approximately 0.09 when there are three candidates and a very large number of voters. This probability increases with the number of candidates.

7. One trial (a Formula One Grand Prix) results in a ranking just like a voting poll. So formally a sports event could correspond to an election, and the competitors to candidates.

$a$ and of $b$. Technically Borda's method violates an axiom which we will later call independence of irrelevant alternatives. All other imaginable methods (organization of primaries, polls, two-round systems, etc.) possess their own inconveniences. This is a consequence of Arrow's famous theorem, which is at the heart of the next section.

## 2.1 Arrow's Theorem

Consider the following very general problem. The set of possible choices is noted $A$. There are $n$ agents $i = 1, \ldots, n$. Using traditional notation (with more common notation in parenthesis), we can represent individual preferences as

- $aP_ib$ if $i$ strictly prefers $a$ to $b$ $[U_i(a) > U_i(b)]$
- $aI_ib$ if $i$ is indifferent between $a$ and $b$ $[U_i(a) = U_i(b)]$
- $aR_ib$ if $i$ likes $a$ at least as much as $b$ $[U_i(a) \geq U_i(b)]$

We can assume that relations $R_i$ are preorders (transitive and complete). Relations $P_i$ and $I_i$ are then obtained from $R_i$ by

- $xP_iy$ iff ($xR_iy$ and not ($yR_ix$))
- $xI_iy$ iff ($xR_iy$ and $yR_ix$)

The aggregation of preferences problem consists in going from the vector (*profile*) of individual preferences $R = (R_1, \ldots, R_n)$ to a collective preference $\hat{R}$ on $A$. The *social welfare function* (SWF) will be the functional $\hat{R} = f(R)$. Several examples of SWFs were given in this chapter's introduction.

Note the considerable generality of this modelization. The description of the possible choices (also called social states) may contain the set of all individual allocations, the production of public goods, governmental orientations, and so on. As for preferences on social states, they can be perfectly selfish or take into account equity concerns. As Arrow (1950, p. 333) states, "It need not be assumed here that an individual's attitude toward different social states is determined exclusively by the commodity bundles that accrue to his lot under each."

First let us examine the most natural case in the development of the neoclassical methods, which was the object of Arrow's founding studies (1950, 1951): that of individual preferences being ordinal and non-comparable among individuals. Where individual preferences are ordinal, it is impossible to determine if $i$ prefers $a$ to $b$ "more" than he prefers $b$ to $c$. Where they are noncomparable, it cannot be said whether or not the preference of $i$ for $a$ over $b$ balances the preferences of $j$ for $b$ over $a$.

Arrow imposed on each SWF a series of four conditions which he thought natural:[8]

1. Transitive criterion: for every $R$, $f(R)$ must be preorder.

2. Pareto (or unanimity) criterion: if $\forall i$, $aR_i b$, then $aRb$.

3. UD (universal domain): $f(R)$ must be defined for every imaginable profile $R$.

4. IIA (independence of irrelevant alternatives). The social choice between $a$ and $b$ must depend only on the individual preferences between $a$ and $b$. More formally, let $R$ and $R'$ be two profiles such that $af(R)b$ and $\{i \mid aR_i b\} = \{i \mid aR_i' b\}$. Then one must get $af(R')b$.

Condition 1 seems quite natural; still, we will see how it can be weakened. Neither does the Pareto criterion of condition 2 seem debatable: if all the individuals prefer $a$ to $b$, it is unclear how the collectivity could be of the opposite opinion. Condition 3 reflects the desire to impose great generality on the model: if individuals have no idea a priori of the nature of their preferences, then the SWF should furnish a universally applicable solution. The independence axiom 4 is the most complicated to express. My discussion above of the Borda method shows why such a criterion is necessary: without it, unforeseen and undesirable phenomena can result. Note that this axiom implies that the sought-after SWF cannot help but take the form of the "generalized vote," where the rank of $x$ in relation to $y$ depends only on the list of $i$ who prefer $x$ to $y$. It particularly prohibits taking into account the "intensity of preferences" which specifies that agent $i$ can prefer $x$ to $y$ "more" than another agent $j$ prefers $y$ to $x$.

Finally an SWF will be called dictatorial if it systematically reproduces an individual's preferences, whatever the individual preference profile:

$$\exists i, \forall R, \quad af(R) \Leftrightarrow aR_i b$$

We can now set forth Arrow's theorem (often called *general possibility theorem*):

---

8. The list resumes pedagogical tradition by which the statements retained differ slightly from Arrow's original conditions.

THEOREM 2.1 (ARROW) If A has at least three elements, every SWF that verifies conditions 1 through 4 is dictatorial.

*Proof* See appendix A.

The conclusion of the theorem is of course quite disappointing (Arrow goes so far as to say it is "the height of bad luck"). The question that will concern us now is the possibility of weakening the hypotheses of the theorem so as to invalidate its conclusion.

First, we note that if A has but two elements, then the simple majority vote satisfies all of Arrow's conditions (other procedures verify these conditions, but a simple majority vote is the only way to satisfy other natural conditions, as formulated by May 1952).

It does not seem very desirable to weaken the Pareto condition: an SWF that would reverse unanimous choices would be quite unsatisfactory.

Conversely, we could imagine weakening condition 1 by no longer insisting that $f(R)$ be an order but that it simply allow maximal elements to be found. It suffices then that in every subset of $A$, there be one or several elements preferred by the social choice. For this, we can show that it is enough for the social preference to be acyclical, in other words, that it verify

$$a_1 P a_2 P \ldots P a_n \Rightarrow a_1 R a_n$$

which is considerably weaker than the transitivity implied by condition 1. Actually this weakening does not eliminate Condorcet's paradox within the bounds of a simple majority vote. Still there are SWFs that verify conditions 2 through 4 and acyclicity, as shown in the following example:

$aRb \Leftrightarrow a$ is not Pareto-dominated by $b$

The inconvenience of this SWF[9] is that its curves of indifference are dense. If neither $a$ nor $b$ Pareto-dominates the other, then $a$ and $b$ are socially indifferent. If, on the other hand, each agent has veto rights, $aP_ib$, then necessarily $aRb$. Indeed, it can be shown that every SWF that verifies conditions 2 through 4 and is quasi-transitive[10] obligatorily gives veto rights to a group of agents that can then be called an

---

9. Aside from its not being transitive.
10. Quasi-transitivity stipulates that only the strict order $P$ is transitive; therefore it is a slightly stronger condition than acyclicity. One can show (see Moulin 1988, ch. 11) that fairly similar results are obtained for acyclical SWFs.

oligarchy. Therefore the weakening of transitivity is not a very promising solution.

The IIA axiom has been greatly disputed. Unfortunately, attempts made to find a weaker version of it are often very technical and have not led far. Its complete suppression would reestablish the existence of nondictatorial SWFs, but they would suffer the aforementioned drawbacks. Conversely, the IIA axiom could be replaced by a fairly natural one of monotonicity (which says that if the ranking of $x$ improves in all $R_i$, then it cannot worsen in $f(R)$) without modifying the conclusion of Arrow's theorem.[11] A better way to consider preference intensity is to suppose that preferences are comparable, as we will see later.

The weakening of the hypothesis of universal domain is more rewarding. It is very possible that in certain situations, one is privy to information on agents' individual preferences a priori. It is fitting then to exploit that information.[12] The most famous example, which dates back to Black (1948), concerns single-peaked or unimodal preferences. Suppose that all individuals agree to arrange the possible choices on one axis and that each individual has single-peaked preferences on that axis, as in figure 2.1.

We could think of political preferences where candidates are naturally categorized as left or right. Under these conditions, it can be illustrated that the simple majority vote leads to a social order that is transitive (the Condorcet paradox cannot then appear with such preferences[13]), and that this order is identified by the preferences of the median voter—whose favorite candidate is in the middle of the axis among all agents' favorites.[14] Note that this SWF is nondictatorial: the median voter varies according to individual preferences, and therefore there is no dictator whose choices are always followed.

This positive result is encouraging, but it allows (at least) two problems to remain. The first is that the rule of simple majority vote is far less appealing in redistribution problems than in electoral contexts. For example, consider the division of a cake among three agents $i$, $j$, and $k$,

---

11. We will find the axiom of monotonicity again in chapter 4.
12. In the framework of an economy, for example, it is possible to limit attention to increasing or convex preferences; unfortunately, it can be shown that this does not invalidate the conclusion of Arrow's theorem.
13. Caplin-Nalebuff (1991) show that this result extends to certain classes of multidimensional preferences, as long as the agents' preferences do not differ too much and the vote requires a majority higher than 64 percent.
14. Strictly speaking, it is necessary that the number of agents be odd in order to enable the definition of a single median agent.

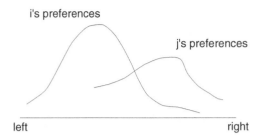

**Figure 2.1**
Single-peaked preferences

each of whom is interested only in his own share. In the social state $a$, $i$ and $j$ each have 40 percent of the cake and $k$ has 20 percent. In state $b$, 10 percent of $k$'s cake has been taken away and divided between $i$ and $j$. State $b$ is clearly preferred to $a$ by a simple majority vote. Nevertheless, this conclusion does not seem fair: $k$, who was already worst off under $a$, is even more impoverished under $b$! It is intuitively clear that the simple majority vote is not a good solution in this context, even with trivial preferences.

Now, it must be remembered that Arrow's conditions constitute only a very minimal set of demands. One could, for example, wish to preserve individual rights in giving each individual final choice in circumstances pertaining to his reserved domain. For example, each individual (at least each unmarried individual!) should be able to decide for himself whether to sleep on his back or his stomach. Sen (1970) formalizes this notion of "minimal liberty" or of "liberalism" insisting that each individual can impose his choices on at least a pair of decisions:

$$\forall i,\ \exists(a,b),\quad af(R)b \iff aR_ib$$

Thus, if $a$ and $b$ are two decisions that differ only in that $i$ sleeps on his stomach in $a$ and on his back in $b$, $i$ must be able to impose his choice on society. It is said then that $i$ is decisive on $(a, b)$.

Unfortunately, there is no Paretian liberal: no SWF (even if only acyclical) satisfies altogether the condition of universal domain, the Pareto principle, and the new condition of liberalism. Sen gives an example of this based on *Lady Chatterley's Lover* (henceforth LCL).[15] Let us concentrate on the two agents $A$, who is prude, and $B$ who is a libertine, and on three possible situations:

---

15. The book by D. H. Lawrence was published in 1928 and scandalized respectable English society with its eroticism.

- $x$: only $A$ reads LCL
- $y$: only $B$ reads LCL
- $z$: neither $A$ nor $B$ reads LCL

$A$, being prudish, prefers that no one read LCL, but if someone must read it, he prefers that it be himself rather than $B$, whom he judges to be much too impressionable. $B$ would like to read LCL, but he would like it even more that the prude $A$ read it and be horrified. Therefore the preferences are

- for $A$: $z > x > y$
- for $B$: $x > y > z$

Conversely, liberalism suggests that $A$ cannot be forced to read LCL, nor $B$ not to read it: $A$ is decisive on $(z, x)$ and $B$ is decisive on $(y, z)$.

In this example the Pareto principle imposes that $x > y$ on a social level, while liberalism imposes $z > x$ and $y > z$; the social preferences are therefore cyclical. Yet it will be observed that this paradox rests on the existence of *nosy preferences*: $A$ and $B$ have simultaneous preferences that dictate not only what they prefer for themselves but also what they prefer for other members of society. It is possible to show that only in such cases does liberalism contradict the Pareto principle.

In fact it seems that in economic situations that interest us the most directly, it is difficult to achieve positive results when individual preferences are ordinal and noncomparable. The path we will take now involves progressively refining the information available on individual preferences.

## 2.2 Noncomparable Cardinal Preferences

It can be shown that switching to noncomparable cardinal preferences does not improve the situation (d'Aspremont-Gevers 1977). I will just give a sketch of this result.

To simplify, we will return to the notation in terms of utility functions. Note that $U = (U_1, \ldots, U_n)$ is a profile of individual utilities and that $\hat{U} = f(U)$ is the corresponding social utility.[16] The fact that the preferences are noncomparable cardinals is translated by the requirement

---

16. Keep in mind that we are working from a *welfarist* perspective, where only the utilities are important; under fairly weak hypotheses, $\hat{U}$ can be represented as a Bergson-Samuelson functional $\hat{U} = W(U_1, \ldots, U_n)$. Therefore the problem lies in studying the restrictions that $W$ must satisfy.

that if all the $U_i$ are submitted to possibly different affine transformations according to

$$U_i' = a_i U_i + b_i$$

then the new social utility $\hat{U}'$ leads to preferences identical to those that subtend the former $\hat{U}$:

$$\hat{U}(x) \geq \hat{U}(y) \Leftrightarrow \hat{U}'(x) \geq \hat{U}'(y)$$

Now let $\phi_i$ be any increasing transformation from IR to IR, and fix two choices $x$ and $y$. It is possible to find coefficients $(a_i)$ and $(b_i)$ such that one gets for each $i$,

$$\begin{cases} \phi_i[U_i(x)] = a_i U_i(x) + b_i \\ \phi_i[U_i(y)] = a_i U_i(y) + b_i \end{cases}$$

since this is a regular system of $2n$ equations with $2n$ unknowns. But as the preferences are noncomparable cardinals, in applying IIA we can deduce that the preferences $\phi_i \circ U_i$ lead to the same social preferences as $U_i$, and we return to the case of ordinal noncomparable preferences.

## 2.3   Comparable Ordinal Preferences

The case of preferences that are comparable between individuals is more promising: It is clear a priori that the comparison between utilities achieved by different agents produces useful information when one examines a redistribution problem. Even in the seemingly simple framework of Formula One racing, we saw that the adopted ranking doesn't satisfy IIA; in turn, the introduction of comparisons (here, the racers' times in the various stage races) would allow for a more satisfying ranking. By the same token, the introduction of a point system in decathlon events allows for an escape from Arrow's theorem. Now let us study the impact of the comparability of individual preferences.

The fact that the preferences are comparable ordinals is illustrated by the requirement that if all the $U_i$ are submitted to the same increasing transformation, then $\hat{U}$ is transformed the same way.

In this setting, several anonymous SWFs[17] exist that verify all of Arrow's conditions. They are all characterized by the existence of a

---

17. An SWF is anonymous when it is indifferent to the identity of individuals, that is, when the order it engenders is unvarying regardless of permutations of individuals.

"positional dictator" defined by its place in the ordained utility vector, which can then be the median agent, or the most advantaged, or the most disadvantaged, or even the 13th most disadvantaged, and so on. One might add one or several conditions in order to arrive at a single characterization. It is in this way that Hammond (1976) adds one condition that he calls equity:

$$\left. \begin{array}{l} U_j(b) < U_j(a) < U_k(a) < U_k(b) \\ \forall i \neq j,k, \quad U_i(a) = U_i(b) \end{array} \right\} \Rightarrow U(b) \leq U(a)$$

This condition states that if the preferences of $j$ and $k$ between $a$ and $b$ are opposed, although all the other agents are indifferent, and if $j$ is more disadvantaged anyways than $k$, then the social preference cannot work against the wishes of $j$. The opinion followed is always that of the most unfortunate—if this individual exists.

Hammond shows that if one adds anonymity and the equity axiom to Arrow's conditions, one obtains a leximin criterion. Without going into too much detail, this preference is a lexicographical generalization[18] of the Rawls criterion, so $U = \min_{i=1,\dots,n} U_i$. Thus a state $a$ is preferred to a state $b$ if the most disadvantaged individual in state $a$ is happier there than the most disadvantaged individual in state $b$ (who of course is not necessarily the same individual). Hammond therefore justifies applying the "difference principle"[19] of Rawls (1971), whose book has had and continues to have considerable influence on political philosophy (see appendix B).

## 2.4   Comparable Cardinal Preferences

When preferences are cardinal and comparable, a like affine increasing transformation of $U_i$ must also be applied to $U$. There then exists only one family of SWFs that verifies Arrow's conditions: the utilitarist family, which is given by

$$U = \sum_{i=1}^{n} \pi_i U_i$$

where the $\pi_i$ possess the properties of a probability vector. If one further insists that the chosen SWF be anonymous, then the only solution is

---

18. It takes into account possible indifferences.
19. The difference principle consists of not admitting inequalities except to the extent that (especially for reasons of incentives) they benefit the individuals who are the least well off.

$U = \frac{1}{n}\Sigma_{i=1}^{n}U_i$. In this way one rediscovers the result of Harsanyi (1955), which justified it by invoking a social contract passed under a "veil of ignorance," before the agents know their identity. It is then reasonable for the agents to be interested in the expectation of their utility. In this sense the criterion of Rawls (whose theory is also tied to the social contract school) corresponds to a case where the agents are infinitely adverse to risk.

Finally, we note that in the extreme case where individual preferences are completely fixed (so that even affine transformations are inadmissible), one again finds the Bergson-Samuelson approach mentioned at the beginning of this chapter: a very large number of compatible SWFs exist under Arrow's conditions. Such a hypothesis is obviously very remote from the framework of neoclassical analysis. However, it can be useful if one is interested only in a unidimensional indicator like income. Thus Atkinson (1970) and Dasgupta-Starrett (1973) show that a distribution of income is preferred to another distribution of equal mean for all strictly quasi-concave and symmetrical SWFs if and only if the corresponding Lorenz curve is nearer the diagonal, which is a customary definition of a more egalitarian distribution of income.

## 2.5  Conclusion

We have seen that the best possible response to the problem posed by Arrow's theorem consists in enriching the available information on individual preferences, in weakening the universal domain hypothesis, or in resorting to interpersonal utility comparisons.

One can go even further, either by enriching the information tied to the utility, as we did in the last two subsections, or by calling on independent utility criteria. The last approach was adopted by Sen in his recent work (e.g., see Sen 1992). This is a fairly vast body of writing that also examines the possibility of introducing equity criteria into the social preferences. Last we saw that the theory of optimal electoral procedures (e.g., see Moulin 1988, ch. 9) also plays a role in the aggregation of preferences.

To conclude, I would like to emphasize that it is impossible to be only interested in distribution questions from the economist's point of view. There are more fundamental philosophical inquiries. The reader can get a brief glimpse of some introductory elements of philosophical-economics writings on social justice in appendix B.

## 2.6   Appendix A: Proof of Arrow's Theorem

The idea for the following proof dates back to Vickrey (1960); it comprises three lemmas.

Denote $I = \{1, \ldots, n\}$.

LEMMA 1   (NEUTRALITY)   Given a division $I = M \cup N$ and $(a, b, x, y) \in A^4$ such that

- $\forall i \in M$, $xP_iy$ and $aP'_ib$
- $\forall i \in N$, $yP_ix$ and $bP'_ia$

then

$$x\hat{P}y \Leftrightarrow a\hat{P}'b \tag{2A.1}$$

$$x\hat{I}y \Leftrightarrow a\hat{I}'b \tag{2A.2}$$

*Proof*   The interpretation of lemma 1 is simple: If $x$ and $y$ are ordered by each individual in $P$ as $a$ and $b$ in $P'$, then this must also be true of social preference; that is, $x$ and $y$ must be ordered by $\hat{P}$ as $a$ and $b$ by $\hat{P}'$. If this weren't the case, then the procedure of aggregation would treat the pairs $(a, b)$ and $(x, y)$ in a nonneutral manner, hence the name of the lemma.

Let us first prove (2A.1). Suppose that $x\hat{P}y$ and that $(a, b, x, y)$ are distinct two by two. Let preferences $P''$ be such that

- $\forall i \in M$, $aP''_ixP''_iyP''_ib$
- $\forall i \in N$, $yP''_ibP''_iaP''_ix$

(such preferences exist because the domain is universal). By IIA, since $x$ and $y$ are ordered individually in $P''$ as in $P$, we have $x\hat{P}''y$. By the Pareto principle, $a\hat{P}''x$ and $y\hat{P}''b$. By transitivity, we get $a\hat{P}''b$. Finally, in reapplying IIA, we find that $a\hat{P}'b$. The cases where $a$ or $b$ coincide with $x$ or $y$ are treated similarly.

Part (2A.2) is obtained directly. If $x\hat{I}y$ but, for example, $a\hat{P}'b$, we find the contradiction $x\hat{P}y$ by (2A.1) in reversing the roles of $(a, b)$ and $(x, y)$.                                                              □

Before stating Lemma 2, two terms must be defined. We say that a set of agents $M$ is almost decisive on $(x, y)$ if for every $\hat{P}$,

$$(\forall i \in M,\ xP_iy \text{ and } \forall i \notin M,\ yP_ix) \Rightarrow x\hat{P}y$$

We say that $M$ is decisive on $(x, y)$ if for every $\hat{P}$,

$$(\forall i \in M, xP_iy) \Rightarrow x\hat{P}y$$

LEMMA 2   If $M$ is almost decisive on $(x, y)$, then it is decisive on $(x, y)$.

*Proof*   Suppose that $\forall i \in M, xP_iy$. By IIA, only individual preferences count on $(x, y)$; the others can be changed. Assume therefore, with no loss of generality, that $z$ exists such that $xP_izP_iy$ if $i \in M$ and $z$ is preferred to $x$ and $y$ by the other agents. Neutrality imposes that $x\hat{P}z$ because the individual preferences are oriented as on $(x, y)$ and $M$ is almost decisive on $(x, y)$. Finally, the Pareto principle implies that $z\hat{P}y$ and transitivity implies the conclusion that $x\hat{P}y$. ☐

Note that neutrality implies that if $M$ is decisive on $(x, y)$, it is decisive on every other pair. We will therefore just say that $M$ is decisive.

LEMMA 3   If $M$ is decisive and contains at least two agents, then a strict subset of $M$ exists that is decisive.

*Proof*   Divide $M = M_1 \cup M_2$, and choose a $\hat{P}$ such that

- on $M_1$, $xP_iyP_iz$
- on $M_2$, $yP_izP_ix$
- outside $M$, $zP_ixP_iy$

As $M$ is decisive, we have $y\hat{P}z$.
One of two things results:

- Either $y\hat{P}x$, and (since $z$ doesn't count by IIA) $M_2$ is almost decisive on $(x, y)$, and therefore decisive by lemma 2
- Or $x\hat{R}y$, and by transitivity $x\hat{P}z$; then ($y$ doesn't count by IIA) $M_1$ is almost decisive on $(x, y)$, and therefore is decisive by lemma 2 ☐

The proof is concluded by noting that by the Pareto principle, $I$ as a whole is decisive. In applying lemma 3, the result is an individual $i$ that is decisive, and this is therefore the sought-after dictator. The attentive reader will have noted that lemma 1 remains valid when there are only two alternatives, contrary to lemmas 2 and 3.

## 2.7   Appendix B: Theories of Justice

For our purposes it will suffice to take a brief historical glimpse at some theories of justice. For readers who are interested in the original or more subtle enlightenments, I encourage them to consult Roemer (1996).

### 2.7.1  Utilitarianism

Modern theories of justice often define themselves in reference (or by opposition) to utilitarianism, which dates back to the writings of Jeremy Bentham at the end of the eighteenth century. Utilitarianism was the dominant doctrine of classical economists at least up to John Stuart Mill. Its hypothesis is based on the notion of "welfarism." It states that for each person and each state of the world, a single index exists to measure welfare, and it is called "utility."

The utilitarianists assumed that these utility indexes were cardinal and comparable among persons, so that one could define their sum. The task of the government then was simply to maximize that sum. Bentham termed this task "the arithmetics of pleasures and pains." The objective was just to maximize (with obvious notation).

$$\sum_{i=1}^{n} U_i(x_i)$$

under the scarcity constraints.

Utilitarianism became subjected to much criticism, however. First it became apparent that the poor and the rich could not be treated in a symmetrical manner, since that meant abandoning all redistributive views. However, Edgeworth showed that this critique is not entirely accurate. Thus suppose that individuals draw no utility except from their income $R_i$, that total income is fixed at $R$, and that the utility indexes are concave. Now utilitarianism calls for equality of marginal utilities $U_i'(R_i)$. If in addition the utility indexes of all individuals coincide, then incomes must all be equalized, and this idea of course corresponds to the most progressive taxation possible.[20]

A second problem of utilitarianism is that it priviledges individuals who easily transform their increments from income into utility. To see this, suppose that the utility $U_i(R_i) = U(R_i, \alpha_i)$ does not depend on $i$ directly but only through a parameter $\alpha_i$, that it is concave, and that the marginal utility of income is increasing in $\alpha$:

---

20. This argument is defective in that total income is independent of the redistributive scheme which neglects all the disincentive aspects of taxes; we will see later in this section that utilitarianism does lead to taxes that are not very progressive when the essential disincentive effects of taxes are reintroduced into the analysis.

$$\frac{\partial^2 U}{\partial R^2} < 0 \quad \text{and} \quad \frac{\partial^2 U}{\partial R \partial \alpha} > 0$$

clearly, a higher $\alpha_i$ corresponds to a greater capacity to transform income into utility. So it is easy to see that equalization of marginal utilities of income leads to giving each individual $i$ an income that increases in his parameter $\alpha_i$. This doesn't seem fair; consider, for example, someone who is disabled or someone who has difficulty transforming a dollar of extra income into utility because, for example, his capacities for leisure consumption are reduced. Then his $\alpha_i$ will be low, and the utilitarian will assign him a lower income.

More generally, all the criticisms of welfarism also apply to utilitarianism: The hypothesis of a sole utility index is reductive, it prohibits the taking into account of liberties and human rights,[21] and sundry other essentials.

But the most important criticism of utilitarianism is philosophical. In adding up the utilities of different individuals, there is implicitly supposed that the happiness of one human being can compensate for the unhappiness of another. This idea violates the Kantian principle that "one cannot treat people as means to an end. This is in fact the main reason that utilitarianism was abandoned by twentieth-century philosophers—though not by economists.

### 2.7.2   Rawls's Difference Principle

John Rawls's 1971 book became the cornerstone of all recent debates on social justice. In Nozick's words, "Political philosophers now must either work within Rawls's theory or explain why not" (1974, p. 183). Rawls chose a framework, which he called the "original situation," that more or less corresponds to Rousseau's pure state of nature. The original situation exists before individuals have concluded a social contract. However, the contribution that earned Rawls his fame is his introduction of the "veil of ignorance": In the original situation, each individual is unaware of who he is and what his place will be in society; he does not even know what wealth and talents he will inherit. Under such circumstances Rawls affirmed that each individual will first of all want to be guaranteed elementary rights and liberties. Hence this is the

---

21. Liberties could be counted as arguments for the utility index, but this runs the risk of bringing back into question the usual properties of the index, and thereby making the result fairly unusable.

first principle, according to which each individual must have access to the most extensive system of liberties that is compatible with an identical system for other individuals.[22]

Another idea that Rawls put forth is that there exist "primary goods" (income surely, but also higher level variables like access to places of responsibility) upon which one can define a utility index that is ordinal and also comparable among individuals. Since individuals are all identical in the original situation, Rawls first affirmed that they will want to equalize these utilities. However, total equalization of primary utilities of goods risks having disincentive effects that will distance the society from a Pareto optimum, so it may be preferable to tolerate certain inequalities if they benefit the most disadvantaged. This brought Rawls to state his famous second principle, often called the "difference principle":[23] "All social primary goods—liberty and opportunity, income and wealth, and the bases of self-respect—are to be distributed equally unless an unequal distribution of any or all of these goods is to the advantage of the least favored" (1971, sec.46).

In mathematical terms what Rawls justifies is the "maximin criterion," according to which society's utility function is given by

$$U(x) = \min_{i=1,\dots,n} U_i(x_i)$$

By way of illustration, I adopt an optimal taxation problem from Roemer (1996). Assume that individuals do not differ except in their marginal productivity $w$, which coincides with their salary in perfect competition and which is distributed among the population according to a uniform on $[0, 1]$. Their utility is $(y - l^2/2)$, where $l$ is their job and $y$ their income, and $y = wl$. The government enacts a purely redistributive affine tax $T(y) = cy + d$. How should parameters $c$ and $d$ be chosen?

First, note that the individual $w$ facing this tax solves

$$\max_l \left[ wl - (cwl + d) - \frac{l^2}{2} \right]$$

which gives $l(w) = w(1 - c)$. The individual $w$ therefore pays a tax

$$t(w) = cw^2(1 - c) + d$$

---

22. This way the allocation of elementary rights eludes welfarism.

23. According to Rawls, this principle has inferior priority to the first principle. The application of the difference principle must not, under any circumstances, lead to a violation of the liberties defined by the first principle.

In order for the tax to be purely redistributive, its balance must be zero. That is, one must have

$$\int_0^1 t(w)dw = 0$$

from which one gets $d = -c(1 - c)/3$. The indirect utility of the individual $w$ becomes

$$v(w) = wl(w) - [cwl(w) + d] - \frac{l(w^2)}{2} = w^2 \frac{(1-c)^2}{2} + \frac{c(1-c)}{3}$$

A Rawlsian government would choose $c$ so as to maximize the indirect utility of the least advantaged:

$$\max_c \min_w v(w)$$

This gives $c = 1/2$, and not $c = 1$ as one might imagine a priori. (An overly confiscatory tax would dissuade the most productive individuals from working and would therefore reduce the mass of income to be redistributed.) On the other hand, a utilitarian government would seek to maximize the expectation of indirect utility:

$$\max_c \int_0^1 v(w)dw$$

which gives $c = 0$, so the government revokes enactment of the tax. This last result is dependent on the hypotheses, and could be modified if redistributive objectives are introduced.[24] Still the conclusion that Rawls's approach leads to a more progressive taxation remains true in general: The poorest individuals (up to $w = \sqrt{2}/3$ here) prefer the Rawlsian tax and the richest prefer the utilitarian tax.

### 2.7.3   Recent Developments

One could summarize Rawls's argument on the allocation of primary goods as follows:

• The inheritance (of wealth and talents) is morally arbitrary

• The ensuing social inequalities must therefore be abolished

• Complete equality must be replaced by the maximin criteria in order to preserve Pareto-optimality

---

24. The reader can easily verify that if the government maximizes $\int_0^1 \mu(w)v(w)dw$, setting $\mu(w) = 1 - w$ to give a higher weight to the utility of the least productive individuals, then it should set $c = 1/3$.

Several authors have been inclined to criticize this reasoning. Sen and Harsanyi, for example, attacked some of its consequences. The maximin criterion risks sacrificing a considerable welfare increase due five billion individuals if it ever so slightly damages the most disadvantaged. Obviously this seems a bit extreme. Moreover there is the opposite argument that has the individuals, in the original situation, not able to tolerate any inequality, so they automatically imagine themselves as among the most disadvantaged and promote behavior that is infinitely adverse to risk. This too does not seem to correspond to reality.

Actually, Rawls's approach does not seem to leave much room for free will. His conclusion proceeds rather directly from the idea that individuals are not morally responsible for their place in society. Certain authors (see Roemer 1996, chs. 7 and 8) have reinterpreted individual responsibility using the general framework of Rawls, but they distinguish morally arbitrary circumstances, among which they categorize the inheritance of wealth and talents, and the free choices of individuals, which include their efforts, and even their tastes insofar as those tastes depend at least in part upon a choice. The maximin criterion then must regard morally arbitrary circumstances so that it can tolerate inequalities that affect an individual's free choice.

This new approach is of course more difficult to model than a straightforward utilitarianism or the maximin criterion. However, it is confirmed to lead to an optimal taxation that is more redistributive than the utilitarist criterion but less so than Rawls's approach.

In this regard it is fitting also to cite the work of Sen (e.g., see Sen 1992). Sen completely rejects welfarism by refusing to accept Rawls's idea on the intercomparable utility of primary goods. Sen criticizes the tendency of earlier theories to focus on a restricted group of variables. He is inspired by the literature on positive rights to define a set of *functionings*: to be well fed, well educated, in good health, and so on. The set of *functionings* available to a human being constitutes his *capability set*, and it is therefore multidimensional. In Sen's view, after taking efficiency into account, it is upon equalization of capability sets that social justice theory must be founded. In practice, this means that we should define an index that takes into account both the *functionings* (which describe an individual's welfare) and the *capabilities* (insofar as freedom of choice has an intrinsic value[25]). Obtaining such an index may seem

---

25. By this Sen means that an individual whose preference is *a* benefits from the possibility of choosing *b*, even if he would never choose it. For example, most people prefer that there be an election rather than the establishment of a dictatorship of their favorite candidate.

to be beyond reach. Nevertheless, Sen's theory has the advantage of considering the diverse talents of individuals. Certain individuals have more difficulty in transforming an allocation of primary goods into welfare, particularly if, for example, they are handicapped or have an inferior social status. Thus the logic is to give more income to disabled individuals, since their other *functionings* are reduced by their handicap.

Sen's approach has considerable real-world consequences. For example, it suggests that the usual measures of the incidence of poverty far underestimate it, since they do not account for the inadequacy of incomes or for other handicaps (e.g., health-related) as being much more widespread among the poor than among the rich. Incidentally, the United Nations was largely influenced by Sen's work in defining their human development indicator, which weighs the statistics of wealth, but also literacy and public health, to rank countries in a way that differs appreciably from the usual ranking of GDP per capita.

### 2.7.4 Nozick's Historical Approach

The theories of Bentham, Rawls, and Sen adopt nonhistorical approaches: an allocation is judged only by its characteristics at the present time. Nozick (1974), inspired by Locke, took the opposite view. He began by justifying the existence of a minimal state, burdened only with defense, police, and justice departments, and showed that in the absence of these services, citizens will refuse to contribute voluntarily to institutions of mutual protection.[26] Next he affirms that any extension of the state's powers beyond the minimal state would be unjust. To demonstrate this, Nozick proposed that an allocation is just if and only if

• the original appropriation of goods respected justice ("justice in appropriation")

• subsequent transfers are likewise conducted according to justice ("justice in transfers")

Nozick's theory obviously has practical value only if one precisely defines the principles of the said justice of appropriation and of transfers. Clearly, in Nozick's mind, the free working of a market economy

---

26. This is the problem of free riding, which we will see again in discussing public goods.

fills the requirement of the justice of transfers. The question of justice in appropriation is more touchy. Since most natural resources are rare, any appropriation of a part of those resources by an individual encroaches on all others by definition and is therefore probably "unjust." Nevertheless, Nozick considers here, too, that a market economy furnishes a good approximation of appropriation justice, insofar as the appropriation of an unused resource by an individual indirectly benefits others by increasing production possibilities. The result is the libertarian philosophy according to which the state must, above all, abstain from intervening in the economy, especially through taxation of individuals (e.g., for redistribution motives) beyond that which is demanded by the functioning of the minimal state.

As brilliant as it may be, Nozick's approach did not convince philosophers, or even most economists. It was difficult to support the statement that in the world in which we live, the principle of justice in appropriation has always been respected; this simple remark considerably reduced the scope of Nozick's practical conclusions. However, we should note that Nozick has widely renounced his former position in recent writings. He now acknowledges a role for government in the economy as a "solemn expression of the values of human solidarity" (see Nozick 1989, ch. 25), though such concerns came under private charity in his earlier book.

### 2.7.5 Conclusion

The recent philosophical debates on the theory of justice have only barely touched most economists, many of whom still hold a very classical conception of utilitarism. Still, Rawls's thinking offers an interesting paradigm from which there can be extracted conclusions on economic policies. This is not an easy task, since there are obvious difficulties in tracing a common boundary between morally arbitrary circumstances and the agents' free will. At the beginning of the third millennium, we can recall from the Bible the famous parable of talents (Matt. 25). The master, leaving on a voyage, entrusts three of his servants with money in direct proportion to their abilities (a none too Rawlsian act, since such an allocation would tend to accentuate innate advantages). Upon his return, he rewards those who show a profit from the money left them but has only these words for the servant who saw fit to bury his portion:

And cast the worthless servant into the outer darkness; there men will weep and gnash their teeth. (Matt. 25:30)

Is this conclusion fair? If the "bad servant" did not make a profit from the money entrusted to him, it is perhaps because he prioritized enjoyment over altruism. On the other hand, it could be that he was born lazy (for which he is not responsible) or that his parents did not instill in him the spirit of initiative or—as the Gospel seems to suggest—the taste for risk (which is not his fault either). To choose one of these explanations, we have to clarify the question of free will, and this has confounded philosophers and theologians alike for time immemorial.

## Bibliography

Arrow, K. 1950. A difficulty in the concept of social welfare. *Journal of Political Economy* 58: 328–46.

Arrow, K. 1951. *Social Choice and Individual Values*. New York: Wiley.

d'Aspremont, C., and L. Gevers. 1977. Equity and the informational basis of collective choice. *Review of Economic Studies* 44: 199–209.

Atkinson, A. 1970. On the measurement of inequality. *Journal of Economic Theory* 2: 244–63.

Black, D. 1948. On the rationale of group decision-making. *Journal of Political Economy* 56: 23–34.

de Borda, J.-C. 1781. *Mémoire sur les élections au scrution*. Paris.

Caplin, A., and B. Nalebuff. 1991. Aggregation and social choice: A mean voter theorem. *Econometrica* 59: 1–23.

Champsaur, P., and G. Laroque. 1981. Fair allocations in large economies. *Journal of Economic Theory* 25: 269–82.

Chipman, J., and J. C. Moore. 1978. The new welfare economics 1939–1974. *International Economic Review* 19: 547–84.

de Condorcet, M. 1785. *Essai sur l'application de l'analyse à la probabilité des décisions rendues à la pluralité des voix*. Paris.

Dasgupta, P., and D. Starrett. 1973. Notes on the measurement of inequality. *Journal of Economic Theory* 6: 180–87.

Foley, D. 1967. Resource allocation and the public sector. *Yale Economic Essays* 7: 45–98.

Hammond, P. 1976. Equity, Arrow's conditions and Rawls' difference principle. *Econometrica* 44: 793–804.

Harrod, R. 1938. Scope and method of economics. *Economic Journal* 48: 383–412.

Harsanyi, J. 1955. Cardinal welfare, individualistic ethics, and interpersonal comparisons of utility. *Journal of Political Economy* 63: 309–21.

May, K. 1952. A set of independent necessary and sufficient conditions for simple majority decision. *Econometrica* 20: 680–84.

Moulin, H. 1988. *Axioms of Cooperative Decision Making*. Cambridge: Cambridge University Press.

Nozick, R. 1974. *Anarchy, State and Utopia*. New York: Basic Books.

Nozick, R. 1989. *The Examined Life*. New York: Touchstone.

Pazner, E., and D. Schmeidler. 1974. A difficulty in the concept of fairness. *Review of Economic Studies* 41: 441–43.

Piketty, T. 1994. Existence of fair allocations in economies with production. *Journal of Public Economics* 55: 391–405.

Rawls, J. 1971. *A Theory of Justice*. Cambridge: Harvard University Press.

Robbins, L. 1932. *An Essay on the Nature and Significance of Economic Science*. London: Macmillan.

Robbins, L. 1938. Interpersonal comparisons of utility: A comment. *Economic Journal* 48: 635–41.

Roemer, J. 1996. *Theories of Distributive Justice*. Cambridge: Harvard University Press.

Sen, A. 1970. The impossibility of a Paretian liberal. *Journal of Political Economy* 72: 152–57.

Sen, A. 1992. *Inequality Reexamined*. Cambridge: Harvard University Press.

Varian, H. 1974. Equity, envy, and efficiency. *Journal of Economic Theory* 25: 217–44.

Vickrey, W. 1960. Utility, strategy, and social decision rules. *Quarterly Journal of Economics* 74: 507–35.

# 3                 Cost-Benefit Analysis

How does one evaluate the social value of a public project? Is it necessary to build a new railroad line in Florida? Must one prohibit the use of asbestos in construction projects? For an economist, all of these questions relate to cost-benefit analysis. For that matter, jurisprudence emphasizes that every public decision must be justified by arguments that show the benefits to exceed the costs. In particular, this has been the case in the United States since the Reagan administration, even if the courts also base their decisions on extra-economic arguments.

I will be content here in summarizing the problems raised by cost-benefit analysis. I refer interested readers to Layard and Glaister (1994) and to their references.

## 3.1 Measures of Welfare

In economics, and especially in this book, there is often a need for calculating welfare variations among agents when prices are changed. For firms this poses no real difficulty: If $\pi(p)$ is a company's profit when the prices are $p$, then

$$\pi(p) = \max_{y \in Y} p \cdot y$$

So it could be said, without ambiguity,[1] that the welfare goes from $\pi(p)$ to $\pi(p')$ when the prices vary from $p$ to $p'$.

Things are not so simple for consumers. It might seem natural to say that the welfare of a consumer is given by his indirect utility, as

---

1. This is the case even if, strictly speaking, only the company's shareholders have a welfare, and so on.

$$V(p,R) = \begin{cases} \max U(x) \\ x \in X \\ p \cdot x \leq R \end{cases}$$

However, such a gauge of welfare depends on the choice of the utility function $U$ and so is not satisfactory. For our purposes a more stable measure must be found that can be expressed, for example, in terms of equivalent income. To this end, in the 1940s, Hicks introduced two measures:[2]

• The equivalent variation of income $E$, which is the sum that must be given to the consumer in the initial state in order for him or her to have the same utility in the final state; that is,

$$V(p', R) = V(p, R+E)$$

• The compensating variation of income $C$, which is the sum that must be deducted from the consumer in the final state in order for him or her to have the same utility as in the initial state; that is,

$$V(p', R-C) = V(p, R)$$

First we note that these two measures are quite independent of the choice of the utility function $U$. If the latter submits to an increasing transformation, the indirect utility function $V$ will be transformed in the same way, since

$$V(p, R) = U[x(p, R)]$$

where $x(p, R)$ is the Marshallian demand function. The variations $E$ and $C$ therefore will be unaffected.

We note also that $C$ and $E$ are expressed very easily in terms of the expenditure function

$$e(p, u) = \begin{cases} \min p \cdot x \\ x \in X \\ U(x) \geq u \end{cases}$$

since the definitions become

---

2. The reader should know that certain authors use different definitions from those that I use. Sometimes $E$ is defined as $-E$ and $C$ as $-C$, and I use Hicks's notation.

$$\begin{cases} C = R - e(p', V(p, R)) \\ E = e(p, V(p', R)) - R \end{cases}$$

Now, suppose that $p'$ is very close to $p$ so that $p' = p + dp$. Then $E$ will also be infinitesimal and to the first-order,

$$\sum_i \frac{\partial V}{\partial p_i} dp_i = \frac{\partial V}{\partial R} E$$

Or, using Roy's identity,

$$E = -\sum_i x_i dp_i$$

The reader will verify that we get exactly the same formula for $C$. Compensatory and equivalent variations coincide then to the first-order, and can then be calculated on the basis of demand and price variations.

This tidy property is of course no longer true for finite price variations. Yet there is a case where $E$ and $C$ coincide. Suppose there exists a good (good 0) such that the marginal rate of substitution between any two goods $i$ and $j$ does not depend on the consumption of this good. Then there is a representation of the utility function such that the marginal utility of the good 0 is constant, and after normalization we can write

$$U(x_0, x_1, ..., x_L) = v(x_1, ..., x_L) + x_0$$

Let $X$ be the vector $(x_1, \ldots, x_L)$, make $p$ the corresponding price vector, and normalize the price of the good 0 to 1.[3] The maximization of utility under budgetary constraints then amounts to

$$\max_X [v(X) + R - p \cdot X]$$

from which $v'[X(p)] = p$. Demands in goods $1, \ldots, L$ are therefore independent of consumer wealth. There is no wealth effect, and the indirect utility is

$$V(p, R) = v[X(p)] + R - p \cdot X(p)$$

Because the utility is linear in $R$, the calculation of variations $C$ and $E$ is extremely simple. Let us set

---

3. The good 0 is often called a *numéraire*, but one must avoid identifying it as money, which in principle does not enter into the utility function.

$$S(p) = v[X(p)] - p \cdot X(p)$$

Then, by the definition of demands $X(p)$, we have

$$S'(p) = -X(p)$$

Immediately this obtains

$$C = E = S(p') - S(p) = \int_{p'}^{p} X(t) \cdot dt$$

So, in the presence of constant marginal utility, variations $C$ and $E$ still coincide. Moreover $C$ and $E$ are easily calculated based on demand functions.[4]

The quantity $S(p)$ is called a *Marshallian consumer surplus*, even though it was actually introduced by Jules Dupuit as early as 1844. It has a very simple graphical representation when $L = 1$. One then has to the nearest constant (making a change of variables and ignoring integral convergence problems)

$$S(p) = \int_{p}^{\infty} X(t)dt = \int_{0}^{X(p)} P(x)dx - pX(p)$$

where $P(x) = v'(x)$ is the inverse demand function, so that $S(p)$ is the hachured area in the usual graph of demand (figure 3.1).

The hypothesis of the absence of wealth effect is of course very strong: There are very few goods for which the demand is not sensitive to income. What can be said in general? Suppose that $p'$ differs from $p$ only by a decrease in price $p_i$, which becomes $p_i' < p_i$. Then a Marshallian surplus variation can still be calculated:

$$\Delta S = \int_{p_i'}^{p_i} x_i(t, R)dt$$

It can be shown that if good $i$ is normal (so that demand increases with income), then we have the inequality

$$C \leq \Delta S \leq E$$

---

4. The mathematician will have noticed that none of the above is defined independently of the path of integration unless $X(t) \cdot dt$ is an exact differential form. For that, it is necessary and sufficient that for every $i$ and $j$,

$$\frac{\partial X_i}{\partial p_j} = \frac{\partial X_j}{\partial p_i}$$

However, this situation obtains in the absence of the wealth effect, since these derivatives then form the Slutsky matrix, which is symmetrical.

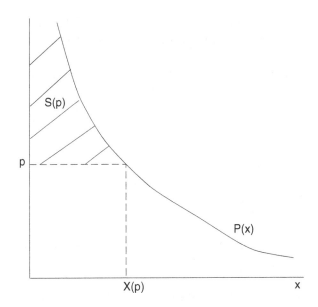

**Figure 3.1**
Consumer suplus

To see this, recall that the derivative of the expenditure function $e(p, u)$ with respect to prices is the compensated demand $X^c(p, u)$. Since $R = e(p, V(p, R)) = e(p', V(p', R))$, one can then write

$$\begin{cases} C = \int_{p_i'}^{p_i} x_i^c[t, V(p, R)]dt \\ E = \int_{p_i'}^{p_i} x_i^c[t, V(p', R)]dt \end{cases}$$

Because good $i$ is assumed to be normal, $x_i(p, R)$ increases in $R$. By the identity $x_i^c(p, u) = x_i(p, e(p, u))$, compensated demand therefore increases in $u$. Now, since $p_i' < p_i$ and $V$ decreases in $p$, one has

$$x_i^c[t, V(p, R)] \leq x_i(t, R) = x_i^c[t, V(t, R)] \leq x_i^c[t, V(p', R)]$$

for every $p_i' \leq t \leq p_i$. This indeed produces (by integration) the sought-after inequality.

The compensatory and equivalent variations thus bracket the surplus variation. Moreover $E$ and $C$ converge toward $\Delta S$ when the wealth effects become negligible.[5]

---

5. More precise inequalities can be obtained in terms of the income elasticity of demand; see Willig (1976).

The use of consumer surplus therefore rests on the hope that wealth effects can be considered small. A simple argument (which can be made more rigorous) in fact shows that this is the case if the good in question represents only a small portion of consumer spending.[6] To see this, we recall Slutsky's equation

$$\frac{\partial x_i}{\partial p_j} = \frac{\partial x_i}{\partial p_j}\bigg|_U - x_j \frac{\partial x_i}{\partial R}$$

Moving on to elasticities, we get

$$\frac{\partial \log x_i}{\partial \log p_j} = \frac{\partial \log x_i}{\partial \log p_j}\bigg|_U - \frac{p_j x_j}{R} \frac{\partial \log x_i}{\partial \log R}$$

which well illustrates that the wealth effect's contribution to demand elasticity becomes negligible if the good whose price varies possesses a small budgetary share ($p_j x_j \ll R$).

In most of our applications, this condition will be approximately verified. Therefore we will be able to use consumer surplus. To obtain the social surplus, the common practice consists in adding the surpluses of different consumers and of firms, possibly weighted to take redistributive objectives into account. Chapter 2, however, shows that this assumes certain ethical judgments that are not universally accepted.

### 3.2  First-Best

Throughout this chapter we suppose that the problem of aggregation of preferences has been settled: There exists a Bergson-Samuelson functional $W(u_1, \ldots, u_n)$ whose maximization gives the social optima.[7] Furthermore in this section we make two assumptions:

• Markets are complete. There is one market for every good, on every possible day, and in every possible state of the world.

• There is no market distortion or failure. No public good, no external effect, no taxes on either income or transactions, all redistribution proceeding from lump-sum transfers.

---

6. Also see the discussion of surplus in the introduction of Tirole's IO book.
7. Otherwise, it would of course be impossible to carry out a cost-benefit analysis, except in the extremely rare cases where all agents agree on a public decision.

These obviously unrealistic hypotheses define a *first-best* problem. We will show that under these conditions, cost-benefit analysis is an extremely simple principle, for it is based on market prices.

To begin, consider a public project that amounts to modifying resources $\omega$ of the economy by a small vector $d\omega$. Certain components of $d\omega$ are positive, and others negative, because some resources are used to produce new ones.

Should this project be carried out? In answer to this question, consider the program defining social optima:

$$\begin{cases} \max_{x_1,\ldots,x_n} & W[U_1(x^1),\ldots,U_n(x^n)] \\ & \sum_{i=1}^{n} x^i \le \omega \end{cases}$$

Let $\lambda$ be the vector of multipliers associated with the scarcity constraints. The first-order conditions give

$$\frac{\partial W}{\partial U_i}\frac{\partial U_i}{\partial x^i} = \lambda$$

But under our hypotheses, the fundamental welfare theorems apply: The optimum is an equilibrium, and the vector $\lambda$ is then proportional to the vector of equilibrium prices $p$. It follows that we get, to the first-order and up to a multiplying constant,

$$dW = p \cdot dw$$

The public project therefore must be evaluated by using market prices to weigh the transformation of resources that it entails, or rather, by simply calculating the increase in national income[8] due to the project.

For noninfinitesimal projects, the calculation is more complicated because market prices depend on economic resources, which are in turn affected by the project. Still, it is simple to show that a project that lowers national income evaluated at initial market prices cannot be desirable in the sense of the Hicks-Kaldor compensation principle (see chapter 2).

Suppose that the initial situation is characterized by resources $\omega_1$, prices $p_1$, and equilibrium consumptions $x_1^i$ (with $\sum_{i=1}^{n} x_1^i = \omega_1$) and that

---

8. This "national income" measure must then (contrary to GDP) take into account the destruction of natural resources, for instance.

the final resources are $\omega_2$, with $p_1 \cdot \omega_2 < p_1 \cdot \omega_1$. Then let $(x_2^i)$ be any final resource allocation. We get

$$p_1 \cdot \sum_{i=1}^{n} x_2^i < p_1 \cdot \sum_{i=1}^{n} x_1^i$$

Therefore a consumer $i$ exists such that $p_1 \cdot x_2^i < p_1 \cdot x_1^i$. Since $x_1^i$ was the preferred consumption of $i$ at prices $p_1$, we can deduce that $U_i(x_2^i) < U_i(x_1^i)$. For every allocation of $\omega_2$, there is at least one consumer whose utility was reduced by the public project. So the Hicks-Kaldor criterion tells us that the project should not be carried out.

## 3.3 Second-Best

Let us consider a more realistic situation. Now the economy is affected by distortions. The fiscal system affects agents' choices, markets are incomplete, and so on. This situation is said to be *second-best*.

### 3.3.1 Shadow Prices

The immediate consequence of this change in perspective is that we can no longer identify $\lambda$ and $p$ as we did in the preceding section. If there are distortions, the market price no longer coincides with the scarcity constraint multiplier. If the markets are incomplete, the situation becomes even worse. By definition, for certain goods there is no longer a market price. So we must calculate the *shadow prices*, $\lambda$ and evaluate $\lambda \cdot d\omega$ in order to assess the social value of an infinitesimal project.

At times it is possible to have an idea of the direction in which $\lambda$ departs from $p$. For example, how can the social cost of a wage-earner's employment in a project be evaluated? Salaries paid an employee simply correspond to transfers between him and taxpayers, so salaries do not then enter social welfare (expect for redistributive considerations). For this reason the social cost of the employment is simply the value of the leisure sacrificed by the employee in order to work. In the first-best, this value coincides with his salary. In the second-best, such as if the economy is in involuntary unemployment, the value of leisure becomes inferior to that of the salary. The shadow price of labor to be used in case of unemployment is then inferior to the market salary.

## 3.3.2   Nonmarket Goods

Certain goods are difficult to assess for lack of a specific market. This is the case, for example, with human life, transportation time, and numerous natural resources (rare animal species, air quality, *etc.*).

Valuing transportation time is crucial to determining whether, for instance, a new railroad line should be built. Under fairly restrictive hypotheses (if labor supply is completely unconstrained), one hour of leisure is worth one hour of salary. Transportation time, at least under these conditions, can then be evaluated by "unearned" salaries.

Noneconomists are often horrified at the explanation that the value of life is not infinite.[9] They generally accept the *cost-effectiveness studies* that calculate by lives saved the cost of diverse public health regulations or measures and that show that some measures are much more effective than others, but they refuse to go so far as to attribute a price to human life. Still, each of us takes risks every day, just by crossing the street. Would we do so if there were an infinite price assigned to our life? Moreover it is readily observed that certain categories of wage-earners choose between high-paying but dangerous professions and those that incur less risk and are also less well-paying. This observation seems to suggest that we do indeed attach a finite price to life.

How can this price be measured? Two main methods are used.

• The method of implicit valuations. This method is founded on the theory of *equalizing differences*, whose principle dates back to Adam Smith. It consists in observing trade-offs on the labor market in terms of the salaries and risks incurred, and in deducing the cost assigned to various risks.

• The method of contingent valuations. This method is very much used, in particular, in the context of renewable resources. It relies on a questionnaire whose subjects are asked to indicate the price they would be willing to pay to have one of the risks that affects them decrease by a given percentage.

---

9. It must be said in their defense that certain economists, and major ones at that, do not go in for half measures. A dozen years ago, Larry Summers had signed a World Bank memo that was destined to remain confidential but became famous. In it was argued that sending waste from industrialized countries to underdeveloped ones was desirable because these countries are much poorer, people's life spans are shorter, and therefore life there has a lesser value. This reasoning is of course quite disputable (e.g., see the analysis of Hausman-McPherson 1996, ch. 2).

One remarkable result of these empirical studies is that these two methods give comparable orders of magnitude: an average subject (neither rich nor poor, neither young nor old) appears to assign to his life a value on the order of two million dollars. This figure is obviously quite fragile. Nonetheless, it suggests that a regulation imposing a cost of 50,000 dollars per life saved should be adopted, while it is advisable to hesitate before a regulation that saves lives at a uniform cost of 100 million dollars. Given the enormous dispersion recorded in costs per life saved (e.g., see tables 1 and 2 in Viscusi 1996), this sort of indication is not as useless as one might, at first, think.

### 3.3.3   Incomplete Markets

In the real world many markets do not exist. This is especially the case with markets for future goods or for state-contingent goods. Insofar as most public projects have uncertain returns that lie in the future, the corresponding shadow prices must be determined.

The interest rate for long-term government bonds is often used to discount future returns on a public project, the rationale being that this interest rate measures the cost of funds for the state. But the ideal rate should reflect the individuals' rates of preference for the present; then the rate would depend on the nature of fiscal distortions or of capital markets distortions. Unfortunately, as is often the case in second-best theory, a general rule cannot be applied.

The situation is slightly more satisfying in regard to uncertainty. The presence of uncertainty should add to the discount rate a term that measures the risk premium. In fact Arrow-Lind (1970) showed that this risk premium can be neglected when the public project concerns a very large number of agents.

### Bibliography

Arrow, K., and R. Lind. 1970. Uncertainty and the evaluation of public investment decisions. *American Economic Review* 60: 364–78.

Dupuit, J. 1844. De la measure de l'utilité des travaux publics. *Annales des Ponts et Chaussées* 8: 332–75. Published in English in P. Jackson, ed. 1996. *The Foundations of Public Finance*. Cheltenham, England: Elgar.

Hausman, D., and M. McPherson. 1996. *Economic Analysis and Moral Philosophy*. Cambridge: Cambridge University Press.

Layard, R., and S. Glaister, eds. 1994. *Cost-Benefit Analysis.* Cambridge: Cambridge University Press.

Viscusi, W. K. 1996. Economic foundations of the current regulatory effort. *Journal of Economic Perspectives* 10: 119–34.

Willig, R. 1976. Consumer's surplus without apology. *American Economic Review* 66: 589–97.

# 4          Implementation

The results obtained in chapter 2, though negative, still allow for the possibility that at least in certain cases, one can effectively aggregate preferences in a satisfactory manner. As Arrow (1951) wrote,[1] it nonetheless remains to collect the necessary information:

> Even when it is possible to aggregate individual preferences into a coherent model of collective ones, one still must define the rules such that individuals actually express their preferences, even when they are reacting rationally.

So it is to the problem of *implementation* that we now turn. Our basic hypothesis, as before, is that agents only act in their own interest. They do not reveal information unless it benefits them to do so. For that they must be offered proper incentives.[2]

We return to the general framework where the set of possible choices is $A$ and each agent $i = 1, \ldots, n$ has a utility function $U_i$ which is known a priori to belong to a set $\mathcal{U}_i$. We will denote $\mathcal{U} = \Pi_{i=1}^{n} \mathcal{U}_i$. We are interested in the implementation of a given *social choice function* (SCF)[3] that associates to any profile of utility functions $U = (U_1, \ldots, U_n)$ a choice $a \in A$ according to $a = f(U)$. Suppose that there exists a "Center" charged with putting a certain social choice function into practice. In the absence of information on the agents' preferences a priori, the Center can only ask them various questions after having announced to them how the information collected will be used. The most general approach consists therefore of searching for a *mechanism*, which comprises spaces

---

1. Even though Arrow had posed the problem in the 1950s, it was not until the 1970s that it received any detailed attention. Hurwicz (1986) provides the many references.
2. We take a view opposite from that of Borda. When someone showed Borda that the method bearing his name could be manipulated, he was offended this response was: "Sir, my method addresses only men of honor!"
3. The SCF could consist in a selection of a set of Pareto optima.

of messages $M_1, \ldots, M_n$ and a rule of the game $g$ which is a function of $M = \Pi_{i=1}^{n} M_i$ in $A$. Each agent $i$ must select a message $m_i \in M_i$. It is understood that if the agents choose $m = (m_1, \ldots, m_n)$, then the choice put to use will be $g(m) \in A$. This defines the game whose set of equilibria will be denoted $h(U) \in M$ ($h$ is a correspondence a priori). Since our goal is to implement the SCF $f$, we will define the following:

• Complete implementation. When $g \circ h = f$, then all equilibria of the game lead to the SCF.

• Weak implementation. When $g \circ h \supset f$, there are then only certain equilibria of the game that lead to the desired SCF.

I have voluntarily remained vague on the concept of equilibrium. Equilibrium is retained for the mechanism-defined game where, as we will see, the results depend heavily on the chosen equilibrium concept.

## 4.1  Dominant Strategy Equilibrium

The strongest concept of equilibrium demands that the strategy (or rather, the message) chosen by agent $i$ be optimal whatever the other agents do. Thus an equilibrium in dominant strategies is a $n$-tuple of messages $m^*$ such that

$$\forall i = 1, \ldots, \forall m \in M, \quad U_i\left[g\left(m_i^*, m_{-i}\right)\right] \geq U_i[g(m)]$$

where I have used the usual notation

$$m_{-i} = \left(m_1, \ldots, m_{i-1}, m_{i+1}, \ldots, m_n\right)$$

If such an equilibrium exists, it is of course quite satisfactory, since then every agent can judge it optimal to conform to his/her equilibrium strategy without even having to wonder which strategies the other will choose. Moreover, the revelation principle (see Myerson 1979), which we will discuss next, shows that it is useless to seek complicated mechanisms; it is better to limit oneself to direct revealing mechanisms. A direct mechanism is such that every agent directly announces a utility function:[4] $\forall i = 1, \ldots, n$, $M_i = U_i$. It is revealing if stating the truth is optimal for all agents.

---

4. Utility functions are generally supposed to be known up to a parameter $\theta_i$; a direct mechanism then corresponds to each agent announcing his $\theta_i$.

THEOREM 3.1 (REVELATION PRINCIPLE) If a mechanism $(M, g)$ weakly implements the SCF $f$ in dominant strategies, then the direct revealing mechanism $(\mathcal{U}, f)$ also implements $f$ weakly in dominant strategies.

*Proof* Let $h_S$ be a selection of the set of equilibria of the mechanism $(M, g)$ such that $g \circ h_S = f$ ($h_S$ exists since $(M, g)$ weakly implements $f$). In dominant strategies, the equilibrium strategies that implement $f$ weakly are therefore given by $m_i^* = h_S^i(U_i)$, since the strategy of agent $i$ cannot depend on that of the other agents. We can proceed ad absurdum. If $(\mathcal{U}, f)$ does not weakly implement $f$, then there exists a utility profile $U'$, an agent $i$ and his utility function $U_i$ such that

$$U_i[\,f(U_i', U_{-i}')\,] > U_i[\,f(U_i, U_{-i}')\,]$$

But since $f = g \circ h_S$, we immediately get

$$U_i\{g[h_S^i(U_i'), h_S^{-i}(U_{-i}')]\} > U_i\{g[h_S^i(U_i), h_S^{-i}(U_{-i}')]\}$$

which contradicts the hypothesis that $(M, g)$ weakly implements $f$, since when the true profile is $(U_i, U_{-i}')$, it is in the agent's $i$ interest to lie by announcing $h_S^i(U_i')$ rather than $h_S^i(U_i)$. $\square$

The revelation principle in fact demonstrates that it is useless to ask agents for more than their own information. Unfortunately, we will expose a very negative result, the Gibbard-Satterthwaite theorem. This theorem shows that the SCFs that are implementable in dominant strategies are too rare to really be useful when the possible utility functions are not restricted.

THEOREM 3.2 (GIBBARD 1973; SATTERTHWAITE 1975) if

- the SCF $f$ is weakly implementable in dominant strategies
- $f(\mathcal{U})$ has at least three elements
- $\mathcal{U}$ is of universal domain

then $f$ is dictatorial.

*Proof* See appendix A.

As the formulation of theorem 3.2 suggests, the result is very close in spirit to Arrow's theorem (which the proof given in appendix A actually uses). It would be possible then to solve the paradox using the path which we saw in chapter 1 was the most promising, and indeed weakening the universal domain hypothesis. Unfortunately, this is not the way to succeed in implementing the correspondence of Walrasian equilibria in an exchange economy, even if it is supposed that preferences are convex. But there are two results that are more positive. The first concerns situations where the choices can be arranged on an axis and where the preferences are unimodal. Then the SCF that selects the preferred choice of the median voter, for example, is implementable. The second positive result refers to quasi-linear preferences. These are written $U_i(x, t) = u(x, \theta_i) + t$, where $x$ is an allocation, $\theta_i$ a known parameter of the agent $i$ alone, and $t$ a monetary transfer. If the preferences are of this type, then optimal decisions can be implemented by a mechanism known as Vickrey-Clarke-Groves, which will be explained in chapter 5.

The second way to avoid negative conclusions to the Gibbard-Satterthwaite theorem is to employ a less demanding concept of equilibrium; that is what we will do now.

## 4.2   Nash Equilibrium

Recall that $m^*$ is a Nash equilibrium if and only if every agent's equilibrium strategy is his best response to the other agents' equilibrium strategies:

$$\forall i = 1, \ldots, n, \forall m_i \in M_i, \quad U_i[g(m^*)] \geq U_i[g(m_i, m_{-i}^*)]$$

The Nash equilibrium is the basic concept of the theory of noncooperative games. It is habitually justified in noting that no agent is interested in deviating from equilibrium if he anticipates that the other agents are conserving their equilibrium strategies. This justification is not convincing here unless we assume that every agent knows the preferences of the other agents. One could imagine an iterative process where every agent repeatedly takes the strategies of the others at iteration $t$ as fixed when he decides his strategy at iteration $(t + 1)$, but this argument merits a more rigorous modelization. It is also flawed in its assumption of myopic behavior on the part of the other agents. The implementation of an SCF through Nash equilibrium must therefore be handled carefully. Here we will suppose that our use of the concept is justified by context.

It is easy to show that if one is limited to direct mechanisms, nothing is gained with respect to dominant strategy equilibrium:

THEOREM 3.3   If $f$ is implementable in Nash equilibrium by a direct mechanism, then it is equally implementable in dominant strategy equilibrium.

*Proof*   It is enough to write the definitions for each utility profile. Weak implementation in Nash equilibrium by a direct mechanism requires that for every profile $U$, every agent $i$, and every $U'_i$,

$$U_i[f(U_i, U_{-i})] \geq U_i[f(U'_i, U_{-i})]$$

But, because this inequality holds for every $U_{-i}$, it implies that $f$ is weakly implementable by a direct mechanism in dominant strategies.                                                                 □

To obtain more satisfactory results than with dominant strategy equilibrium, it is necessary for us to resort to spaces of messages $M_i$ "larger" than $\mathcal{U}_i$. In fact one can demonstrate a revelation principle that stipulates that if $f$ is weakly implementable in Nash equilibrium, then it is also implementable by a mechanism where $M_i = \mathcal{U}$. The proof is identical to that of the principle of revelation in dominant strategy equilibriums. In both cases it is sufficient for each agent to give out all of his information—which here means the whole utility profile.

Unfortunately, weak implementation is not a very useful concept in Nash equilibrium. To see this, consider any SCF $f$ and the following mechanism:

- $\forall i = 1, \ldots, n, M_i = \mathcal{U}$
- $g(m) = f(U)$ if $\forall i = 1, \ldots, n, m_i = U$
- Or else, "everybody's dead"[5]

The idea of this mechanism is that if the agents succeed in coordinating themselves on a statement of the profile of the utilities, the corresponding social choice is put to use. In the opposite situation, all of the agents are severely punished. It is easy to see that the statement of the true utility profile is a Nash equilibrium of this game, so this mechanism weakly implements $f$. But many other Nash equilibria exist: all those where the agents are coordinated on the same lie. Clearly, it is a very weak form implementation, where $g \circ h$ contains $f$ but also a whole $n$-dimensional continuum of other equilibria.

---

5. A dissuasive fine is inflicted on all agents.

Therefore we had better study complete implementation. As in all of this literature, we will henceforth assume that $f$ is a correspondence. In this regard we must slightly extend the revelation principle, which stipulates (henceforth) that it suffices to limit oneself to mechanisms where every $M_i$ is $\mathcal{U} \times A$. Maskin (1977, only published in 1999) used this type of mechanism to completely characterize the implementable SCF's in Nash equilibrium.[6] We begin by introducing two conditions:

• $f$ is *monotone* if and only if

if there is a profile $U$ and $a \in f(U)$, and a new profile $U'$ such that

$$\forall i = 1, \ldots, n, \forall b \in A, \quad [U_i(a) \ge U_i(b) \Rightarrow U'_i(a) \ge U'_i(b)]$$

then $a \in f(U')$.

• $f$ verifies NVP (*no veto power*) if and only if

$$\forall a \in A, \forall i = 1, \ldots, n, \quad [\forall j \ne i, \forall b \in A, U_j(a) \ge U_j(b) \Rightarrow a \in f(U)]$$

These conditions are less complicated than they may appear. On the whole the condition of monotonicity states that if one passes from one utility profile under which $a$ was socially chosen to another profile where $a$ has not gone down in the preferences of any agent, then $a$ will continue to be chosen. This is easily seen by defining the set of choices to which $i$ prefers $a$ by

$$L_i(a, U_i) = \{b \in A \mid U_i(a) \ge U_i(b)\}$$

Then the premise of the condition of monotonicity expresses that for every $i$, $L_i(a, U'_i)$ contains $L_i(a, U_i)$. As for the NVP condition, it simply states that if $a$ is the preferred choice of all the agents except one, then $a$ will be chosen.

Maskin's theorem gives a necessary condition and a set of sufficient conditions for complete implementation in Nash equilibrium:

THEOREM 3.4   (MASKIN)

• If $f$ is completely implementable, then $f$ is monotone
• If $f$ is monotone, verifies NVP, and if $n \ge 3$, then $f$ is completely implementable

---

6. For technical reasons, often mechanisms are used that also comprise the statement of an integer (see appendix B).

*Demonstration*   It is easy to see that the monotonicity of $f$ is a necessary condition. First, assume that $f$ is not monotone; then there exist two utility profiles $U$ and $U'$ and a choice $a$ such that

- $a \in f(U)$
- $\forall i = 1, \ldots, n, L_i(a, U'_i) \supset L_i(a, U_i)$
- $a \notin f(U')$

If $f$ is completely implementable, there exist a mechanism $(M, g)$ and a Nash equilibrium $m^*$ of that mechanism for the profile $U$ such that $g(m^*) = a$. One deduces from this that for every $i$ and $m'_i$,

$$U_i(a) \geq U_i\left[g\left(m'_i, m^*_{-i}\right)\right]$$

But since $L_i(a, U'_i) \supset L_i(a, U_i)$, one gets for every $i$ and $m'_i$,

$$U'_i(a) \geq U'_i\left[g\left(m'_i, m^*_{-i}\right)\right]$$

which shows that $a = g(m^*)$ remains a Nash equilibrium for $U'$, and therefore contradicts the hypothesis that $a \notin f(U')$. □

The construction of the mechanism that implements $f$ when the latter verifies the sufficient conditions is a bit more complex; it is given in appendix B.

Note that when there are two agents, the implementation is more difficult. The mechanism found by Maskin is based on the detection of an agent who makes a false statement upon the confrontation of all statements. When there are conflicting statements from only two agents, it is obviously considerably more difficult to identify the agent who cheats.[7] In other respects the NVP condition is very strong with two agents. It is easy to see that when there are three or more agents, the NVP condition is rather weak, quite simply because it is rare that two agents' preferred choices coincide.[8]

The opposite can be observed in the condition of monotonicity. Take the example of the construction and financing of a bridge. The utility profile is summed up in a $n$-tuple of provisions to pay for the bridge. We start from a profile such that the bridge is constructed and financed according to some nonrandom apportioning of costs, and suppose that

---

7. Moore and Repullo (1990) study the case of $n = 2$; they also give a necessary and sufficient (albeit a bit complicated) condition when $n \geq 3$.

8. If, as in the example of an exchange economy of private goods, each agent covets the economy's resources, then the NVP condition is satisfied rather trivially.

the propensity to pay of agent $i$ increases. Then monotonicity imposes that the bridge construction continue (fortunately!) but above all that the division of costs remain the same—which doesn't seem very reasonable. This difficulty is present in all problems involving a redistributive element.

Moore's (1992) excellent review provides another example.[9] It is the biblical case where monotonicity is violated by Solomon's famous judgment (I Kings 3:16–28). Solomon's solution falls under Nash equilibrium implementation, since each woman knows who is the real mother. His solution, which consisted in threatening to cut the baby in two, is not entirely foolproof: What would he have done if the impostor had had the presence of mind to scream like a real mother? We will attempt to reexamine Solomon's dilemma via our general framework.

Two women quarrel over the baby: Anne and Beatrice. There are two states: state $\alpha$, where Anne is the real mother, and state $\beta$, where it is Beatrice. Solomon has three possibilities: give the baby to Anne ($a$), give it to Beatrice ($b$), or kill it ($t$). He would of course like to implement the SCF $f$ which gives the baby to its real mother: $f(\alpha) = a$ and $f(\beta) = b$. The following are the individual preferences that correspond to the biblical parable:

- For Anne,

  in state $\alpha$: $a \succ b \succ t$

  in state $\beta$: $a \succ t \succ b$
- For Beatrice,

  in state $\alpha$: $b \succ t \succ a$

  in state $\beta$: $b \succ a \succ t$

Each woman wishes, above all, to get the baby. If she is the mother, she prefers to give the baby away rather than see it die. In the opposite case, she would prefer the baby's death to its being given to her rival.

Note that $f(\alpha) = a$ and that $a$ is better placed for Anne and Beatrice under $\beta$ than under $\alpha$. According to the condition of monotonicity, one should therefore get $f(\beta) = a$, which is obviously not what we want. The SCF then is not monotone, and by the necessary condition of the Maskin theorem, it is not implementable in Nash equilibrium. Solomon's judgment is a more difficult problem than it appears in reading the Bible.

---

9. Adapted from Glazer and Ma (1989).

If the reader finds this example to be a bit far-fetched, here is another, borrowed from Moulin (1988, ch. 9). Consider the method of the two-round election (which well defines an SCF $f$ when the agents vote sincerely), such as is used for presidential elections in France, for example. In such a vote, the two best-placed candidates after the first ballot face each other in a second round. Suppose that there are three candidates $a$, $b$, and $c$ and 17 electors. The preferences $U$ are

- $a > b > c$ for 6 electors
- $c > a > b$ for 5 electors
- $b > c > a$ for 4 electors
- $b > a > c$ for 2 electors

With these preferences, $a$, $b$, and $c$ receive, respectively, 6, 6, and 5 votes in the first round, which eliminates $c$. In the second round, $a$ is elected by 11 votes against 6 for $b$. In our notation then we have $a \in f(U)$. Now change the preferences of the last group of two electors to $a > b > c$. This causes $a$ to come back up in the new preferences $U'$, and $a$ should then always be elected if $f$ is monotone. However, this is not the case; now $a$ wins 8 votes, $b$ 4 votes, and $c$ 5 votes in the first round, which eliminates $b$; and $c$ is elected over $a$ by 9 votes against 8 in the second round, even though the relative majority of $a$ in the first round increased. Incidentally, this enables us to illustrate the possibilities of manipulation in such an election method: If the preferences are given by $U$ and if the voters of the first two groups and of the last group vote sincerely, the four electors of the third group (whose preferred candidate $b$ does not survive the first ballot if they vote sincerely) have every interest in voting for $c$ in the first round, which permits them to avoid the election of $a$, to whom they prefer $c$.

A last example is: Can the Walrasian equilibrium be implemented in Nash equilibrium? It can be shown that in an exchange economy with convex preferences, every completely implementable SCF must contain the correspondence of Walrasian equilibria. Can this be taken further, in other words, to implement this correspondence and nothing but? Without going into details, the response is globally positive.

## 4.3 Refinements of the Nash Equilibrium

If the situation is therefore more encouraging in Nash equilibrium than in dominant strategy equilibrium, some negative results remain. To overcome them, recent research (see Moore 1992 and Palfrey 1998) has shown interest in refining the Nash equilibrium concept, in particular, using subgame perfect equilibrium.[10] Moore and Repullo (1988) show that the condition of monotonicity necessary (and nearly sufficient) for subgame perfect implementation is much weaker than for implementation in Nash equilibrium, to the point that in economic environments, "almost anything can be implemented".[11] One gets a comparable result by using an equilibrium concept that eliminates weakly dominated strategies (Palfrey and Srivastava 1991).[12]

One problem with the mechanisms used is that they are sometimes based on methods that do not seem very realistic (like stating an integer). Still one can often exploit the particular characteristics of an implementation problem to construct simpler mechanisms (e.g., see Jackson, Palfrey, and Srivastava 1994). Virtual implementation, which is content to implement approximately a social choice function, also seems to be a path of fruitful research (see Abreu and Sen 1991. The underlying idea is that if $f$ is not monotone, quite often there exists a lottery $\tilde{f}$ "close" to $f$ which is monotone.[13]

Another drawback of certain mechanisms is that they do not resist renegotiation. During implementation of the mechanism, it is possible that the agents find themselves in a situation where they would prefer, by mutual agreement, to modify the mechanism so as to implement an allocation preferred by all. In such situations it is difficult to see what can keep agents from renegotiating. If they do renegotiate, the incentive properties of the mechanism will be modified. Maskin and Moore (1999) characterize the SCFs that can be implemented by a renegotiation-proof mechanism.

### 4.4   Bayesian Equilibrium

The most simple justification in considering implementation in Nash equilibrium concerns situations where every agent knows the identity of all other agents. Without going that far, it is reasonable to assume

---

10. In a game with several stages, a Nash equilibrium is subgame perfect if it induces a Nash equilibrium in each subgame, even out of the equilibrium path. This equilibrium concept permits us to eliminate noncredible threats and therefore reduce the multiplicity of equilibria.

11. This still does not solve the problem of Solomon's judgment.

12. Now the judgment of Solomon is implementable.

13. It is nevertheless possible that $\tilde{f}$ puts weight on suboptimal choices.

that each agent possesses probabilist "beliefs" on the utilities of the others. To simplify the notation, we assume that the utility function of an agent is known up to one parameter: The utility of agent $i$ is thus $U_i(a, \theta_i)$. All agents (and the government) know that the vector of the "types," $\theta = (\theta_1, \ldots, \theta_n)$, is distributed according to a $q(\theta)$ a priori on a set $\Theta$, which I will assume to be finite. Every agent knows his type $\theta_i$ and can therefore compute the conditional distribution of the types of the other agents:

$$q(\theta_{-i} \mid \theta_i) = \frac{q(\theta_i, \theta_{-i})}{\sum_{\theta'_{-i}} q(\theta_i, \theta'_{-i})}$$

As is usual, a mechanism is a pair $(M, g)$. An equilibrium in Bayesian strategies will be a $n$-tuple of strategies $\sigma_i^*(\theta_i)$ such that for all $i$, $\theta_i$, and $m_i$,

$$\sum_{\theta_{-i}} q(\theta_{-i} \mid \theta_i) U_i \left\{ g \left[ \sigma_i^*(\theta_i), \sigma_{-i}^*(\theta_{-i}) \right], \theta_i \right\} \geq \sum_{\theta_{-i}} q(\theta_{-i} \mid \theta_i) U_i \left\{ g \left[ m_i, \sigma_{-i}^*(\theta_{-i}) \right], \theta_i \right\}$$

It is therefore, so to speak, a Nash equilibrium "in expectation."

It is easily shown that the principle of revelation applies here again: Anything that is implementable is implementable in revealing direct mechanisms, where each agent truthfully announces his type in equilibrium. (Interested readers can refer to Palfrey 1992 or Palfrey-Srivastava 1993 for a study of Bayesian implementation.) For implementation in Nash equilibrium, the central difficulty is to eliminate parasite equilibria. Here again, a property of monotonicity is necessary (and nearly sufficient) for complete implementation.

## 4.5  Appendix A: Proof of the Gibbard-Satterthwaite Theorem

Several proofs of the Gibbard-Satterthwaite theorem exist. The proof presented here is due to Schmeidler-Sonnenschein (1978). It has the advantage of bringing to light a close relationship to Arrow's theorem.

To simplify the exposition, we will return to the notation used in pre-orders of preferences. Thus $aP_ib$ means that $i$ strictly prefers $a$ to $b$. We will also assume that the individual preferences are all strict, in other words, that there is never a situation of indifference. For all $i$, $a$ and $b$, one gets perforce $aP_ib$ or $bP_ia$ (this hypothesis is hardly restrictive if $A$ is finite).

Recall that the revelation principle allows us to limit ourselves to direct mechanisms $(\mathcal{P}, f)$. We want to prove that if such a mechanism is revealing, then $f$ is dictatorial. We say that $f$ is *manipulable* by $i$ in $P$ if and only if $P_i'$ exists such that

$$f(P_i', P_{-i})P_i f(P)$$

put differently, it behooves $i$ to lie. A manipulable mechanism of course cannot be revealing.

The demonstration comprises two lemmas; it consists of starting from an implementable SCF $f$ (which is implementable by a direct mechanism, therefore, and is not manipulable) and of constructing from it an SWF $F$ that verifies Arrow's conditions. One concludes from this that $F$ is dictatorial, which implies that $f$ also is.

LEMMA 1    Suppose that $f(P) = a_1$ and $f(P_i', P_{-i}) = a_2$, where $a_2 \neq a_1$. Then

1. $f$ is manipulable by $i$ in $(P_i', P_{-i})$ if $a_1 P_i' a_2$
2. $f$ is manipulable by $i$ in $P$ if $a_2 P_i a_1$

*Proof*   In both cases it is sufficient to write the definition of manipulability.                                                                              □

We will need the notation $P_i^j$, which, for a profile $P$ and given agents $i < j$, will represent the vector $(P_i, \ldots, P_j)$.

LEMMA 2    Let $B$ be a subset of the image of $f$ and $P$ a profile such that

$$\forall a_1 \in B, \ \forall a_2 \notin B, \ \ \forall i = 1, \ldots, n, \ a_1 P_i a_2$$

Then $f(P) \in B$.

*Proof*   This can be shown by contradiction. Let $a_2 = f(P)$, and suppose that $a_2 \notin B$. Let $P'$ be a profile such that $f(P') = a_1 \in B$ (such a profile does exist, since $B$ is included in the image of $f$ and given the universal domain hypothesis). Now construct a sequence $(a_3^i)_{i=0,\ldots,n}$ by

- $a_3^0 = a_2 \notin B$
- for $i = 1, \ldots, n - 1, a_3^i = f(P_1'^i, P_{i+1}^n)$
- $a_3^n = a_1 \in B$

Let $j$ be the first integer such that $a_3^j \in B$. We then get

- $f(P_1'^j, P_{j+1}^n) = a_3^j \in B$
- $f(P_1'^{j-1}, P_j^n) = a_3^{j-1} \notin B$

and by the hypothesis of the lemma, $a_3^i P_i a_3^{i-1}$. Lemma 1 then implies that $f$ is manipulable. □

Now construct an SWF $F$. Let $P$ be any profile and $a_1$, $a_2$ two choices in $A$. Define a new profile (using UD) $\tilde{P}$ such that for each $i$,

- $\tilde{P}_i$ coincides with $P_i$ on $\{a_1, a_2\}$
- $\tilde{P}_i$ coincides with $P_i$ on $A - \{a_1, a_2\}$
- $\{a_1, a_2\}$ is placed at the top of the preferences $\tilde{P}_i$

(Strictly speaking, $\tilde{P}$ of course depends on $a_1$ and $a_2$, and the notation should reflect this.)

Lemma 2 implies that $f(\tilde{P}) \in \{a_1, a_2\}$ (taking $B = \{a_1, a_2\}$ and replacing $P$ by $\tilde{P}$ in the statement of the lemma). $F$ can therefore be defined by

$$a_1 F(P) a_2 \Leftrightarrow f(\tilde{P}) = a_1$$

Now we can verify Arrow's conditions:

- There are surely at least three choices.
- $F$ is, by construction, of universal domain.
- $F$ satisfies the Pareto principle: if for every $i$, $a_1 P_i a_2$, then $a_1$ is at the top of all preferences $\tilde{P}_i$. By taking $B = \{a_1, a_2\}$ in the statement of lemma 2, we indeed get $f(\tilde{P}) = a_1$.
- $F$ satisfies IIA: if this were not the case, there would exist $P$, $P'$, $a_1$ and $a_2$ such that

for every $i$, $a_1 P_i a_2 \Leftrightarrow a_1 P'_i a_2$

$a_1 F(P) a_2$ and $a_2 F(P) a_1$

Now define a sequence $(a_3^i)_{i=0,\dots,n}$ by

$$a_3^0 = a_1$$

for $i = 1, \dots, n-1$, $a_3^i = f(\tilde{P}_1^{\prime i}, \tilde{P}_{i+1}^n)$

$$a_3^n = a_2$$

Lemma 2 implies that $a_3^i \in \{a_1, a_2\}$ for every $i$. Therefore let $j$ be the first integer such that $a_3^j = a_2$. This gives $f(\tilde{P}_1^{\prime j}, \tilde{P}_{j+1}^n) = a_2$ and $f(\tilde{P}_1^{\prime j-1}, \tilde{P}_j^n) = a_1$. Now one of two things can result:

$a_1 P_j a_2$

This implies $a_1P_j'a_2$ and therefore $a_1\tilde{P}_j'a_2$, so lemma 1 implies that $f$ is manipulable.

$a_2P_ja_1$

This implies $a_2\tilde{P}_ja_1$, so lemma 1 again implies that $f$ is manipulable.

But there is contradiction in both results: for every $P$, $F(P)$ is clearly a complete and asymmetrical binary relation. What remains for us is to verify that it is transitive.

Take the opposite case so that we have a cycle on a triplet $\{a_1, a_2, a_3\}$. For every $i$, let $P_i'$ which coincides with $P_i$ on $\{a_1, a_2, a_3\}$ and on $A - \{a_1, a_2, a_3\}$ be such that $\{a_1, a_2, a_3\}$ is at the top of $P'_i$ (using UD). Lemma 2 implies that $f(P') \in \{a_1, a_2, a_3\}$; without any loss of generality, we can assume that $f(P') = a_1$. Since $F(P)$ has a cycle on $\{a_1, a_2, a_3\}$, we necessarily get $a_2F(P)a_1$ or $a_3F(P)a_1$. Here again, without loss of generality, we can assume that $a_3F(P)a_1$. Now modify $P'$ in $P''$ by making $a_2$ move into third place in each individual preference ($P''$ is admissible by UD). Note that $a_3P_ia_1$ if and only if $a_3P_i''a_1$; in applying IIA (which we have just shown is satisfied), we get $a_3F(P'')a_1$, which again implies $a_3 = f(P'')$.

At the risk of seeming redundant, we now define a sequence $(a_4^i)_{i=0,...,n}$ by

$a_4^0 = a_1$

for $i = 1,..., n-1$, $a_3^i = f\left(\tilde{P}_1''^i, \tilde{P}_{i+1}'^n\right)$

$a_4^n = a_3$

Lemma 2 implies that $a_4^i \in \{a_1, a_2, a_3\}$ for every $i$. Therefore let $j$ be the first integer such that $a_4^i \neq a_1$. One of two things results:

$a_4^j = a_2$

but $a_1P_j''a_2$, since $a_2$ is only in third position in $P_j''$. Therefore $f(\tilde{P}_1''^{j-1}, \tilde{P}_j'^n)P_j''f(\tilde{P}_1''^j, \tilde{P}_{j+1}'^n)$, so $f$ is manipulable.

$a_4^j = a_3$

Now, if $a_1P_j'a_3$, we also have $a_1P_j''a_3$. Therefore $f(\tilde{P}_1''^{j-1}, \tilde{P}_j'^n)P_j''f(\tilde{P}_1''^j, \tilde{P}_{j+1}'^n)$, and $f$ is manipulable. If $a_3P_j'a_1$, we directly get $f(\tilde{P}_1''^j, \tilde{P}_{j+1}'^n)P_j'f(\tilde{P}_1''^{j-1}, \tilde{P}_j'^n)$, and $f$ is still manipulable. We are led therefore to a contradiction in every case, which shows that $F(P)$ is transitive.

Since $F$ verifies all of Arrow's conditions, $F$ must be dictatorial; let $i$ be the dictator. Let $P$ be any profile and arrange the choices in such a way that $a_1 P_i a_2 P_i \ldots$ Since $i$ is the dictator, more precisely we have $a_1 F(P) a_2$ and therefore $f(\tilde{P}) = a_1$. But, by construction, $\tilde{P}$ coincides with $P$ and $f(P)$ is therefore $a_1$, the preferred choice of $i$, which concludes the proof showing that $i$ is also a dictator for $f$. $\square$

### 4.6 Appendix B: Proof of Maskin's Theorem

Recall from the text the necessity of monotonicity. To see the (near) reciprocal, we can depend on the simplest construction of Maskin's mechanism, which is due to Repullo (1987).

In Repullo's mechanism the message $m_i$ sent by each agent consists of

- a statement $U_i$ of the utility profile
- a choice $a_i$
- an integer $k_i \in \mathbb{N}$

The allocation procedure $g$ consists of two rules:

1. If there is a $i$ such that for each $j \neq i$, $m_j = (U, a, k)$, then $g(m)$ is $a_i$ if $a_i \in L_i(a, U_i)$ and $a$ if not.

2. Otherwise, $g(m) = a_i$, where $i$ is the smallest integer such that $k_i = \max_{j=1,\ldots,n} k_j$.

This mechanism deserves some explanations. First note that it does implement $f$ weakly: $U$ is the true profile, $a \in f(U)$, and $k$ is any integer. The statement $(U, a, k)$ by all agents ends in $g(m) = a$, and it is clearly a Nash equilibrium: if an agent $i$ deviates, the first rule of $g$ applies, and the implemented choice is either $a$ or the statement $i$ if the latter is less favorable. It is in no one's interest to lie; any unilateral deviation is sanctioned.

The second rule of $g$ is more subtle; it comes into play if there are at least three different statements. The effect is called an *integer game*. Each agent, in order to win, must announce the largest possible integer, which is of course an impossible task.

Now let us prove that every Nash equilibrium implements $f$. Let $U$ be the true utility profile and $m$ a corresponding Nash equilibrium. We will use a familiar lemma:

LEMMA    If $m$ is a Nash equilibrium for $U$ and $g(m) = a$, let $m'_i$ be a deviation of $i$ such that $g(m'_i, m_{-i}) = b$. Then $b \in L_i(a, U_i)$.

Proof   Since $m$ is a Nash equilibrium for $U$, we have, in particular,

$$U_i[g(m)] \geq U_i[g(m'_i, m_{-i})]$$

which is the definition of $b \in L_i(a, U_i)$.                                      □

Three cases may present themselves:

• All agents announce the same $m_i = (U', a, k)$ with $a \in f(U')$. By rule 1, we have $g(m) = a$, so we want to prove that $a \in f(U)$. Let $b \in L_i(a, U'_i)$, so the new message for $i$ is $m'_i = (U', b, k)$. Then $g(m'_i, m_{-i}) = b$ by rule 1. Now, since $m$ is a Nash equilibrium for $U$, the lemma implies that $b \in L_i(a, U_i)$. From this we can conclude that $L_i(a, U_i) \supset L_i(a, U'_i)$, so the monotonicity of $f$ indeed implies that $a \in f(U)$.

• All agents announce a same $m_i = (U', a, k)$, but $a \notin f(U')$. Let $b$ be any choice of an agent $i$ whose deviation is $m'_i = (U', b, k')$, where $k' > \min_{j \neq i} k_j$. Rule 2 applies, and $g(m'_i, m_{-i}) = b$. By the lemma above, we get $b \in L_i(a, U_i)$. Since $b$ and $i$ are unconstrained, $a$ is the preferred choice of all the agents under $U$, and NVP implies that $a \in f(U)$.

• In all other cases, two agents may send different messages. We can call them 1 and 2, without loss of generality. Let $i > 2$, $b \in A$, and the deviation $m'_i = (U, b, k')$, where $k' > \min_{j \neq i} k_j$. Rule 2 applies, and $g(m'_i, m_{-i}) = b$. The lemma implies that $b \in L_i(g(m), U_i)$, and $g(m)$ is therefore the preferred choice of all the agents $i \neq 1, 2$ under $U$. In order to apply NVP, we must prove that $g(m)$ is also the preferred choice of either 1 or 2. To do this, let $i \neq 1, 2$; we inevitably get $m_i \neq m_1$ or $m_i \neq m_2$. Without loss of generality, we can assume that $m_i \neq m_1$. Now consider a deviation $m'_2 = (U, b, k')$ for 2, where $b$ is any choice and $k' > \min_{j \neq 2} k_j$. The application of rule 2 gives $g(m'_2, m_{-2}) = b$, and the lemma gives $b \in L_2(g(m), U_2)$. NVP can therefore be used to show that $g(m) \in f(U)$.

To conclude, we have proved that if $m$ is a Nash equilibrium for $U$, then we inevitably get $g(m) \in f(U)$. We can deduce from this fact that the mechanism constructed above completely implements $f$.                    □

# Bibliography

Abreu, D., and A. Sen. 1991. Virtual implementation in Nash equilibrium. *Econometrica* 59: 997–1021.

Arrow, K. 1951. *Social Choice and Individual Values.* New York: Wiley.

Gibbard, A. 1973. Manipulation of voting schemes: A general result. *Econometrica* 41: 587–601.

Glazer, J., and C.-T. Ma. 1989. Efficient allocation of a prize—King Solomon's dilemma. *Games and Economic Behaviour* 1: 223–33.

Hurwicz, L. 1986. Incentive aspects of decentralization. In K. Arrow and M. D. Intriligator, eds., *Handbook of Mathematical Economics*, vol. 3. North-Holland, Amsterdam.

Jackson, M., T. Palfrey, and S. Srivastava. 1994. Undominated Nash implementation in bounded mechanisms. *Games and Economic Behavior* 6: 474–501.

Maskin, E. 1977. Nash equilibrium and welfare optimality. Published in the *Review of Economic Studies* (1999), 66: 23–38.

Maskin, E., and J. Moore. 1999. Implementation and renegotiation. *Review of Economic Studies* 66: 39–56.

Moore, J. 1992. Implementation, contracts, and renegotiation in environments with complete information. In J.-J. Laffont, ed., *Advances in Economic Theory*, vol. 1. Cambridge: Cambridge University Press.

Moore, J., and R. Repullo. 1990. Nash implementation: A full characterization. *Econometrica* 58: 1083–99.

Moore, J., and R. Repullo. 1988. Subgame perfect implementation. *Econometrica* 56: 1191–220.

Moulin, H. 1988. *Axioms of Cooperative Decision Making.* Cambridge: Cambridge University Press.

Myerson, R. 1979. Incentive compatibility and the bargaining problem. *Econometrica* 47: 61–73.

Palfrey, T. 1992. Implementation in Bayesian equilibria: The multiple equilibrium problem in mechanism design. In J.-J. Laffont, ed., *Advances in Economic Theory*, vol. 1. Cambridge: Cambridge University Press.

Palfrey, T. 1998. Implementation theory. In R. Aumann and S. Hart, eds., *The Handbook of Game Theory*, vol. 3. Amsterdam: North-Holland.

Palfrey, T., and S. Srivastava. 1991. Nash implementation using undominated strategies. *Econometrica* 59: 479–501.

Palfrey, T., and S. Srivastava. 1993. *Bayesian Implementation.* New York: Harwood Academic.

Repullo, R. 1987. A simple proof of Maskin's theorem on Nash implementation. *Social Choice and Welfare* 4: 39–41.

Satterthwaite, M. 1975. Strategy-proofness and Arrow's conditions: Existence and correspondence theorems for voting procedures and social welfare functions. *Journal of Economic Theory* 10: 187–217.

Schmeidler, D., and H. Sonnenschein. 1978. Two proofs of the Gibbard-Satterthwaite theorem on the possibility of a strategy-proof social choice function. In H. Gottinger and W. Ensler, eds., *Proceedings of a Conference on Decision Theory and Social Ethics at Schloss Reisenberg.* Dordrecht: Reidel.

# II    Public Economics

The next three chapters highlight public economics, but they do not exhaust this domain. Traditionally public economics is defined as "the positive and normative study of government action over the economy." This definition is probably too wide, since it seems to include, for example, the analysis of macroeconomic policies. My objective is much more limited. For one thing, I will confine myself to microeconomic aspects of the subject; for another, I will discuss taxation and the effects of public spending only as potential remedies for market failures. Therefore my approach will treat rather what is called *welfare economics*.

I will give little room to taxation questions, which really deserve an entire book. For these issues I could do no better than advise the interested reader to refer to the works of Atkinson-Stiglitz (1980) or Myles (1995), or to that of Stiglitz (1988) for a less formal approach.

## Bibliography

Atkinson, A., and J. Stiglitz. 1980. *Lectures on Public Economics*. New York: McGraw-Hill.

Myles, G. 1995. *Public Economics*. Cambridge: Cambridge University Press.

Stiglitz, J. 1988. *Economics of the Public Sector*. New York: Norton.

# 5          Public Goods

The private goods that so far have been the theme of this book possess two properties that distinguish them. The first is that these goods are *rivals*: consumption by an agent reduces the possibilities of consumption by other agents (usually to nothing). For example, if I eat an apple, no other agent can consume it after me. The second is *economic*. Private goods are subject to *exclusion*, in other words, it is necessary to pay to consume them.

There are other types of goods that do not necessarily possess these properties. A nonrival good is called a public good. *Pure public goods*, which are at the heart of this chapter, are therefore nonrival by definition; moreover they are not subject to exclusion.[1] The standard example concerns the services of national defense, the police, or emission standards for air quality.

Of course there are numerous intermediary cases. Thus research protected by a patent is subject to exclusion, since a royalty must be paid to access it, but it is nonrival, since several agents can buy the rights. A similar situation exists with coded or cable television or with a toll road.[2] The opposite is the case of a free parking space which is a good without exclusion (because it is free) but a rival good (because two cars cannot occupy it simultaneously). On the other hand, many public goods are submitted to external effects (see chapter 6). Take highways congested by heavy traffic, for example; clearly, their use value diminishes. We will dismiss these complications in this chapter; our interest in pure public goods suffices to relieve us of the particularities of public goods in general.

---

1. It is sometimes also assumed that their use is obligatory: no agent can choose not to consume them.
2. This type of good is often called a *club good*.

The reader should not confuse public goods and publicly provided private goods. To explain the latter case, in many countries (a large part of) education and health care are provided by the public sector. Education is not a public good: one can make access to it exclusive by asking that a tuition be paid, and it is a rival good insofar as the cost of educating an extra child is not negligible. The same can be said about health care. This does not mean that there is no market failure in education or health care but rather that such failures are due to external effects. For example, contagion for health and the positive social effect of a well-educated population.

The most simple test for determining whether a good is a public good consists of asking

• whether its use can be rationed (i.e., whether it can be denied a given agent)

• whether it is desirable to ration it (whether, on the contrary, the marginal cost of an additional consumer is zero; then, as we will see in chapter 7, the price of the good should be zero at the optimum)

The good is public if the response to both questions is negative. This test is not perfectly foolproof, but it permits us to forge a reasonable idea of what is a public good. The reader will verify that education and health do not pass the test.

## 5.1 The Optimality Condition

This section studies Pareto optima in an economy that comprises public goods. To simplify things, we will consider an economy where only two goods exist: a private good $x$ (e.g., which may aggregate all private goods) and a public good $z$. The consumer $i = 1, \ldots, n$ has a utility function $U_i(x_i, z_i)$ that is assumed to be increasing in its two arguments. The public good is produced from the private good according to a technology given by $z = f(x)$, where $f$ is increasing and concave. The initial resources of the economy boil down to $X$ units of the private good.

The big difference between public and private goods resides in the scarcity constraints. Assume that a quantity $x$ of private good is set aside to produce a quantity $z$ of public good. Then, as usual, the scarcity constraint for the private good expresses that the sum of consumptions must not exceed what remains of the private good, or

$$\sum_{i=1}^{n} x_i \leq X - x$$

On the other hand, the consumption of $i$ in public goods is limited only by the total disposable quantity since the public good is by definition nonrival. One therefore gets

$$\forall i = 1, \ldots, n, \quad z_i \leq z$$

One obtains, as usual, the Pareto optima by fixing the utility of the last $n - 1$ consumers and by maximizing the utility of $i = 1$ under the feasibility constraints, or

$$\begin{cases} \max_{\substack{x_1, \ldots, x_n, x \\ z_1, \ldots, z_n, z}} \quad U_1(x_1, z_1) \\ \\ \quad \forall i = 2, \ldots, n, \quad U_i(x_i, z_i) \geq \overline{U}_i \\ \quad \sum_{i=1}^{n} x_i \leq X - x \\ \quad \forall i = 1, \ldots, n, \quad z_i \leq z \\ \quad z \leq f(x) \end{cases}$$

Recall that in this program $x$ represents the quantity of the private good set aside for the production of the public good and $z$ the quantity of the public good produced. Since utility functions are increasing, one gets $\forall i = 1, \ldots, n, z_i = z = f(x)$. Hereafter we will denote $g$ the cost in the private good for the production of the public good:

$$z = f(x) \Leftrightarrow x = g(z)$$

Obviously $g$ is an increasing and convex function. The program is then simplified to

$$\begin{cases} \max_{x_1, \ldots, x_n, z} \quad U_1(x_1, z_1) \\ \quad \forall i = 2, \ldots, n, \quad U_i(x_i, z_i) \geq \overline{U}_i \quad (\lambda_i) \\ \quad \sum_{i=1}^{n} x_i \leq X - g(z) \quad\quad (\mu) \end{cases}$$

where the $\lambda_i$ and $\mu$ are multipliers attached to different constraints. The Lagrangean can be written

$$\mathcal{L} = U_1(x_1, z) + \sum_{i=2}^{n} \lambda_i (U_i(x_i, z) - \overline{U}_i) + \mu \left( X - g(z) - \sum_{i=1}^{n} x_i \right)$$

Normalizing $\lambda_1 = 1$ to make the formulas symmetrical, the first-order conditions are

$$\begin{cases} \sum_{i=1}^{n} \lambda_i \dfrac{\partial U_i}{\partial z} = g'(z) \\ \lambda_i \dfrac{\partial U_i}{\partial x_i} = \mu, \quad \forall i = 1, \dots, n \end{cases}$$

From the second group of conditions we can derive

$$\lambda_i = \frac{\mu}{\partial U_i / \partial x_i}$$

whence, by substituting in the first condition the Pareto-optimality condition which sets the level of public good production,

$$\sum_{i=1}^{n} \frac{\partial U_i / \partial z}{\partial U_i / \partial x_i} = g'(z) = \frac{1}{f'(x)} \qquad \text{(BLS)}$$

The expression above is called the *Bowen-Lindahl-Samuelson condition*, which we will denote (BLS) (see Samuelson 1954).

Notice that

$$\frac{\partial U_i / \partial z}{\partial U_i / \partial x_i} = -\frac{dx_i}{dz}\bigg|_{U_i}$$

is simply the marginal rate of substitution of consumer $i$, that is, his propensity for sacrificing his private good consumption to instigate growth in the level of his public good consumption. But as an increase of public good production by definition benefits all consumers, its marginal cost $g'(z)$ must be compared to the sum of all propensities for paying, not to that of a sole consumer as the case would be for a private good. One must therefore equalize marginal cost and the sum of propensities to pay, which is the aim of the (BLS) condition.[3]

The rest of this chapter will be devoted to examining different modes of economic organization which are liable to lead to a Pareto-optimal allocation a priori.

## 5.2  Implementing the Optimum

To simplify notation in what follows, we will take the private good as the numéraire; that is, its price will be normalized to one.

---

3. The careful reader will note that we have only used nonrivalry to achieve the (BLS) condition.

## 5.2.1    The Subscription Equilibrium

The first solution to consider consists of asking consumers to subscribe part of their wealth to contribute to public good production. Assume that the wealth of consumer $i$ is $R_i$. He can then subscribe $s_i$ to public good production, thus consuming $x_i = R_i - s_i$ private good units. The total quantity of public good produced will be simply $f(\Sigma_{i=1}^n s_i)$.

The choice of $i$ of the quantity $s_i$ is made according to the principles of the Nash equilibrium: $i$ will take the quantity subscribed by other consumers $s_{-i}$ as given and will resolve the program

$$
\begin{cases}
\max_{x_i, s_i, z} \; U_i(x_i, z) \\
\quad x_i + s_i = R_i \\
\quad z = f\left(\sum_{i=1}^n s_j\right)
\end{cases}
$$

or again, after obvious simplifications,

$$
\max_{s_i} U_i\left[R_i - s_i, f\left(s_i + \sum_{j \neq i} s_j\right)\right]
$$

This leads to

$$
\frac{\partial U_i / \partial z}{\partial U_i / \partial x_i} = \frac{1}{f'\left(\sum_{j=1}^n s_j\right)}
$$

which clearly does not coincide with the optimality condition (BLS). In effect, when a consumer decides to subscribe to the public good, he takes into account only the increase of his own consumption of public good. In his calculations he neglects the subsequent growth of the utility of all other consumers, so the equilibrium cannot be optimal. Under reasonable conditions, subscription equilibrium leads to a sub-production of public good which is all the larger when consumers are more numerous.

## 5.2.2    Voting Equilibrium

A variant of the preceding procedure consists in asking the agents to vote for their preferred level of public good.[4] To simplify things,

---

4. Historically this procedure was the first proposed by economists having studied public goods; in particular, it was studied by Bowen.

suppose that the public good is produced at a constant marginal cost, that is, $g'(z) = c$ for every $z$. It is conceivable to have a mechanism by which each consumer announces a public good level $z_i$ knowing that public good production is $Z(z_1, \ldots, z_n)$ and that its financing will be distributed following a scheme $t_i(z_1, \ldots, z_n)$. Such a mechanism would give rise to all of the difficulties set out in chapter 4. We will limit ourselves here to a simpler approach. It will be supposed, though it may be irrational, that each consumer believes it is his statement that will determine the level of public good production, and that the production cost will then be distributed equally among all the consumers. Therefore each consumer chooses $z_i$ in such a way as to maximize

$$F_i(z_i) = U_i\left( R_i - \frac{cz_i}{n}, z_i \right)$$

It is easy to verify that if $U$ is concave in its two arguments, $F_i$ is equally concave and thus unimodal. The analyses in the first part of this book show that the voting equilibrium consists, for planning purposes, of choosing the median agent's preferred level of production. With $m$ as the median agent, the retained level of production is therefore $z_m$ such that $F'_m(z_m) = 0$. So after these immediate substitutions we have

$$\frac{\partial U_m/\partial z}{\partial U_m/\partial x_m}\left( R_m - \frac{cz_m}{n}, z_m \right) = \frac{c}{n}$$

This result of course does not coincide with the BLS condition, except in the miraculous case where the marginal rate of substitution of the median agent is equal to the average of the marginal rates of substitution of all consumers. Still, note that contrary to the subscription equilibrium, the voting equilibrium does not necessarily lead to a subproduction of the public good: the direction of the comparison depends on fine characteristics of the distribution of the marginal rates of substitution.

### 5.2.3   The Lindahl Equilibrium

Assume that personalized prices for the public good can be established. Every consumer $i$ must pay $p_i$ per unit of public good that he consumes. The producer of the public good would then perceive a price $p = \sum_{i=1}^{n} p_i$ and produce up to the level where his marginal cost equals $p$:

$$g'(z) = p$$

Every consumer chooses to equate his marginal substitution rate to his personalized price:

$$\frac{\partial U_i/\partial z}{\partial U_i/\partial x_i} = p_i$$

At equilibrium the amount of public good in demand by each consumer must equal the amount produced, or

$$\forall i = 1, \ldots, n \quad z_i\left(p_i^*\right) = z\left(p^*\right)$$

From this result it is then deduced that

$$\sum_{i=1}^{n} \frac{\partial U_i/\partial z}{\partial U_i/\partial x_i} = \sum_{i=1}^{n} p_i = p = g'(z)$$

so the BLS condition is verified this time. Now the Lindahl equilibrium (so named after the Swedish economist who came up with the idea in 1919) leads to a Pareto optimum.[5]

The disadvantage to this process is that it assumes as a matter of fact the existence of $n$ "micromarkets" upon which a sole consumer buys the public good at his personalized price. In such circumstances it is difficult to maintain the competitive hypothesis unless one can assume that the consumers are divided in homogeneous groups from the point of view of their propensity to pay for the public good—one market (and one price) per group would then suffice. In the opposite case, it is in every consumer's interest to underestimate his demand, hoping that the others will be more honest and that the level of produced public good will then be high enough to meet his needs; this is the famous *free-rider* problem which was evidenced for the first time by Wicksell in 1896.

### 5.2.4 Personalized Taxation

Now suppose that every consumer $i$ is taxed by the state in terms of his consumption $z_i$ of public good: the budgetary constraint of the consumer $i$ then becomes

$$x_i + t_i(z_i) = R_i$$

---

5. It can be shown that the Lindahl equilibrium exists under the usual conditions and that each Pareto optimum is decentralizable in a Lindahl equilibrium.

The consumer then will equate his marginal rate of substitution with the private marginal cost of the public good, whence

$$\frac{\partial U_i / \partial z}{\partial U_i / \partial x_i} = t_i'(z_i)$$

If the state chooses taxes of the form $t_i(z_i) = p_i^* z_i$, where $p_i^*$ is the personalized price of $i$ in the Lindahl equilibrium, it is clear that the condition of optimality will hold. Unfortunately, this operation assumes that the state is privy to very detailed information about the tastes of all consumers, which in general is not realistic.[6] In practice, the financing of a public good is accomplished by fiscal resources which the state levies on agents (taxes on income, consumption, etc.). Insofar as these taxes bring on economic distortions and affect agents' decisions, the BLS condition must be modified. Under reasonable hypotheses, after taking into account the fiscal distortions, this *second-best* problem reduces the optimum production level of the public good.

### 5.2.5   A Planning Procedure

Malinvaud (1971) and Drèze and de la Vallée Poussin (1971) devised the MDP method by which a planning office could, without using decentralized information on consumers or even on the function of production of the public good, implement the Pareto optimum. Their procedure takes place in continuous time $t \in [0, +\infty]$. At each instant $t$, for a given allocation $(x_1(t), \dots , x_n(t), z(t))$,

• every consumer $i$ evaluates his marginal rate of substitution

$$S_i(t) = \frac{\partial U_i / \partial z}{\partial U_i / \partial x_i}(x_i(t), z(t))$$

and announces it to the planning office

---

6. In regard to implementation, it can still be shown that the Lindahl equilibrium (or personalized taxation) possesses properties comparable to those of the Walrasian equilibrium: it is not implementable in dominant strategy equilibria, but it is implementable in Nash equilibrium. However, the core of an economy comprising public goods is not reduced to the set of Lindahl equilibria when the number of consumers tends toward infinity. Since any coalition that decides to pull out of the game in order to constitute its own subeconomy sacrifices the contribution of other consumers to the financing of the public good, the core must be quite large.

- the company announces its marginal cost $g'(z(t))$
- the planning office readjusts the current allocation according to the differential equations

$$\begin{cases} z'(t) = \sum_{i=1}^{n} S_i(t) - g'(z(t)) \\ x_i'(t) = -S_i(t)z'(t) + \theta_i z'(t)^2 \quad \forall i = 1, \ldots, n \end{cases}$$

where the $\theta_i$ are positive constants whose sum equals 1

Let us try to interpret these differential equations. The right-hand side of the first equation is zero at the optimum, by the BLS condition. This equation describes therefore a process of trial and error by which the level of public good continually draws nearer to the optimum. As for the second group of equations, note that

$$x_i'(t) + S_i(t)z'(t) = \frac{dU_i/dt}{\partial U_i/\partial x_i}$$

So the differential system can be rewritten as

$$\frac{dU_i}{dt} = \frac{\partial U_i}{\partial x_i} \theta_i z'(t)^2$$

which shows that the utility of each consumer is an increasing function of time, and that the increase in social surplus is divided according to the choice of the $\theta_i$.

Let us show that the MDP method converges toward a Pareto optimum. For this we note first that every stationary point of the process (for which $z' = x_1' = \ldots = x_n' = 0$) is necessarily a Pareto optimum, since the BLS condition applies. Let the function

$$F(t) = \sum_{i=1}^{n} U_i(t)$$

The preceding expression shows that $F$ is an increasing function. However, $F$ cannot rise above a certain point (the economy's resources are finite). Finally $F'$ is only zero under BLS, that is when the system reaches a Pareto optimum. We deduce from this that $F$ is a Lyapounov function for the process, which therefore converges toward a Pareto optimum.

We can also prove that the MDP procedure is *neutral* in the sense that it favors no Pareto optimum: for every Pareto optimum, there exists a choice of constants $(\theta_i)$ that leads to that optimum.

This method assumes that the agents announce their characteristics without cheating. In fact it can be shown that even if the agents manipulate their statements, the statement of truth is a maximin strategy for each. In other words, to announce the truth is the best solution for an agent who is infinitely adverse to risk and who thus fears that the other agents will choose statements that are the most unfavorable for him. This property of course is not perfectly satisfying. We must conclude that in general, agents may well lie, and thus we put back into question the optimality of the process.

### 5.2.6   The Pivot Mechanism

We encountered in chapter 3 the Vickrey-Clarke-Groves (VCG) mechanism which permits implementation of an optimal social decision in a dominant strategy equilibrium when the utility functions are quasi-linear. Consider an indivisible public good of which 0 or 1 unit can be consumed (e.g., the decision to build a bridge) and for which the unit costs $C$. The utilities of the agents are assumed to be quasi-linear: if $x_i$ represents the consumption of the sole private good and $z$ that of the public good, we get

$$U_i(x_i, z) = x_i + u_i z$$

where $u_i$ is a parameter of propensity to pay for the public good which is known only by consumer $i$, who has initial resources $R_i$ in private good at his disposal.

The decision to build a bridge brings a benefit of $\Sigma_{i=1}^{n} u_i$ and a cost of $C$. In the Pareto optimum the bridge should be built if and only if the sum of propensities to pay exceeds the bridge's cost: $\Sigma_{i=1}^{n} u_i \geq C$.

A first possible mechanism consists of asking consumers to vote on the opportunity of building the bridge, knowing (for example) that each will contribute equally to its financing. Then the consumer $i$ will vote for the construction if and only if $u_i \geq C/n$. Let $F$ be the cumulative distribution function of the characteristics $u_i$ in the population. The bridge therefore will be constructed if and only if $F(C/n) \geq 1/2$, that is if $C/n$ does not exceed the median of $F$. The comparison with the Pareto-optimal decision rule immediately shows that this mechanism is only optimal if the median of $F$ coincides with its average, which has no particular reason to be true.[7]

---

7. If, for example, the $u_i$ are correlated with wealth $R_i$, they risk having an asymmetrical distribution, since it is known that the distribution of wealth has a median distinctly

Now I will present a direct revealing mechanism that implements this optimal decision rule. The intuition of this mechanism can be understood by referring to the theory of auctions. Assume an indivisible object is proposed to buyers $i = 1, \ldots, n$ whose propensities to pay $u_i$ are known only to themselves. First, consider a first price auction, where the winner (the one who bid the highest) pays the price he indicated. If any consumer $i$ announces a price $v_i$, he will have a utility $u_i - v_i$ if he wins and zero if not. He can then guarantee himself a positive utility in expectation by announcing a price $v_i$ inferior to his true disposition to pay $u_i$, for he can win the bid if the other consumers are not very tempted by the object.

Following the terminology of chapter 4, the first price auction is a direct but nonrevealing mechanism. Vickrey (1961) showed that on the contrary, the second price auction is revealing. The second price auction consists of making the winner (who is still the one who indicated the highest price) pay the price indicated by the person immediately after him. Consider still consumer $i$, and let $\bar{v}_i$ be the highest price announced by the other consumers. If $I$ announces $v_i > \bar{v}_i$, he will win the bid and will have a utility $u_i - \bar{v}_i$; if he bids $v_i < \bar{v}_i$, he will lose and will have a zero utility. Thus he with choose to bid some $v_i > \bar{v}_i$ if $u_i > \bar{v}_i$ and some $v_i < \bar{v}_i$ if $u_i < \bar{v}_i$. In both cases his utility is independent of his bid, and it is therefore not in his interest to lie.

In order to interpret this result, consider the social surplus created when $i$ buys the object. The price paid is simply a transfer that does not intervene in the social surplus. If $P$ is the price at which the seller values the object, the social surplus is therefore $u_i - P$. But if the other consumers tell the truth, the increase of utility of $i$ in the second price auction when he raises his bid in order to win is $u_i - \bar{u}_i$, which coincides with the increase in the social surplus. The second price auction is a revealing mechanism because it leads consumers' objectives to align themselves on the social objective.

Now let us return to the bridge's construction. The VCG mechanism does nothing but generalize the idea of the second price bid. The theoretical importance of this mechanism is such that Green-Laffont (1979) devoted an essential part of their book to it. We will be content here to look at some of its properties. To simplify the notation, I will subtract from the $u_i$ the per capita cost $C/n$, which lets us rid ourselves of the

---

lower than its average. A vote would then sometimes lead to not constructing the bridge even when it would be socially optimal.

cost $C$ of the problem;[8] the new $u_i$ can therefore be either positive or negative, and the Pareto-optimal decision rule amounts to constructing the bridge when $\Sigma_{i=1}^{n} u_i \geq 0$. Let $d(u)$ be the indicator of that event.

Social surplus, with which the utility of each consumer must be identified, is $\Sigma_{i=1}^{n} u_i d(u)$. Let $v = (v_1, \ldots, v_n)$ be the statements of the agents. In equilibrium, all consumers must tell the truth; the consumer $i$ therefore evaluates the social surplus at

$$\left( \sum_{j \neq i} v_j + u_i \right) d(v)$$

If a transfer $t_i(v)$ is deducted from him, we then have (up to a constant)

$$R_i - t_i + u_i d(v) = \left( \sum_{j \neq i} v_j + u_i \right) d(v)$$

which implies (still up to a constant)

$$t_i(v) = -\sum_{j \neq i} v_j d(v)$$

In fact, we can even add to the transfers of every agent any quantity independent of his statement. The category of VCG mechanisms is therefore characterized by

• $d(v) = 1$, that is, the bridge is constructed if and only if

$$\sum_{i=1}^{n} v_i \geq 0$$

• the consumer $i$ pays a transfer

$$t_i(v) = -\sum_{j \neq i} v_j d(v) + h_i(v_{-i})$$

where $h_i(v_{-i})$ is any sum depending only on statements of the other consumers

Groves-Loeb (1975) proved that all of these mechanisms are revealing in dominant strategies. The proof is very simple. The utility of $i$ under this mechanism is written

---

8. This transformation can be interpreted by assuming that if the bridge is built, each consumer contributes $C/n$ even before the transfers linked to the VCG mechanism are put into place.

$$R_i + \left( \sum_{j \neq i} v_j + u_i \right) d(v) - h_i(v_i)$$

which depends on the statement $v_i$ of $i$ only through $d(v)$. The agent $i$ must then choose his statement in such a way as to maximize the second term, which gives

$$d(v) = 1 \quad \text{iff} \quad \sum_{j \neq i} v_j + u_i \geq 0$$

But by definition,

$$d(v) = 1 \quad \text{iff} \quad \sum_{j=1}^{n} v_j \geq 0$$

and $v_i = u_i$ is therefore one of the solutions of the program of agent $i$, whatever the statements of the other agents may be.

Clarke (1971) proposed a particularly interesting VCG mechanism. Choose

$$h_i(v_{-i}) = \max \left( \sum_{j \neq i} v_j, 0 \right)$$

Then there are four cases to consider:

1. If $\Sigma_{j \neq i}\, v_j > 0$ and $\Sigma_{j=1}^{n}\, v_j > 0$, $t_i(v) = 0$
2. If $\Sigma_{j \neq i}\, v_j > 0$ and $\Sigma_{j=1}^{n}\, v_j < 0$, $t_i(v) = \Sigma_{j \neq i}\, v_j > 0$
3. If $\Sigma_{j \neq i}\, v_j < 0$ and $\Sigma_{j=1}^{n}\, v_j > 0$, $t_i(v) = -\Sigma_{j \neq i}\, v_j > 0$
4. If $\Sigma_{j \neq i}\, v_j < 0$ and $\Sigma_{j=1}^{n}\, v_j < 0$, $t_i(v) = 0$

In cases 1 and 4, the statement of agent $i$ does not change the decision to build the bridge, and he pays a zero transfer. On the contrary, in cases 2 and 3, agent $i$ modifies the decision with his statement, and he then pays a positive transfer; he is called a "pivot" agent. This property gave its name to Clarke's mechanism.

It is immediately ascertained that the pivot mechanism is not "balanced": no transfer is negative, and their sum is strictly positive if there is at least one pivot agent. This property is unfortunately common to all VCG mechanisms. To see this, consider the case of two agents ($n = 2$) and assume the existence of a balanced VCG mechanism, in other words a choice of functions $h_1(v_2)$ and $h_2(v_1)$ such that for every $v = (v_1, v_2)$,

$t_1(v) + t_2(v) = 0$

Assume three statements $v_1'$, $v_1''$, and $v_2$ such that

$v_1' + v_2 > 0$   and   $v_1'' + v_2 < 0$

The result clearly is $d(v_1', v_2) = 1$ and $d(v_1'', v_2) = 0$, whence the two conditions of the budget balance

$$\begin{cases} h_1(v_2) + h_2(v_1') = v_2 + v_1' \\ h_1(v_2) + h_2(v_1'') = 0 \end{cases}$$

By subtracting the second condition from the first, we get

$h_2(v_1') - v_1' = v_2$

which cannot be satisfied systematically, since the left-hand side, but not the right-hand side, is independent of $v_2$.

How are we to interpret this budgetary imbalance? It cannot be redistributed to the agents, since the incentive properties of the mechanism would be modified. The VCG mechanisms therefore do not allow a true Pareto optimum to be attained, since such an optimum requires budget balance as well as efficient decision making. This conclusion is sometimes summed up by saying the VCG mechanisms are only "satisfactory." Unfortunately, we can prove (see this chapter's appendix) that VCG mechanisms are the only mechanisms that are satisfactory when the $u_i$ can assume all real values. Therefore it seems that we have arrived at an impasse. In fact the situation is salvageable. On the one hand, the pivot mechanism can be shown to be asymptotically balanced: when the number of agents tends toward infinity, budget imbalances become negligible[9] and if they are redistributed to the agents, stating the truth is nearly optimal for them. On the other hand, we can imagine only proposing the mechanism to a representative sample of agents, and redistributing the eventual surpluses to the nonparticipatory agents. Finally d'Aspremont-Gérard-Varet (1979) showed that if we only ask for implementation in Bayesian equilibriums (and no more in dominant strategies), a fully Pareto-optimal mechanism exists, which then simultaneously ensures efficient decision making and budget balance.

---

9. This result is easy to understand: when there are many agents, the number of pivot agents becomes quite small, since it is improbable that an agent can change the decision on his own.

It is fitting to note that even if these mechanisms have abstract satisfactory properties, at times they can give counterintuitive taxation schemes. Such schemes tend to be very advantageous for the agents with high propensities to pay.[10]

To conclude, return to the hypotheses. The fact that the good is indivisible simplifies the exposition, but actually matters little. If the quantity of public good $z$ could assume values in a set $Z$, it would be necessary to write the agents' utilities as

$$U_i(x_i, z) = x_i + u_i(z)$$

The optimal decision rule would then be given by

$$z^*(u) = \arg\max_{z \in Z} \sum_{i=1}^{n} u_i(z)$$

and we can easily see that the pivot mechanism, for example, would be associated with transfers

$$t_i(v) = \sum_{j \neq i} v_j[z^*(v_{-i})] - \sum_{j \neq i} v_j[z^*(v)]$$

On the other hand, the quasi-linearity of the agents' utility functions is absolutely crucial. It behooves us then to inquire in each particular case whether this quasi-linearity indeed constitutes a good approximation of reality.

## 5.3   The Property of Public Goods

If is often asserted that public goods should be provided by the public sector, as is effectively the case for defense, police, or the justice system. The underlying argument is that if the public good was provided by a market mechanism, a consumer who would buy some (and would then stimulate its production) would not take into account the benefit that he would unwittingly give to other consumers. This is what is called a positive externality in chapter 6; this phenomenon of course leads to a suboptimal production of the public good. Coase (1974) has

---

10. Henry (1989) provides a good example of this. Consider the pivot mechanism and suppose that the first $n/2$ agents are ready to pay 1, $9C/n$ and the last $n/2$ are ready to pay only 0, $19C/n$. Then the bridge will still be built, but we can easily see that if $n \geq 20$, no agent either pays or receives any transfer (on top of $C/n$)—this is obviously advantageous for the first group.

nevertheless brought this reasoning into question. Consider the example of a lighthouse showing the way for ships. The service rendered is clearly a public good, since it is nonrival: the fact that a ship sees the lighthouse beam of course does not keep any other ship from seeing it also. For the same reason it is seemingly very difficult to exclude ships from the service rendered by the lighthouse, which makes their profitability quite doubtful for a private firm. Adam Smith already thought that in such a situation, the state itself must provide the service in question (*The Wealth of Nations*, bk. V, ch. 1):

The third and last duty of the sovereign or commonwealth is that of erecting and maintaining those publick institutions and those publick works, which, though they may be in the highest degree advantageous to a great society are, however, of such a nature, that the profit could never repay the expence to any individual or small number of individuals, and which it, therefore, cannot be expected that any individual or small number of individuals should erect or maintain.

After Smith, numerous classical authors, from John Stuart Mill to Paul Samuelson, illustrated this principle through the lighthouse example. Coase remarks, however, that through the vicissitudes of history, British lighthouses were generally the responsibility of private national organizations, and they perceived a fixed right which was compulsorily discharged by any ship landing in a British port. That arrangement does not seem to have had tragic consequences for British naval commerce. Coase considers that private provision gives better incentives to lighthouse keepers: since shipowners are more conscious of paying for this service than if they financed it (like all other citizens, only through general taxation), they will take to heart the need to verify that the service is indeed rendered.

The fact remains that private provision of the service rendered by lighthouses violates the condition of equality of price and marginal cost which is necessary for the optimum (see chapter 7). Insofar as the marginal cost of lighting the way for an additional ship is zero, the price of the service should also be zero. Making the ship pay may dissuade it from visiting British ports, which would be inefficient.

In the specific example of lighthouses, we wonder whether this theoretical argument actually carries weight in the real world. This discussion nonetheless illustrates the difficulty of clearly expressing general principles in public economics: each situation must be studied in terms of its own characteristics.

## 5.4   The Importance of the Free-Rider Problem

The problem of the free rider is at the heart of the analysis of public goods. It is then crucial to thoroughly determine its theoretical and empirical relevance. First on the theoretical plane, note that in an economy lacking public goods, the consumers—if they are very numerous—gain nothing by trying to manipulate the Walrasian mechanism (Roberts-Postlewaite 1976). In effect no consumer is "big" enough to influence prices appreciably on his own. The situation is quite different in an economy comprising public goods (Roberts 1976). This time, a free rider who would announce a very small demand of public goods would participate very little in the financing but would hardly suffer from it, since the production level of the public good is practically independent of his statement. One can then expect the free-rider problem to be more important when the number of agents affected by the public good is higher.

On the empirical plane now, there are good reasons to doubt the importance of the free-rider problem. The first is that honesty is a social norm that molds the behavior of individuals. The second is that at least in a small group, where each consumer has a notable influence on the level of public good, it is difficult for each agent to calculate the best way to underevaluate its demand. Moreover the majority of decisions of public goods production are made by elected representatives who may have less tendency to announce levels that are very low.

An oft-quoted study of Bohm (1972) seemed to confirm this skepticism. Bohm put into operation several different financing schemes for a television program in Sweden. He then showed that the propensities to pay announced by groups to whom he had submitted these different schemes varied only little across schemes, which would imply that the agents have a tendency to announce their true preferences.

Bohm's experience has been criticized by numerous authors, who set up their own experiments. Ledyard (1995) surveys this literature, from which he gleans conclusions. The most recent experiments mitigate Bohm's conclusions quite a bit. In the current state of our understanding, it seems that

• the majority of subjects announce a propensity to pay that is intermediary between the Nash equilibrium (behavior of the free rider) and the Pareto optimum
• they contribute less if the game is repeated

- they contribute more if they are allowed to communicate with each other before making their decision

These results are consistent with the theory, even if the theory certainly exaggerates the extent of the free-rider problem in predicting negligible voluntary contributions. This problem is more acute when the agents accumulate experience and can thus realize their capacity to manipulate the financing plan; it also grows in importance when the number of agents concerned is higher, since it then becomes more difficult for them to communicate.

## 5.5 Local Public Goods

Up to this point we have assumed that public goods concern the community as a whole. In fact, quite a few public goods apply only to the inhabitants of a given geographical area. For example, this is the case with water (whose distribution usually is under communal supervision), garbage collection, or urban transports in some countries. Such goods are called local public goods. Tiebout (1956) was the first to study this theory. A fundamental feature of local public goods is that consumers can decide in which local community they will establish themselves. If the production level of local public goods or the conditions of their financing are not satisfying, they can "vote with their feet" by moving to another community. Tiebout showed that under certain hypotheses, this process has an equilibrium that is efficient. The most recent literature (e.g., see Rubinfeld 1987) comes back to Tiebout's hypotheses: perfect information and perfect mobility of the consumers, existence of a large number of communities, absence of land tax, a very gross modeling of the supply of local public goods, and so on. It shows that once these hypotheses are relaxed, the situation becomes much more complex, owing particularly to the emergence of nonconvexities: it is possible for equilibrium not to exist, and it is possible for it to be inefficient when it does exist.

## 5.6 Appendix: Characterization of VCG Mechanisms

Consider a direct revealing satisfactory mechanism $\{d(v), [t_1(v), \ldots, t_n(v)]\}$, which therefore allows effective decision making: $d(v) = 1$ if and only if $\Sigma_{i=1}^{n} v_i \geq 0$. The proof that this mechanism is necessarily a VCG mechanism relies on two lemmas.

LEMMA 1 (INDEPENDENCE OF TRANSFERS) If $d(v_{-i}, v_i') = d(v_{-i}, v_i)$, then $t_i(v_{-i}, v_i') = t_i(v_{-i}, v_i)$. The transfer paid by $i$ cannot therefore change except when its statement modifies the decision.

*Proof* If, for example, $t_i(v_{-i}, v_i') > t_i(v_{-i}, v_i)$, then assume that $i$'s true propensity to pay is $u_i = v_i'$. We get

$$u_i d(v_{-i}, u_i) - t_i(v_{-i}, u_i) < u_i d(v_{-i}, v_i) - t_i(v_{-i}, v_i)$$

so that the mechanism cannot be revealing.

LEMMA 2 (PRINCIPLE OF COMPENSATION)

$$t_i(v_{-i}, v_i') - t_i(v_{-i}, v_i) = \left( \sum_{j \neq i} v_j \right) [d(v_{-i}, v_i) - d(v_{-i}, v_i')]$$

*Proof* Assume, without loss of generality, that

$$t_i(v_{-i}, v_i') - t_i(v_{-i}, v_i) = \left( \sum_{j \neq i} v_j \right) [d(v_{-i}, v_i) - d(v_{-i}, v_i')] + \varepsilon$$

where $\varepsilon$ is a positive real. Lemma 1 implies that we inevitably get $d(v_{-i}, v_i) \neq d(v_{-i}, v_i')$ (otherwise the transfers would be equal). Still, without loss of generality, assume that

$$d(v_{-i}, v_i) = 1 \quad \text{and} \quad d(v_{-i}, v_i') = 0$$

Define a statement $v_i'' = -\Sigma_{j \neq i} v_j - \varepsilon/2$. We get $\Sigma_{j \neq i} v_j + v_i'' < 0$ and therefore $d(v_{-i}, v_i'') = 0 = d(v_{-i}, v_i')$, and lemma 1 gives $t_i(v_{-i}, v_i'') = t_i(v_{-i}, v_i')$. We deduce from this that

$$t_i(v_{-i}, v_i'') - t_i(v_{-i}, v_i) = \sum_{j \neq i} v_j + \varepsilon = -v_i'' + \frac{\varepsilon}{2}$$

Now, if the true propensity to pay of $i$ is $u_i = u_i''$, we get

$$u_i d(v_{-i}, v_i) - t_i(v_{-i}, v_i) = u_i d(v_{-i}, u_i) - t_i(v_{-i}, u_i) + \frac{\varepsilon}{2}$$

So the mechanism is not revealing.

The proof concludes simply by "integrating" lemma 2 (i.e., by fixing $v_i'$), whence

$$t_i(v_{-i}, v_i) = -\sum_{j \neq i} v_j d(v_{-i}, v_i) + h_i(v_{-i})$$

which is precisely the definition of VCG mechanisms.

# Bibliography

d'Aspremont, C., and L.-A. Gérard-Varet. 1979. Incentives and incomplete information. *Journal of Public Economics* 11: 25–45.

Bohm, P. 1972. Estimating demand for public goods: An experiment. *European Economic Review* 3: 111–30.

Clarke, E. 1971. Multipart pricing of public goods. *Public Choice* 2: 19–33.

Coase, R. 1974. The lighthouse in economics. *Journal of Law and Economics* 17: 357–76.

Drèze, J., and D. de la Vallée Poussin. 1971. A tâtonnement process for public goods. *Review of Economic Studies* 38: 133–50.

Groves, T., and M. Loeb. 1974. Incentives and public inputs. *Journal of Public Economics* 4: 311–26.

Henry, C. 1989. *Microeconomics for Public Policy: Helping the Invisible Hand.* Oxford: Clarendon Press.

Ledyard, J. 1995. Public goods: A survey of experimental research. In J. Kagel and A. Roth, eds., *The Handbook of Experimental Economics.* Princeton University Press, Princeton.

Malinvaud, E. 1971. A planning approach to the public good problem. *Swedish Journal of Economics* 11: 96–112.

Roberts, J. 1976. The incentives for correct revelation of preferences and the number of consumers. *Journal of Public Economics* 6: 359–74.

Roberts, J., and A. Postlewaite. 1976. The incentives for price-taking behavior in large economies. *Econometrica* 44: 115–27.

Rubinfeld, D. 1987. The economics of the local public sector. In A. Auerbach and M. Feldstein, eds., *Handbook of Public Economics*, vol. 2. Amsterdam: North-Holland.

Samuelson, P. 1954. The pure theory of public expenditure. *Review of Economics and Statistics* 36: 387–9.

Tiebout, C. 1956. A pure theory of local expenditures. *Journal of Political Economy* 64: 416–24.

Vickrey, W. 1961. Counterspeculation, auctions and competitive sealed tenders. *Journal of Finance* 16: 1–17

# 6                        External Effects

We say that there is an external effect, or an externality, when an agent's actions *directly* influence the choice possibilities (i.e., the production set or consumption set) of another agent. The word "directly" is very important in this definition. We must not confuse genuine externalities and what are at times improperly called "pecuniary externalities," which pass through the intermediary of the market and fit perfectly within the framework of the most basic general equilibrium model.[1] Even if this distinction dates back to Scitovsky (1954), it is at times neglected in the applied literature.

Examples of externalities are many. The most famous one in the literature is that of Meade, who considers a beekeeper and a nearby located orchard. The beekeeper's bees contribute to the productivity of the orchard in fertilizing the flowers of the trees; in return, the trees provide the bees with pollen which enters into the production of the beekeeper's honey. In each case one agent's production function moves upward because of another agent's actions. It is therefore a matter of positive crossexternalities of production.

All externalities are not so favorable. Pollution constitutes a typical example of negative production (and also consumption) externality; noise or cigarette smoke are negative consumption externalities.[2] To make up for this, the network effects tied to the extension of a telephone network are positive consumption externalities. The arrival of a new subscriber on the network allows all existing subscribers to call an

---

1. Pecuniary externalities so far create no inefficiency in the public economics framework of this book. Such is no longer the case when competition is imperfect, as we will see in chapter 10.
2. To take another example, if I derive a particular pleasure from seeing that my consumption is superior to that of my neighbors, as in the (heterodox) theories of Veblen, then their consumption inflicts on me a negative consumption externality.

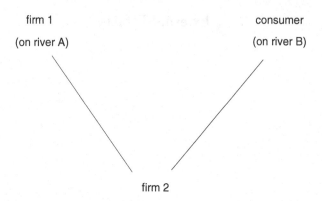

firm 1                                          consumer

(on river A)                                    (on river B)

firm 2

**Figure 6.1**
River pollution

extra correspondent and therefore contributes positively to their welfare.[3] Scientific research also constitutes a positive externality, from the moment it falls into the public domain.

At times it is difficult to separate externalities from other market failures. An agent who contributes to the financing of a public good exerts a positive consumption externality over all other agents who can benefit from an increased production of public good. Even the incompleteness of markets refers to external effects (see chapter 13).

## 6.1 The Pareto Optimum

As in the preceding chapter, our first task consists in characterizing the Pareto optimum in the presence of externalities. Consider here again a simplified example that comprises two goods (1 and 2), two firms, and one consumer. Good 1 is supposed to be polluting and good 2 nonpolluting.

As shown in figure 6.1, firm 1 is situated on river $A$ and produces good 1 from good 2 according to $y_1 = f(x_2)$. The consumer is on river B and has a utility function $U(x_1^c, x_2^c)$. Now firm 2, situated beyond the confluence of the two rivers, produces good 2 from good 1. Since it is downstream from firm 1 (which ejects its wastes into river $A$) and from

---

3. The literature on the economics of networks has developed dramatically in recent years, in connection with the explosion of telecommunications and the Internet. The reader can find its principal themes in the symposium published in the *Journal of Economic Perspectives* (spring 1994) or in the survey of Economides (1996).

consumer 1 (who pollutes river $B$), its production suffers from two negative externalities, so its production function

$$y_2 = g(x_1, y_1, x_1^c)$$

is increasing and concave in its first argument but decreases in its last two arguments. Denote $(\omega_1, \omega_2)$ the initial resources of the economy.

The Pareto optima of this economy are given by the following program:

$$\left\{ \begin{array}{ll} \max_{x_1, x_2, y_1, y_2, x_1^c, x_2^c} U(x_1^c, x_2^c) & \\ \quad x_1^c + x_1 \leq \omega_1 + y_1 & (\lambda_1) \\ \quad x_2^c + x_2 \leq \omega_2 + y_2 & (\lambda_2) \\ \quad y_1 \leq f(x_2) & (\mu_1) \\ \quad y_2 \leq g(x_1, y_1, x_1^c) & (\mu_2) \end{array} \right.$$

where $\lambda_1$, $\lambda_2$, $\mu_1$, and $\mu_2$ are four multipliers. The first-order conditions are

$$\left\{ \begin{array}{ll} \dfrac{\partial U}{\partial x_1} - \lambda_1 + \dfrac{\partial g}{\partial x_1^c} \mu_2 = 0 & \\[2ex] \dfrac{\partial U}{\partial x_2} & = \lambda_2 \\[2ex] \lambda_1 & = \mu_2 \dfrac{\partial g}{\partial x_1} \\[2ex] \lambda_2 & = \mu_1 \dfrac{\partial f}{\partial x_2} \\[2ex] \lambda_1 & = \mu_1 - \dfrac{\partial g}{\partial y_1} \mu_2 \\[2ex] \lambda_2 & = \mu_2 \end{array} \right.$$

By eliminating the multipliers, we obtain

$$\frac{(\partial U/\partial x_1) + (\partial U/\partial x_2)(\partial g/\partial x_1^c)}{(\partial U/\partial x_2)} = \frac{\partial g}{\partial x_1} = \frac{1}{\partial f/\partial x_2} - \frac{\partial g}{\partial y_1}$$

Although this condition of optimality may seem complicated, it is interpreted quite easily. The left-hand member is the marginal rate of substitution of the consumer, corrected by the fact that his consumption of good 1 entails pollution downstream. This is called the social marginal rate of substitution of the consumer, and it takes into account all of the consequences of his consumption on social welfare. In the same way the right-hand member is the marginal rate of transformation of firm 1, corrected by the effect of its pollution on firm 2. As for the central term, this is the usual marginal rate of transformation of firm 2. In effect the firm 2 does not pollute, and its social marginal rate of transformation coincides therefore with its private marginal rate of transformation.

The principle to remember is therefore the following: in the presence of external effects, the usual optimality condition of equality between the marginal rates of substitution of consumers and the marginal rates of transformation of firms bears on the *social* values of these quantities. The social values take into account the external effects of each agent's decisions on the rest of the economy. This principle is due to Arthur Pigou in the 1920s. Its application permits us to justify, for example, the establishment of toll booths on highways in the face of excess traffic (when the arrival of one more vehicle reduces traffic speed): the social marginal cost of this new vehicle is positive even if its private marginal cost is practically nothing. The toll right then represents the marginal cost that the vehicle entering the highway imposes on other vehicles.[4]

In our simplified economy, the consequences of externalities are clear. At the optimum, firm 1 must produce less, and the consumer must consume less of good 1 than in the absence of externalities. This is perfectly intuitive: if a firm pollutes, it is advisable that its level of production be reduced.

## 6.2   Implementing the Optimum

Now let us see what are the means at our disposal for implementing the optimum; this is often called *internalizing externalities*.

### 6.2.1   The Competitive Equilibrium

Assume that firm 2 takes the pollution factors $y_1$ and $x_1^c$ as given. Then, if the prices of goods are $p_1$ and $p_2$, the agents' choices will lead to

$$\frac{(\partial U/\partial x_1)}{(\partial U/\partial x_2)} = \frac{p_1}{p_2} = \frac{\partial g}{\partial x_1} = \frac{1}{\partial f/\partial x_2}$$

---

4. Logically it should depend on the degree of highway congestion at the location and hour in question.

which is inefficient. In competitive equilibrium the agents only take into account the consequences of their choices on their own welfare, in equating the *private* marginal rates of substitution and of transformation. Under usual conditions, one can show that there is too much of good 1 being produced and consumed.

This analysis permits us to explain the phenomenon of overfishing, that is, the overexploitation of fisheries resources by fishermen. The quantity of fish in the oceans is the archetypal example of a "common resource" that belongs to everyone and to no one.[5] Every fisherman, in pulling a fish from the water, reduces the capacity of the species' reproduction and therefore future stocks; in so doing, he exerts a negative production externality on other fishermen. The preceding results lead us to think that the competitive equilibrium will indeed exhibit a phenomenon of overfishing. It can easily be verified in a single-period model, even if a dynamic framework would obviously be more appropriate. Normalize the price of a fish at 1. We will model the negative externality by assuming that the cost of extracting $P_i$ fish by the fisherman $i$ when the set of fishermen takes $S = \Sigma_{i=1}^{n} S_i$ fish from the ocean is $cS_iS$. As more fish are caught, they become more rare, so it becomes more costly to find them. The private marginal cost of extracting a fish is the derivative of $cS_i$ $(S_i + \Sigma_{j \neq i}S_j)$ in $S_i$, that is, $c(S_i + S)$. On the other hand, the social marginal cost must take into account the derivatives in $S_i$ of the costs of the other fishermen $j \neq i$, which is $cS_j$. When all fishermen are identical, we get $S = nS_i$. The competitive equilibrium $E$ is therefore given by the equality of the price and of the marginal private cost so that

$$1 = c\left(\frac{S^E}{n} + S^E\right)$$

Now at the social optimum $O$ price equals social marginal cost,

$$1 = c\left(S_i^O + S^O + \sum_{j \neq i} S_j^O\right) = 2cS^O$$

So we get

$$S^O = \frac{1}{2c} < S^E = \frac{n}{c(n+1)}$$

---

5. This is also the case with air quality or the climate (i.e., global warming).

and the equilibrium clearly leads to overfishing, as compared to the social optimum.

### 6.2.2 Quotas

The simplest way to arrive at a Pareto optimum is of course for the government to set quotas specifying that the externality-inducing activities should be set at their optimal level. This is certainly an authoritarian solution and one that assumes a very fine knowledge of the characteristics of the economy. In the example studied here, it would amount to calculating the Pareto-optimal levels of $y_1$ and $x_{1,}^c$ which we denote $y_1^*$ and $x_1^{c*}$, and to forbid firm 1 from producing more than $y_1^*$ and the consumer from consuming more than $x_1^{c*}$ of good 1. It is nevertheless an oft-adopted solution, under a slightly less brutal form, that consists of limiting the quantity of a certain type of pollutants emitted by firms, or even by consumers (as in carbon emissions of automobiles).

### 6.2.3 Subsidies for Depollution

It is sometimes possible to install dispositions to reduce pollution. Suppose that firm 1 can invest in depolluting a quantity $a$ of good 2 which, without affecting its production, reduces its pollution as if $y_1$ were $y_1 - d(a)$.

First, let us look for the Pareto optimum. The scarcity constraint for good 2 becomes

$$x_2^c + x_2 + a \leq \omega_2 + y_2$$

while the production constraint of firm 2 becomes

$$y_2 \leq g[x_1, y_1 - d(a), x_1^c]$$

The quantity $a$ also becomes a maximand of the program. We easily see that the optimality conditions obtained above are unchanged, but that we must add to them a condition to determine the optimal depollution level $a^*$:

$$d'(a^*) = -\frac{1}{\partial g/\partial y_1}$$

What happens here with the competitive equilibrium? If firm 1 is not prompted to depollute, it will of course choose not to do so. It still seems reasonable for the government to subsidize such an expense by paying firm 1 a sum $s(a)$. The profit maximization program of firm 1 then becomes

$$\max_{x_2,a}[p_1 f(x_2) - p_2 x_2 - p_2 a + s(a)]$$

while firm 2 maximizes in $x_1$

$$p_2 g[x_1, y_1 - d(a), x_1^c] - p_1 x_1$$

The condition of profit maximization of firm 1 implies that

$$s'(a) = 1$$

So choosing subsidy $s(.)$ such that $s'(a^*) = 1$ induces the firm to realize the socially optimal expenditures of depollution. Unfortunately, the first-order conditions also entail

$$\frac{\partial g}{\partial x_1} = \frac{1}{\partial f / \partial x_2}$$

So the subsidized equilibrium is still not Pareto optimal.

### 6.2.4   The Rights to Pollute

Meade (1952) suggested a solution to the problem of external effects which has generally found favor with economists (and more rarely with decision makers). It rests on the finding that externalities contribute to inefficiency only because no other market exists upon which they may be exchanged. Therefore assume that the state (or any other institution) creates a "rights to pollute" market: a right to pollute gives the right to a certain number of pollution units. The polluters (firm 1 and the consumer) can then pollute with the proviso that they buy the corresponding rights to pollute. Thus

- firm 1 pays $q$ to firm 2 for each unit of $y_1$
- the consumer pays $r$ to firm 2 for each unit of $x_1^c$

The consumer's program gives

$$\frac{\partial U / \partial x_1}{\partial U / \partial x_2} = \frac{p_1 + r}{p_2}$$

while the profit maximization of firm 1 implies that

$$\frac{p_1 - q}{p_2} = \frac{1}{\partial f / \partial x_2}$$

As for firm 2, it must take into account payments it receives for determining the number of pollution rights it is ready to sell; it solves therefore

$$\max_{x_1, y_1, x_1^c} \left[ p_2 g(x_1, y_1, x_1^c) - p_1 x_1 + r x_1^c + q y_1 \right]$$

whence

$$\begin{cases} \dfrac{p_1}{p_2} = \dfrac{\partial g}{\partial x_1} \\[2mm] \dfrac{q}{p_2} = -\dfrac{\partial g}{\partial y_1} \\[2mm] \dfrac{r}{p_2} = -\dfrac{\partial g}{\partial x_1^c} \end{cases}$$

All of these equalities amount to

$$\frac{(\partial U / \partial x_1) + (\partial U / \partial x_2)(\partial g / \partial x_1^c)}{\partial U / \partial x_2} = \frac{\partial g}{\partial x_1} = \frac{1}{\partial f / \partial x_2} - \frac{\partial g}{\partial y_1}$$

which is the condition of efficiency. The creation of markets for rights to pollute thus implements a Pareto optimum.[6] In other respects, it is a system far less demanding than the imposition of pollution quotas, since the calculation of such quotas implies that the state knows the preferences and technologies of all agents. It is enough here for the state to open pollution rights markets and let equilibrium establish itself.[7]

This result merits some comments. First, note that the consumer and firm 1 do not necessarily pay the same price to pollute at equilibrium. We

---

6. Neglected here are second-order conditions, which Starrett (1972) has shown are problematic. In effect, function $g$ cannot be concave in $y_1$ or $x_1^c$ on all of $\mathbb{R}^+$, since it is decreasing and positive. The program of firm 2 is therefore nonconvex, and this can cause difficulties for equilibrium, as we will see in chapter 7.

7. We assume that the pollutees are authorized to sell pollution rights, which results in an optimal pollution level. In practice, these markets are often reserved to the polluters. The pollution level attained depends then on the number of rights put into circulation, which poses the problem of the government's capacity to calculate the optimal pollution level, to issue the correct number of rights to pollute, and to resist the pressure of agents who would like to see that number modified.

would get $q = r$ only if the pollution was impersonal in the sense that $g(x_1, y_1, x_1^c) = G(x_1, y_1 + x_1^c)$. Second, there is but one sole applicant and one sole supplier on each open pollution rights market in this example, which raises the problem of strategic behaviors. This solution is therefore better adapted to situations where the pollution is of collective origin—we can imagine similarly disposed polluters around the same lake.[8]

Finally, we have implicitly adopted the polluter-pays principle made popular by the OECD in a 1972 report. In fact optimality does not at all require that polluters make amends to the pollutees. One could easily take a situation of serious pollution as a reference point and impose "depollution rights" whereby the pollutees buy from the polluters to reestablish optimality.[9] Of course the distribution of utility at equilibrium would not be the same.

### 6.2.5 Taxation

It is conceivable to tax the production of the good 1 at the rate $\tau$ and its consumption at the rate $t$. It is easy to see that if one chooses $\tau = q$ and $t = r$, where $q$ and $r$ are the equilibrium prices on virtual markets of pollution rights, we again find a Pareto optimum. These tax levels are often called Pigovian taxes, in honor of Pigou (1928). The disadvantage to this remedy is that like the imposition of pollution quotas, one needs extraordinarily detailed information on the primitive data of the economy, since the government must be able to calculate the equilibrium prices on pollution rights markets.

### 6.2.6 The Integration of Firms

For simplicity's sake assume that the consumer does not pollute, so $\partial g / \partial x_1^c = 0$. In this case one can envision the two firms as merging (in economic terms, we speak of "integrating"). The new firm thus formed will maximize the joint profit as

---

8. One of the most spectacular applications of the pollution rights market functions in the San Francisco bay area (see Henry 1989). The regulation of thermal power stations and of sulfur dioxide emissions in the United States offers other examples. More recently the summit on global warming held in Kyoto in 1997 decided to study the use of rights markets at the world level.

9. A famous example is that of a city-dweller who retires to the country, settling next to a farm. The question is, Does he have ground to ask for compensation if the farmer's rooster wakes him at the crack of dawn? A French court has decided that he is entitled to compensation, but this judgment is much debated.

$$\begin{cases} \max_{x_1,x_2,y_1} [p_1 f(x_2) + p_2 g(x_1, y_1) - p_2 x_2 - p_1 x_1] \\ \qquad y_1 \le f(x_2) \end{cases}$$

which gives

$$\frac{p_1}{p_2} = \frac{\partial g}{\partial x_1} = \frac{1}{\partial f / \partial x_2} - \frac{\partial g}{\partial y_1}$$

Again we have the Pareto optimum. The solution is obviously radical, and it shows little regard for property rights. We often see in industrial economics that the market power confered upon mastodons is not without inconveniences. Nevertheless, the integration of firms is not to be discarded entirely.

### 6.2.7   A Compensation Mechanism

Varian (1994) proposed a mechanism that implements the optimum when every agent (but not the regulator) is informed of the parameters of the whole economy. Suppose again that the consumer does not pollute. If the regulator knows the production functions, he could still calculate the Pareto optimum $(x_1^*, x_2^*)$ and impose a Pigovian tax on firm 1:

$$t^* = -p_2 \frac{\partial g}{\partial y_1} [x_1^*, f(x_2^*)]$$

Firm 1 would then choose the socially optimal level of pollution $y_1^* = f(x_2^*)$.

Now suppose that each firm knows the two production functions but that the regulator does not have this information at his disposal. The compensation mechanism has two stages:

1. Firm 1 announces a tax level $t_1$ and firm 2 a tax level $t_2$.

2. The regulator imposes transfers on both firms such that their profit functions become

$$\begin{cases} \pi_1 = p_1 f(x_2) - p_2 x_2 - t_2 y_1 - \alpha(t_1 - t_2)^2 \\ \pi_2 = p_2 g(x_1, y_1) - p_1 x_1 + t_1 y_1 \end{cases}$$

where $\alpha$ is any positive parameter. The two firms make their production decisions based on these modified profit functions.

There exist multiple Nash equilibria in this game. In every equilibrium, $t_1$ and $t_2$ are equal, but they may differ from the Pigovian tax $t^*$, so the optimal allocation is not implemented. On the other hand, we can show that there exists a unique subgame-perfect equilibrium and that it implements the Pareto optimum.

A subgame-perfect equilibrium is, by definition, a Nash equilibrium in every subgame. Subgame-perfect equilibria are obtained by backward induction, that is in starting from the end of the game, here at the second stage. Therefore suppose that as $t_1$ and $t_2$ are announced, firm 1 maximizes its profit by choosing $x_2$ such that

$$(p_1 - t_2) f'(x_2) = p_2 \tag{1}$$

The solution to this equation is a decreasing function of $t_2$, which we will denote $x_2(t_2)$. As for firm 2, it chooses $x_1$ such that

$$\frac{\partial g}{\partial x_1} = \frac{p_1}{p_2} \tag{2}$$

In the first stage of the game, certainly it is optimal for firm 1 to choose $t_1 = t_2$, considering the quadratic penalty. Company 2 must choose $t_2$ in order to maximize its profit, which indirectly depends on $t_2$ by the intermediary of $y_1$ and therefore on the function $x_2(t_2)$. By differentiating, we get

$$\frac{\partial \pi_2}{\partial t_2} = \left( p_2 \frac{\partial g}{\partial y_1} + t_1 \right) f'(x_2) x_2'(t_2)$$

Since $f$ is increasing and $x_2$ decreasing, $t_2$ must be chosen at the level where

$$p_2 \frac{\partial g}{\partial y_1} \{ x_1, f[x_2(t_2)] \} + t_1 = 0 \tag{3}$$

By combining (1), (2), (3), and the equality $t_1 = t_2$, we again easily find the optimality conditions

$$\frac{p_1}{p_2} = \frac{\partial g}{\partial x_1} = \frac{1}{\partial f / \partial x_2} - \frac{\partial g}{\partial y_1}$$

and the equality of $t_1$ and $t_2$ with the Pigovian tax $t^*$. This mechanism effectively allows for the solution of the problem caused by the externality. The fact that it rests on the agents' perfect knowledge of their technologies can be a bit bothersome. Doubtless this situation is more

probable in cases of local pollution, where the parameters of the polluter and the pollutee can be well known, even though the regulator
has difficulty obtaining unbiased information.

### 6.3   Must Prices or Quantities Be Regulated?

We have seen that regulation by quantities (e.g., in the form of emission quotas) and regulation by prices (e.g., by taxation) both permit the
restoration of Pareto-optimality of the equilibrium and are therefore
equivalent. Let us follow Weitzman (1974) and consider a pollutant
production $q$. The firm has costs $C(q)$ and its profit is then $(pq - C(q))$ if
the price is $p$. The production entails "benefits" $B(q)$ and a consumer
surplus $B(q) - pq$.

This modeling suggests two comments. The first is of a semantic
nature: many times students are amazed that pollutant production
can be beneficial. In reality there is often joint production of a useful
good and of pollution; what we call "benefits" of the pollutant production is the value of useful production minus the cost inflicted by
pollution. The difference between benefits and costs is generally
maximal for a positive level of pollution; as was judged by a medieval
English court in the case of a candlemaker accused of smoking out his
neighborhood:

*Le utility del chose excusera le noisomeness del stink.* (The item's usefulness excuses
the annoyance of the odor.)

The reader will note that in this interpretation,[10] the social production
cost at once comprises the production cost $C(q)$ and the pollution cost,
which was deducted from the value of production to get $B(q)$.

The second comment is more technical. In the example we have
studied so far, $q$ would be $y_1$, the production of firm 1. This production
permits the consumer to raise his consumption of good 1, but it reduces
the production possibilities of firm 2. The sum of these two effects constitutes the "benefits" of $y_1$, which has moreover a cost given by the
technology of firm 1. Unfortunately, it is not possible to describe the
result in the form of a benefit minus a cost. Such a breakdown is in fact
more reasonable when the pollution injures consumers. In the interest
of not straying too far from our needs, we will disregard this con-

---

10. We could resort to a dual interpretation where $q$ represents the nonpolluted good,
like air quality.

sideration here. We will also make the usual hypotheses that $B(q)$ is increasing and concave and $C(q)$ increasing and convex.

When information is perfect, the optimal emission quota is calculated by maximizing the social surplus $(B(q) - C(q))$. We then get

$$B'(q^*) = C'(q^*)$$

As for the optimal tax rate, it is fixed in such a way that the prices verify

$$p^* = B'(q^*) = C'(q^*)$$

Then the firm effectively produces the optimal pollution level $q^*$.

At this stage the two modes of regulation are perfectly equivalent. Still, opinions on their respective advantages are generally quite clear-cut. As noted by Weitzman (1974, p. 477):

I think it is a fair generalization to say that the average economist in the Western marginal tradition has at least a vague preference toward indirect control by prices, just as the typical noneconomist leans toward the direct regulation of quantities.

The introduction of an imperfection of government information on the costs and benefits will let us compare the two modes of regulation. Thus suppose that either because the agents benefit from private information or because the future is uncertain, the cost and benefit functions are affected by independent shocks $\theta$ and $\eta$ so that they become $C(q, \theta)$ and $B(q, \eta)$.

Ideally price or quantity would be fixed conditionally to realizations of shocks in such a way as to verify

$$p^*(\theta,\eta) = \frac{\partial B}{\partial q}[q^*(\theta,\eta),\, \eta] = \frac{\partial C}{\partial q}[q^*(\theta,\eta),\, \theta]$$

and regulations by prices and by quantities would remain strictly equivalent.

In practice, this *first-best* solution is beyond reach, since the government must make decisions knowing only the distributions of $\eta$ and $\theta$ and not their realizations. In this *second-best* situation, the government chooses the emissions quota $\hat{q}$ so as to maximize the expected social surplus

$$E(B(q,\eta) - C(q,\theta))$$

Things are only slightly more complicated for regulation by price. If the government fixes a price $p$, the firm will choose a production $Q(p, \theta)$ such that

$$p = \frac{\partial C}{\partial q}[Q(p,\theta),\theta]$$

The government must then fix the price at the level $\hat{p}$ that maximizes

$$E\{B[Q(p,\theta),\eta] - C[Q(p,\theta),\theta]\}$$

This time there is no more reason that the two modes of regulation be equivalent. In fact it is easily checked (using second-order calculations for small uncertainties) that the advantage (in terms of expected social surplus) of regulation by prices on regulation by quantities is

$$\Delta \approx \frac{\sigma^2}{2(C'')^2}\left(\frac{\partial^2 B}{\partial q^2} + \frac{\partial^2 C}{\partial q^2}\right)$$

where $\sigma^2$ is the variance of the marginal cost $\partial C/\partial q$. Since $B$ is concave and $C$ convex, the sign of $\Delta$ is ambiguous a priori. Note that if marginal costs are almost constant, then regulation by quantities will dominate regulation by prices. In effect a small error in price setting can lead to a large error in the level of pollution attained.

It is clear that this purely normative perspective on the regulation of polluters is insufficient. It must be completed by a more descriptive analysis of the game that brings together polluters, consumer organizations, and the administration. Finkelshtain-Kislev (1997) show that in such a game, the two modes of regulation are no longer equivalent, even with perfect information.

## 6.4   Coase's Theorem

In a famous article Coase (1960) doubted the necessity of any governmental intervention in the presence of externalities. His reasoning is very simple: let $b(q)$ be the benefit that the polluter draws from a level of pollutant production $q$ and $c(q)$ the cost thus imposed on the pollutee.[11] When $b$ is concave and $c$ increasing and convex, the optimal pollution level is given by

$$b'(q^*) = c'(q^*)$$

Suppose that the status quo $q_0$ corresponds to a situation where $b'(q_0) < c'(q_0)$, and thus the pollution level is too high. Then the polluter and

---

11. Be careful not to identify this notation with that of the preceding section.

the pollutee have an interest in negotiating. Let $\varepsilon$ be a small positive number, and assume that the polluter proposes to lower the pollution level to $(q_0 - \varepsilon)$ against a payment of $t\varepsilon$, where $t$ is comprised between $b'(q_0)$ and $c'(q_0)$. Since $t > c'(q_0)$, this offer raises the polluter's profits; and it is equally beneficial for the pollutee, since $t < b'(q_0)$. Therefore the two parties will agree to move to a slightly lower pollution level. The reasoning does not stop here: so long as $b' < c'$, it is possible to lower the pollution level against a well-chosen transfer from pollutee to polluter. The end result is the optimal pollution level. A very similar argument applies in the case where $b'(q_0) > c'(q_0)$. The "Coase theorem" can thus be set forth as follows:

If property rights are clearly defined and transaction costs are zero, the parties affected by an externality succeed in eliminating any inefficiency through the simple recourse of negotiation.

Stated in this way, the theorem becomes more a tautology: if nothing keeps the parties from negotiating in an optimal manner, they will arrive at a Pareto optimum. In fact Coase (1988) explained in a collection of his articles that above all he wanted at the time to bring attention to the importance of property rights and of transaction costs. Unfortunately, it is more than anything his "theorem" that has passed into posterity.

What happens if the hypotheses of the theorem do not hold? First of all note that in many industrial pollution cases, property rights are not defined. For a common resource like ocean fish, for example, it is impossible to identify the polluters and the pollutees and then put a negotiation into place; Coase's theorem is therefore of no great help to us in attacking overfishing. Even if property rights are clearly defined, transaction costs are rarely negligible. For example, these costs include expenses incurred during negotiation (lost time, necessary recourse to lawyers, etc.). In the argument above, an elementary negotiation improves the social surplus by $(c'(q_0) - b'(q_0))\varepsilon$. If the salary of the retained lawyer is higher, the parties will renounce this stage of the negotiation and will stop before having attained the optimal level.

Recent literature has above all insisted on the transaction costs due to asymmetrical information.[12] If the polluter has private information on $b'(q_0)$ and the pollutee has private information on $c'(q_0)$, each will try

---

12. Farrell (1987) offers a good discussion of this topic.

to "hog the blanket," thereby manipulating the transfer $t$. Myerson-Satterthwaite (1983) show that under these conditions the parties will not be able to achieve a Pareto optimum. When the concerned parties become more numerous, it is of course much more difficult for each to them to manipulate the "prices" $t$. In fact the negotiation becomes again asymptotically efficient when the number of agents tends toward infinity (Gresik-Satterthwaite 1989). One can still wonder about the capacity of a large number of polluters and pollutees to negotiate together, since other transaction costs then risk coming out.

These critiques do not reduce the interest in the Coase theorem to nothing. In fact Cheung (1973) shows that in the case of the beekeeper-orchard crossexternality made popular by Meade, there exist in the United States contracts between two parties that seek to internalize the externality. It is therefore reasonable to think that under certain conditions the private agents, left to themselves, can effectively negotiate to arrive at a level of externality that, if not optimal, is at least more satisfying. The imperfections of such a solution to the externality problem must in any case be compared to those of the Pigovian solutions in a world where governmental information is quite imperfect.

## Bibliography

Cheung, S. 1973. The fable of the bees: An economic investigation. *Journal of Law and Economics* 16: 11–33.

Coase, R. 1960. The problem of social cost. *Journal of Law and Economics* 3: 1–44.

Coase, R. 1988. *The Firm, the Market, and the Law*. Chicago: University of Chicago Press.

Economides, I. 1996. The economics of networks. *International Journal of Industrial Organization* 14: 673–99.

Farrell, J. 1987. Information and the Coase theorem. *Journal of Economic Perspectives* 1: 113–29.

Finkelshtain, I., and Y. Kislev. 1997. Prices vs. quantities: The political perspective. *Journal of Political Economy* 105: 83–100.

Gresik, T., and M. Satterthwaite. 1989. The rate at which a simple market converges to efficiency as the number of traders increases: An asymptotic result for optimal trading mechanisms. *Journal of Economic Theory* 48: 304–32.

Henry, C. 1989. *Microeconomics for Public Policy: Helping the Invisible Hand*. Oxford: Clarendon Press.

Meade, J. 1952. External economies and diseconomies in a competitive situation. *Economic Journal* 62: 54–67.

Myerson, R., and M. Satterthwaite. 1983. Efficient mechanisms for bilateral trading. *Journal of Economic Theory* 28: 265–81.

Pigou, A. 1928. *A Study of Public Finance.* New York: Macmillan.

Scitovsky, T. 1954. Two concepts of external economies. *Journal of Political Economy* 62: 143–51.

Starrett, D. 1972. Fundamental nonconvexities in the theory of externalities. *Journal of Economic Theory* 4: 180–99.

Varian, H. 1994. A solution to the problem of externalities when agents are well-informed. *American Economic Review* 84: 1278–93.

Weitzman, M. 1974. Prices vs. quantities. *Review of Economic Studies* 41: 477–91.

# 7            Nonconvexities

Certain results that I recalled in chapter 1 strongly rest on the absence of nonconvexities in the economy. This is particularly the case for the theorem on the existence of equilibrium and the theorem on the decentralization of Pareto optima (the second fundamental welfare theorem), for which it must be assumed that preferences and production sets are convex.

In the first part of this chapter (sections 7.1 and 7.2), I present various theoretical elements on the treatment of nonconvexities. In the second part (section 7.3) I focus on natural monopolies, their pricing and their regulation.

## 7.1   Consequences of Nonconvexities

### 7.1.1   Nonconvex Preferences

We will begin by looking at the effect that nonconvexities have on the existence of equilibrium.[1] The hypothesis that preferences are convex has a long history. Originally the marginalists expressed utility under an additively separable form: $U(x) = \Sigma_{k=1}^{l} u_k(x_k)$. The convexity of preferences then referred to the concavity of each utility index $u_k$. The latter could be justified by appealing to introspection or to experimental psychology (and particularly to the Fechner-Weber law, which states that the response to a stimulus grows less and less quickly when the intensity of the stimulus increases). In the more modern framework where utility is not separable, the convexity of

---

1. Nonconvexities of course not only affect the existence of the equilibrium; the second fundamental welfare theorem rests in a crucial way on a theorem of separation of convexes, which is no longer applicable *a priori* when the preferences or the production sets are not all convex.

preferences has been presented by arguments that bear on the monotonicity of marginal rates of substitution: if, for example, there are only
two goods, bread and water, the quantity of bread that the consumer
will be ready to sacrifice for a glass of water is smaller when his thirst
is already slaked.

Even if such reasonings seem intuitive in a simple world, they are not
necessarily so in the real world where very many goods coexist. The
convexity of preferences implies that if the consumer is indifferent to
two baskets of goods $x$ and $x'$, he will like any convex linear combination $(\lambda x + (1 - \lambda)x')$ of those two baskets at least as much. The reader will
have no difficulty imagining counterexamples. Now, if the preference
convexities cannot be affirmed, the indifference curves can be shaped in
such a way that demand is discontinuous, as shown in figure 7.1. In a
two-good economy a small change in relative prices (symbolized by
budget lines in the figure) makes the tangency point pass from one side
of the nonconvexity to the other, thereby creating a discontinuity of
demand, which becomes a correspondence with nonconvex values. The
discontinuity of demand can directly result in the nonexistence of equilibrium if the supply function intersects the segment.

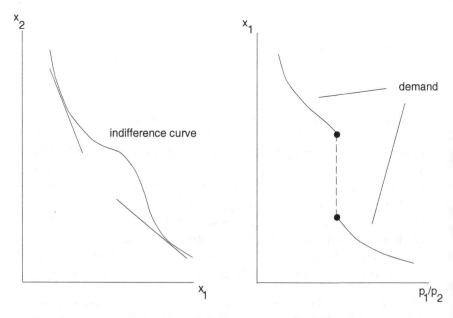

**Fiugre 7.1**
Nonconvex preferences

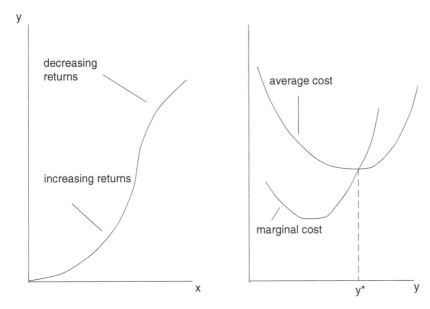

**Figure 7.2**
Small nonconvexity in production

## 7.1.2   Nonconvex Sets of Production

Now consider production. Here the convexity hypothesis particularly implies that returns to scale are decreasing. This is a strong hypothesis. At least two different cases may present themselves. In the first, which we will call the "small nonconvexity"[2] case, returns are increasing (possibly with a fixed cost) for small-scale production and then become decreasing. The production function has the aspect given in figure 7.2. This is the classic textbook case since Marshall where the average cost curve is U-shaped. Recall that there then exists a finite "efficient scale," which is the scale of firms in the long-term (free-entry) equilibrium of the industry: this scale $y^*$ is given by the minimum of the average cost in figure 7.2—and it is also the point where marginal and average costs are equal.

The second case is that of "large nonconvexities," where returns to scale are constantly increasing.[3] The production functions in both

---

2. The reader should be forewarned that in this chapter I adopt my own preferred terminology.
3. The efficient scale of the firm then is infinite; in fact it would be sufficient for it simply to be larger than the size of the market.

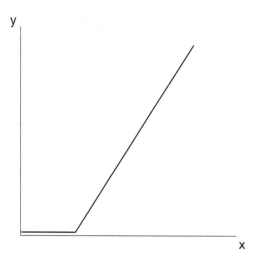

**Figure 7.3**
Large nonconvexities of production, I

figures 7.3 and 7.4 illustrate this case. In the first figure there are fixed costs, and then a constant marginal cost. In the second figure, marginal costs are stubbornly decreasing. The first case obviously can only be an approximation, but this approximation seems to be realistic in numerous cases,[4] which confers upon it a central role in models of regulation (see section 7.3) and of industrial organization.

The consequences of these nonconvexities on supply functions are very different. In the case of small nonconvexities, the supply curve is discontinuous. In effect, the necessary first-order condition, which equates price and marginal cost, only defines the firm's supply if it does not bring on losses. The supply curve therefore coincides with the marginal cost curve only for prices high enough to make production profitable, as presented in figure 7.5. There is a threshold price for which supply is either nil or equal to the efficient scale.

When there are large nonconvexities, the situation is more catastrophic: depending the respective values of the price and of the marginal cost at infinity, supply can only be zero or infinite, and the supply curve therefore degenerates completely.

In any case, the nonconvexity of the production set always implies that the supply curve is discontinuous, and that equilibrium is

---

4. For a software producing firm, for example, the costs are essentially due to research and development, so they are fixed. The marginal cost of manufacturing a copy of software can be considered as a constant. The pharmaceutical industry has similar characteristics.

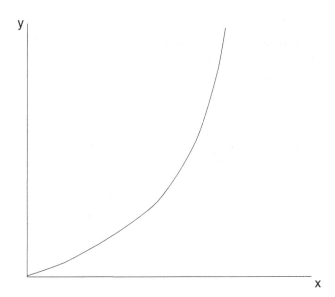

**Figure 7.4**
Large nonconvexities of production, II

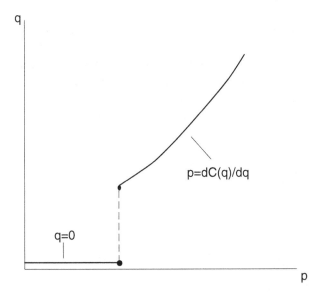

**Figure 7.5**
Supply in the presence of a small nonconvexity

therefore compromised. In the case of large nonconvexities, there cannot be an equilibrium; for small nonconvexities and a fixed number of firms, equilibrium only exists if the efficient scale is small enough in relation to the market scale.

## 7.2   Convexification by Numbers

In this section we will show that the impact of certain nonconvexities becomes negligible when the number of agents rises to infinity. The suitable mathematical tool is the Shapley-Folkman theorem, which inserts itself into a gamut of remarkable results on convex sets. We will note co $D$ the convex envelope of $D$, which is the smallest convex set containing $D$.

THEOREM 7.1   (SHAPLEY-FOLKMAN)   Let $D_1, \ldots, D_n$ be any nonempty sets of $\mathbb{R}^l$ and a point $z \in co \, \Sigma_{i=1}^n D_i$. Then

$$\exists x_1, \ldots, x_n, \begin{cases} \forall i = 1, \ldots, n, \quad x_i \in coD_i \\ \sum_{i=1}^n x_i = z \\ \{i = 1, \ldots, n | x_1 \notin D_i\} \quad \text{has at most } l \text{ elements} \end{cases}$$

This theorem tells us that in order to attain a point of the convex envelope of the sum of $n$ sets, it suffices to add $n$ well-chosen points of the convex envelopes of these sets, of which at most $l$ do not belong to the sets themselves. The interest of this result stems from the case where, $l$ being fixed, $n$ tends toward the infinite. Consider now the case where aggregate excess demand $z(p)$ is discontinuous, so equilibrium does not exist. It is easy to show that in compensation, a pseudoequilibrium $p^*$ exists which verifies $0 \in co \, z(p^*)$, as we see in figure 7.6.

But, if there are $l$ goods and $n$ agents, application of the Shapley-Folkman theorem shows that

$$\exists x_1, \ldots, z_n, \begin{cases} \forall i = 1, \ldots, n, \quad z_i \in co \, z_i(p^*) \\ \sum_{i=1}^n z_i = 0 \\ \{i = 1, \ldots, n | z_1 \notin z_i(p^*)\} \quad \text{has at most } l \text{ elements} \end{cases}$$

Therefore an approximate equilibrium is obtained where only $l$ of at the most $n$ agents are not situated on their excess demand curve. When $n$ becomes very large, the proportion of these agents becomes negligible in the economy, since the number of goods $l$ is fixed. It is in this

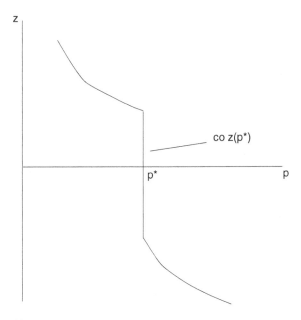

**Figure 7.6**
Pseudoequilibrium

sense that the multiplication of the number of agents makes the economy convex.

Let us look at the two examples more closely. Figure 7.7 corresponds to nonconvex preferences. In figure 7.8 we see how the problem posed by small nonconvexities in production is (approximately) solved. Note the interpretation of this second example: to obtain an approximate equilibrium, it is sufficient to have a well-chosen number of firms produce at their efficient scale and allow the others to close. This will be indifferent to these firms because they would all have zero profit anyway.

## 7.3  Regulation of Natural Monopolies

Convexification by number solves nothing in the presence of large non-convexities: the supply function is not clearly defined, so there does not even exist pseudoequilibrium. Since equilibrium concepts are no help to us, we must resort to optimality concepts. Now, what is the best way to organize production? Assume an industry where a sole

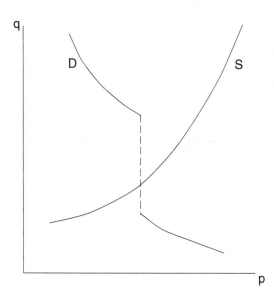

**Figure 7.7**
Convexification of preferences

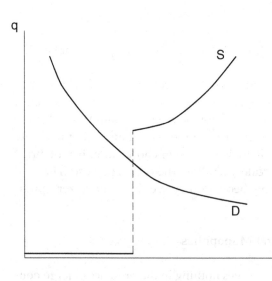

**Figure 7.8**
Convexification in production

technology exists that is characterized by a cost function $C(q)$. If we determine that the optimum requires a production $Q$, productive efficiency supposes that the total production cost is minimized. Therefore we must solve the program

$$\begin{cases} \min_{n,q_1,...,q_n} \sum_{i=1}^{n} C(q_i) \\ \qquad \sum_{i=1}^{n} q_i \geq Q \end{cases}$$

which jointly determines the number of operating firms and the distribution of production among them.

When marginal costs are increasing, the efficient scale $q^*$ is zero, and it would be fitting therefore to multiply small production units. In the presence of small nonconvexities, it is easy to see that the solution is $n = Q/q^*$ (to the nearest integer): a certain number of firms are closed and the others are made to produce at the efficient scale. The case that interests us here is that of large nonconvexities. Then the cost function is subadditive; that is, we get

$$\forall n, \forall i = 1,...,n, \quad C\left(\sum_{i=1}^{n} q_i\right) \leq \sum_{i=1}^{n} C(q_i)$$

and $n = 1$ at the optimum. Clearly, it would be better if a single firm produced, rather than production being shared among several firms.[5] It is then said that the sector in question is a *natural monopoly*. For purely technological reasons, it is fitting to grant a monopoly to one of the firms. However, the firm may then behave as a monopoly, which is socially harmful as we will see in chapter 9. Even economists the least prone to intervention have traditionally thought that in such a situation, adequate regulation is called for.[6] Habitually cited are transportation, telecommunications, and what are called *utilities* in the United States: water, electricity, and so on. All these sectors operate with high fixed costs (or heavy infrastructure). For example, it seems that even if competition is desirable, it would be absurdly costly to double the number of railroad lines.

The problem that interests us in this section therefore is how this type of sector must be regulated. Both economists' opinions and adopted

---

5. This is fairly obvious when there are large nonconvexities of the first type ($C(q) = F + cq$), since then adding firms reverts to the multiplication of fixed costs without gaining in efficiency in other respects.
6. The maxim followed is: "Competition where possible, regulation where necessary."

policy measures have far evolved in the course of recent years, and we will try to understand why.

### 7.3.1   Marginal Cost Pricing

As we well know, in any interior Pareto optimum, the marginal rates of substitution and the marginal rates of transformation must be equal. As an example, consider an economy with two goods $x$ and $y$, with $y$ produced from $x$ with a production function $y = f(x)$. If the consumer has a utility function $U(x, y)$, this amounts to

$$\frac{\partial U/\partial x}{\partial U/\partial y} = f'(x)$$

But at the consumer's optimum, it takes the form

$$\frac{\partial U/\partial x}{\partial U/\partial y} = \frac{p_x}{p_y}$$

Now the cost function is $C(y) = p_x f^{-1}(y)$, which gives a marginal cost $C'(y) = p_x/f'(x)$. From this we can deduce the rule according to which any good produced must be priced at the marginal cost, regardless of the conditions of its production:

$$p_y = C'(y)$$

This rule is due in its general form to Hotelling (1938),[7] who expressed it like this:

The optimum of the general welfare corresponds to the sale of everything at marginal cost.

Note that if Hotelling's rule is applied, a firm subject to large nonconvexities will necessarily make losses since its average cost is always higher than its marginal cost (e.g., a firm with cost function $C(y) = F + cy$ will lose its fixed costs). The firm must therefore be subsidized, preferably with lump-sum transfers in order not to distort the agents' choices—which would take the economy away from the Pareto optimum.

Marginal cost pricing was the object of a long debate until the end of the 1950s. Certain authors judged that it was an unattainable

---

7. Even if Dupuit (1844) had already stated it in the case of pricing bridge use.

optimum, particularly because the lump-sum transfers destined to finance firm losses are difficult to implement. They suggested that one be content with average cost pricing, the firm then making zero profit by construction. Maurice Allais's famous allegory of the mine and the forest illustrates the inefficiency of this solution, even in the absence of nonconvexities. Suppose that the inhabitants of a town can warm themselves one of two ways: by extracting coal from a mine or by chopping down trees in a forest on a neighboring hill. The coal is mined at a constant marginal cost, while the woodcutting has an increasing marginal cost—for example, because it is necessary to climb higher and higher to find slopes that have not yet been cleared of trees. Of course the production optimum consists of cutting trees until the marginal cost of this activity coincides with that of the coal mining. What happens if one then prices at the average cost?

• The average cost of coal mining coincides with its marginal cost

• The average cost of chopping down trees is lower than its marginal cost

For a given price of energy (independent of its origin), average cost pricing implies therefore that the trees are cut beyond the point where their marginal cost meets that of the coal. This leads then to a waste of labor and distances the economy from the production optimum.[8]

It is clear that average cost pricing is almost never optimal, but that marginal cost pricing loses its character of optimality in the presence of tax distortions. The choice of pricing then becomes a second-best problem, which one can only study by modeling the sources of distortion. This is what we will do below.

### 7.3.2   Second-Best Pricing of Regulated Firms

Many natural monopolies are state-owned firms (or are state-regulated in some way). We will study two models that emphasize two aspects of regulation. The Ramsey-Boiteux model[9] studies optimal pricing of a part of the regulated sector submitted to budgetary equilibrium when only unit taxes are possible. Baron-Myerson (1982) analyze the problem

---

8. Another possible example is that a bridge should be constructed because it engenders a positive net surplus, but no toll rights level exists that could finance its construction.
9. Ramsey (1927) was the first to solve the optimal taxation problem; Boiteux (1956) was more interested in the problem posed in the text. Their two models are formally equivalent, as is evident by the fact that the two authors are joined in its name.

of the regulator when the regulated firm possess private information on its costs.

*The Ramsey-Boiteux Formula*

Here we take a set of regulated firms as one big firm. This firm produces goods $(x_1, \ldots, x_l)$ at a cost $(C + c_1 x_1 + \ldots + c_l x_l)$. The product $k$ is taxed at a rate $t_k$, so its consumption price is $p_k = c_k + t_k$. The firm faces a budgetary constraint[10]

$$C = \sum_{k=1}^{l} t_k x_k (p_1, \ldots, p_l)$$

where the $x_k$ are demand functions.

In the economy there is a numéraire good $y$ and a representative consumer endowed with an income $R$ whose utility function is quasi-linear (absence of wealth effect) and additively separable: $U = \Sigma_{k=1}^{l} u_k(x_k) + y$. With these specifications, the demand functions are simply given by

$$u_k'(x_k(p_k)) = p_k$$

The regulator problem consists in maximizing the utility of the consumer under the budgetary constraint:

$$\begin{cases} \max(p_1, \ldots, p_l) \left( \sum_{k=1}^{l} u_k(x_k(p_k)) + R - \sum_{k=1}^{l} p_k x_k(p_k) \right) \\ C = \sum_{k=1}^{l} (p_k - c_k) x_k(p_k) \qquad (\lambda) \end{cases}$$

where $\lambda$ is the multiplier attached to the constraint.

The first-order conditions give

$$\forall k = 1, \ldots, l, \quad u_k' x_k' - p_k x_k' - x_k + \lambda x_k + \lambda(p_k - c_k) x_k' = 0$$

Put differently, after utilization of $u_k' = p_k$ and rearrangement of the terms,

$$\forall k = 1, \ldots, l, \quad \frac{p_k x_k'}{x_k} \frac{p_k - c_k}{p_k} = \frac{1 - \lambda}{\lambda}$$

If we denote $\varepsilon_k = -p_k x_k'/x_k$, the demand elasticity for good $k$ and $\tau_k = (p_k - c_k)/p_k$, the tax rate on this good, finally we get the Ramsey-Boiteux formula:

---

10. The results will be qualitatively the same if one assigns only to the transfers given to the firm a cost that takes into account the distortions entailed by their collection.

$$\forall k = 1,\ldots,l, \quad \varepsilon_k \tau_k = \frac{\lambda - 1}{\lambda}$$

The formula shows that the tax rate on a good must be inversely proportional to the elasticity of demand for that good. This result is easily understood: it is advisable to limit the distortions linked to non-lump-sum taxation and therefore to tax more vigorously goods that are the least sensitive to price variations. For that matter, the Ramsey-Boiteux formula implies that at first-order, consumptions of all goods are discouraged in the same way: simple calculations show that if the fixed costs (and therefore the tax rates necessary to finance them) are very small, the relative drop in the consumption of good $k$ is given by

$$-\frac{\delta x_k}{x_k} = -\frac{x'_k t_k}{x_k}$$

$$= -\frac{x'_k p_k \tau_k}{x_k} \frac{\lambda - 1}{\lambda}$$

$$= \frac{\lambda - 1}{\lambda}$$

which is independent of the good $k$. Therefore an effective second-best taxation must not equalize the tax rates but rather equally discourage consumptions of different goods.[11] Unfortunately, goods with high price elasticities are often those with high income elasticity, that is, luxury goods. Contrary to what common sense suggests, luxury goods must therefore be taxed less heavily than necessities. Insofar as this leads to taxing the consumption of the poor more heavily than that of the rich, it is advisable to take into account the distributive concerns in this model. Then the objective to maximize is no longer the utility of a representative consumer but a weighted sum of the consumers' utilities: $\Sigma_{i=1}^{n} \alpha_i U_i$, where $\alpha_i$ is the weight of the consumer $i$ in the social utility (and $\Sigma_{i=1}^{n} \alpha_i = 1$). Very similar calculations to those above show that we get at the second-best optimum

$$\tau_k \varepsilon_k = \frac{\lambda - \rho_k}{\lambda}$$

where $\varepsilon_k$ is the price elasticity of aggregate demand $X_k$ for good $k$ and $\rho_k$ is the "distributive factor" of that good:

---

11. This result remains valid in the presence of income effects and cross-elasticities of demand.

$$\rho_k = \frac{\sum_{i=1}^{n} \alpha_i x_k^i}{\sum_{i=1}^{n} x_k^i}$$

We note that $\rho_k$ is one in the absence of redistributive objectives (all $\alpha_i$ being equal); it is more than one if the consumers whose weight in social utility is the highest (which are generally the "poor") consume more of good $k$ than the others. The modified Ramsey-Boiteux formula says therefore that for given elasticities, the tax rate must be smaller on goods that are consumed mostly by the poor. This could also be interpreted in noting that consumptions of the poor must be less discouraged than those of the rich.[12]

It should be noted that the Ramsey-Boiteux formula is quite remote from the situation of public transportation which operates on the basis that each mode must be entirely financed by its users. Nothing in the Ramsey-Boiteux model suggests a budgetary equilibrium on each good is desirable. By comparison, a French report cited by Henry (1989) calculated that given the estimated elasticities, three-quarters of the fixed costs of rail transport should be financed by taxes on highway traffic.

As suggested by the public transportation example above, Ramsey-Boiteux pricing has not had much impact on decision makers, perhaps because it gives no simple rule. Scott (1986) studies the example of the United States Postal Service to show how real-world decision makers try to draw inspiration from the Ramsey-Boiteux formula while taking into account other extra-economic constraints.

*Asymmetrical Information Regulation*
Recent literature on the regulation of firms has insisted on the strategic importance of private information at the disposal of regulated firms. For example, it is clear that it behooves such a firm to overestimate its costs to obtain a more favorable treatment. The regulator must, in order to avoid this snag, construct a revealing mechanism which delegates as much of the decision-making to the firm as possible. Formally, this is a Principal-Agent problem where the regulator is the Principal and the firm is the Agent.

Consider then a natural monopoly of cost function $C(q, \theta) = K + \theta q$. The firm is brought to budgetary equilibrium by a subsidy $t$ levied on

---

12. The numerical applications conducted on developing countries show that the consumption of certain basic foods should in fact be subsidized.

the consumers, the social unit cost of which is $\lambda$: when the government collects a tax $t$, the utility of the consumers decreases by $(1 + \lambda)t$ because of tax management costs and the economic distortions which accompany taxes.[13] The firm's profit is therefore

$$t - C(q, \theta)$$

while the consumer surplus is

$$S(q) - (1 + \lambda)t = \int_0^q P(x)dx - (1 + \lambda)t$$

where $P$ is the inverse demand function. We will assume that the regulator's objective is social welfare, or the nonweighted sum of the consumer surplus and of firm profit:

$$S(q) - C(q, \theta) - \lambda t$$

*First-Best*
Suppose that the regulator observes $\theta$. Then it would suffice him to solve

$$\begin{cases} \max_{(q,t)} [S(q) - C(q, \theta) - \lambda t] \\ \quad t - C(q, \theta) \geq 0 \end{cases}$$

whose solution is of course $t = C(q, \theta)$ and $S'(q) = P(q) = (1 + \lambda)\theta$, that is we see again the marginal cost pricing rule, corrected here for the cost of public funds $\lambda$.[14]

*Second-Best*
In fact it is more realistic to suppose that information is asymmetric: the firm obviously knows $\theta$, but the regulator simply has a Bayesian a priori such that $\theta$ follows a cumulative distribution function $F$ with density $f$ on an interval $[\underline{\theta}, \overline{\theta}]$. The revelation principle introduced in chapter 4 applies here: the regulator must find a direct mechanism $(q(\theta), t(\theta))$ that maximizes the objective

$$\int_{\underline{\theta}}^{\overline{\theta}} \{S[q(\theta)] - C[q(\theta), \theta] - \lambda t(\theta)\} dF(\theta)$$

---

13. Empirical estimates suggest that the value of $\lambda$ can be on the order of 0.2.
14. It is therefore the *social* marginal cost $(1 + \lambda)\theta$ that we must consider here.

under the incentive constraints (IC) and under the participation constraints (IR). The incentive constraints state that the firm $\theta$ chooses the pair $(q(\theta), t(\theta))$ destined to it and are written as

$$\forall \theta, \theta', \quad t(\theta) - C(q(\theta), \theta) \geq t(\theta') - C(q(\theta'), \theta) \quad \text{(IC)}$$

The participation constraints guarantee a nonnegative profit to the firm:

$$\forall \theta, \quad t(\theta) - C[q(\theta), \theta] \geq 0 \quad \text{(IR)}$$

Denote by $r(\theta) = t(\theta) - C(q(\theta), \theta) = t(\theta) - \theta q(\theta) - F$ the *informational rent* of the firm $\theta$. This is the profit that it succeeds in obtaining thanks to its private information. The incentive constraints can be written

$$\forall \theta, \theta', \quad r(\theta) \geq r(\theta') - (\theta - \theta') q(\theta') \quad \text{(IC)}$$

By exchanging the roles of $\theta$ and $\theta'$, we get a second inequality that can be combined with the first. It is written as

$$\forall \theta, \theta', \quad (\theta - \theta') q(\theta) \leq r(\theta') - r(\theta) \leq (\theta - \theta') q(\theta')$$

which implies, in particular, that $(\theta - \theta')(q(\theta') - q(\theta)) \geq 0$ and therefore that $q$ is decreasing. Moreover, by assuming that $\theta \leq \theta'$ and by dividing by $(\theta' - \theta)$, we get

$$-q(\theta) \leq \frac{r(\theta') - r(\theta)}{\theta' - \theta} \leq -q(\theta')$$

So at every point where $q$ is continuous,[15] $r$ may be differentiated and $r' = -q$. We can then deduce that $r$ is convex since $q$ is decreasing.

Since $q$ is positive, $r$ decreases, and the constraints of participation amount to just $r(\bar{\theta}) = 0$. Therefore we get

$$r(\theta) = \int_{\theta}^{\bar{\theta}} q(t) \, dt$$

which, incidentally, gives transfers $t$ in terms of $q$:

$$t(\theta) = C(q(\theta), \theta) + \int_{\theta}^{\bar{\theta}} q(t) \, dt$$

Having eliminated the transfers, it only remains for us to maximize

---

15. It is easily shown that $q$, being a strictly decreasing function, can only have a countable set of points of discontinuity.

$$\int_{\underline{\theta}}^{\bar{\theta}} \left( S[q(\theta)] - (1+\lambda)\theta q(\theta) - \lambda \int_{\theta}^{\bar{\theta}} q(t)\,dt \right) dF(\theta)$$

under the sole constraint $q'(\theta) \leq 0$.

To solve this program, we should first neglect the constraint that $q$ be decreasing. The optimum is then found by integrating the objective by parts, whence

$$\int_{\underline{\theta}}^{\bar{\theta}} \left( S[q(\theta)] - (1+\lambda)\theta q(\theta) - \lambda \frac{F(\theta)}{f(\theta)} q(\theta) \right) dF(\theta)$$

This result is simply maximized point by point, whence finally

$$S'[q(\theta)] = P[q(\theta)] = (1+\lambda)\theta + \lambda \frac{F(\theta)}{f(\theta)}$$

If $(\theta + F(\theta)/f(\theta))$ is an increasing function (which is a hypothesis verified by the majority of usual distributions), then the right-hand member is increasing,[16] and since $P$ is decreasing, the solution $q(\theta)$ verifies the constraint $q'(\theta) \leq 0$.

Therefore the price this time is higher than the social marginal cost; the supplementary term is used to compel the firm to reveal its type. It leads to underproduction: $q$ is smaller than in the first-best. This underproduction stems from the fact that if a regulator wants to augment production of a $\theta$ while maintaining the incentives to reveal their type for all the other types, what also must be augmented is the informational rent of all types more efficient than $\theta$ (the $\theta' < \theta$). In more intuitive terms, the regulator must keep the $\theta$-type firm from posing as a less efficient firm $\theta' > \theta$ and thus from pocketing a higher subsidy. The most economical way to do this is to reduce the production of inefficient firms, so that they get smaller subsidies, and more efficient firms are not tempted to lie.

The reader should note here that the hypothesis that costs are unobservable is not always the most realistic. Laffont-Tirole (1986) introduced a slightly different model where the costs $C$ of the firm depend simultaneously on an efficiency parameter and on a level of effort, both of which are unobserved though the costs are (imperfectly) observable. They show that the optimal incentive mechanism then consists in offering a menu of linear prices $t = a + bC$ where there are as many (well-chosen) pairs $(a, b)$ as possible parameters of efficiency. The most

---

16. For the study of the general case, I refer the reader to Salanié (1997, ch. 2).

efficient firm chooses a *fixed-price* contract (a tariff with $b = 0$, which assures the firm a transfer independent of its costs), and the less efficient firms choose a tariff corresponding to a higher $b$.[17]

## 7.4 Deregulation

The regulation of natural monopolies has greatly evolved over the last few years as numerous firms of these industries were privatized and often faced fierce competition. The designation of this movement as "deregulation" is somewhat inaccurate, since one form of regulation was being displaced by another.[18] This has proved to be a fertile field of application for the models of section 7.3.2.

Deregulation is based on a triad of beliefs:

• Technological innovations make natural monopolies more expendable: even where the fixed costs remain high at the infrastructure level, infrastructures can be separated from the actual service activity, where returns to scale are rarely increasing.[19]

• The diversified product range of these sectors (one need only think of the new telecommunication products), makes detailed regulation problematic.

• Competition in itself is an effective regulator.

The first two statements do not call for any further comment. Concerning the third belief, there is the idea proposed a number of decades ago by Demsetz (1968). Demsetz argued that rather than regulate the distribution of utilities like electricity, the right to distribute electricity could be put up for auction and then granted to the highest bidder. In this way the monopoly rents would transfer to the taxpayer who could select the most efficient operator. The most recent literature insists on the use of competition to reduce informational rents: the underlying idea is that if the industry is left to several firms whose costs are correlated, the observation of their behavior in the

17. A similar contract menu was effectively used in the United States for regulating the "Baby Bells," the seven local telephone firms created by the breakup of AT&T.
18. Kay and Vickers (1988) provide a good explanation of how deregulation has replaced *structural* regulation (which defines the marketplace and the number of firms that can operate there) by regulation of the *behavior* of firms.
19. This distinction particularly applies to network industries like transportation, telecommunications, and energy.

framework of the Baron-Myerson model permits their costs to be better understood.

Clearly, it is incorrect to say that deregulation is a uniform and universal movement. Still we can point to certain common themes (aside from privatization, which would merit special treatment):

• Infrastructures and the services used by these infrastructures are separated. This permits the activity with increasing returns to be isolated. The infrastructures have sometimes been regrouped in a firm created for that purpose; in other cases (e.g., telecommunications) one firm has conserved all the property or infrastructure but has allowed its competitors access, subject to the payment of a fee.

• Increasing returns are a negligible phenomenon in the opening of services to competition in the market.

• *Price-cap* type of regulation formula is adopted. The most popular was recommended by the 1983 Littlechild Report in the United Kingdom and is called RPI − *X*; it consists of limiting the growth rate of a weighted average of the firm's prices to the increase of the retail price index after deduction of an expected productivity growth rate.

## Bibliography

Baron, D., and R. Myerson. 1982. Regulating a monopoly with unknown costs. *Econometrica* 50: 911–30.

Boiteux, M. 1956. Sur la gestion des monopoles publics astreints à l'équilibre budgétaire. *Econometrica* 24: 22–40.

Demsetz, H. 1968. Why regulate utilities? *Journal of Law and Economics* 9: 55–65.

Dupuit, J. 1844. De la mesure de l'utilité des travaux publics. *Annales des Ponts et Chaussées* 8: 332–75. Published in English in P. Jackson, ed. *The Foundations of Public Finance*. Elgar, Cheltenham, England, 1996.

Henry, C. 1989. *Microeconomics for Public Policy: Helping the Invisible Hand*. Clarendon Press, Oxford.

Hotelling, H. 1938. The general welfare in relation to problems of taxation and of railway and utility rates. *Econometrica* 6: 242–69.

Kay, J., and J. Vickers. 1988. Regulatory reform in Britain. *Economic Policy* 7: 286–351.

Laffont, J.-J., and J. Tirole. 1986. Using cost observation to regulate firms. *Journal of Political Economy* 94: 614–41.

Ramsey, F. 1927. A contribution to the theory of taxation. *Economic Journal* 37: 47–61.

Salanié, B. 1997. *The Economics of Contracts: A Primer*. MIT Press, Cambridge.

# III  Industrial Organization

The next five chapters are devoted to industrial organization. Industrial organization theory, or simply IO, applies to the operation of isolated markets as opposed to general equilibrium theory, which is concerned with the global operation of an economy. IO theory rests on a fairly detailed description of strategic interactions among agents.

The terms "imperfect competition" and "industrial organization" are nearly synonymous. They can be defined by antithesis in recalling the four classical conditions for perfect competition:

• The number of each market's buyers and sellers is very high

• There are no barriers to entering the market

• The exchange concerns a homogeneous good

• The information on prices is perfect

One enters the domain of industrial organization as soon as one of these conditions ceases to be verified.

The classical economists were interested, above all, in perfect competition. Their aversion to what they called "monopolies" had to do more with the existence of barriers to entry than with the modern concept of a monopoly.[1] The theory of imperfect competition came from Cournot (1838)[2] and its criticism from Bertrand (1883). Unfortunately, both contributions did not receive the welcome they deserved,

1. Thus Adam Smith under the name "monopoly" deplored the existence of professional corporations that regulated the behavior of participants on the market.
2. I can't praise highly enough Cournot's little book. In it one finds a strong plea for the use of mathematics in economics (introduction), the discovery of demand curves and (with very few exceptions) of elasticity (chapter IV), the resolution of the monopoly problem (chapter V), a theory of oligopoly (chapter VII) and its competitive limit (chapter VIII). All this appeared at least fifty years ahead of its time, and in a form that remains quite modern.

so Alfred Marshall's (1890) famous manual in this domain really redis-covered Cournot's theory of monopoly.

Three important contributions must be noted between the two World Wars. Hotelling (1929) invented the horizontal differentiation model which remains at the foundation of numerous developments in indus-trial and spatial organization. Chamberlin (1933) and Robinson (1933) had both ambitiously planned to re-establish microeconomics around a theory of imperfect competition: monopolistic competition for Chamberlin, and monopoly for Robinson.

Industrial organization developed more fully in the 1950s. It was first dominated by Harvard, where the central figure was Joe Bain.[3] The work of the Harvard economists was hinged by the triptych *structure–conduct–performance*: it went from the organization of a sector of the economy, to its consequences on the behavior of firms, and then to their profits. A typical application of this type of analysis was a regression of the profit rates of different sectors on a measure of the sectors' concentration. In the 1960s Chicago economists, grouped around George Stigler, offered a more Popperian approach of indus-trial organization, which consisted of proposing different theories and then attempting to choose from among them on the basis of empirical tests.[4] In the 1970s the torch was taken up by economists who system-atically applied to industrial organization tools of game theory by constructing more elaborate theoretical models which often contained an explicit dynamic component. This part of the book is situated in the theoretical models of this last school. The reader should not presume to find an exhaustive treatise on industrial organization. Only the basics are given with illustrations using concrete examples. Readers not satiated by the contents of the next few chapters can refer to Tirole's manual cited in the introduction.

The reader will notice a certain analytical rupture between parts II and III. In part III we effectively exit the framework of general equi-librium and interest ourselves in partial equilibrium models. Chapter

---

3. We should note also the work of Schumpeter (1942), which led among other things to the rehabilitation of large firms as essential vectors of "creative destruction." Schumpeter argued that innovative firms constantly replaced those that had exhausted their innovation potential. Unfortunately, we do not yet have sufficiently sophisticated dynamic models to test Schumpeter's intuitions, but we will but touch upon them in chapter 11.
4. The Chicago school is also associated with an optimistic vision of the principle of laissez-faire and with deep skepticism about the government's capacity for worthwhile intervention.

8 attempts to explain why it is difficult to construct a theory of general equilibrium of imperfect competition.

## Bibliography

Bertrand, J. 1883. Théorie des richesses. *Journal des Savants*, 499–508. Published in English in A. Daughety, ed. *Cournot Oligopoly: Characterization and Applications.* Cambridge: Cambridge University Press (1988).

Chamberlin, E. 1933. *The Theory of Monopolistic Competition.* Cambridge: Harvard University Press.

Cournot, A. 1838. *Recherches sur les principes mathématiques de la théorie des richesses.* Published in English as *Mathematical Principles of the Theory of Wealth,* James and Gordon, San Diego, CA 1995.

Hotelling, H. 1929. Stability in competition. *Economic Journal* 39: 41–57.

Marshall, A. 1890. *Principles of Economics.* London: Macmillan.

Robinson, J. 1933. *The Economics of Imperfect Competition.* London: Macmillan.

Schumpeter, J. 1942. *Capitalism, Socialism and Democracy.* New York: Harper and Brothers.

# 8    General Equilibrium of
       Imperfect Competition

While models of welfare economics are set in a general equilibrium framework, those of industrial organization are partial equilibrium models. The study of the complexity of strategic interactions is a sufficiently difficult problem without our adding in general equilibrium considerations. Moreover, if we limit ourselves to the most simple strategic concepts—what is called Cournot or Bertrand competition—their immersion in a framework of general equilibrium poses delicate problems for which no satisfactory solution has yet been found. This chapter is dedicated to this second point. Without sinking into overly technical digressions, we will get an idea of the difficulties entailed when attempts are made to construct models of general equilibrium in imperfect competition. It will be worthwhile for those interested in these questions to refer to Bénassy (1991), Bonanno (1990), or Hart (1985).[1]

## 8.1    Three Difficulties

Each model of general equilibrium in imperfect competition harbors its own difficulties. The objective of this section is to discuss three problems that intervene in all of these models: the ambiguity of the objective of noncompetitive firms, the noninvariance of equilibrium in relation to the price normalization rule, and the impossibility of finding conditions that ensure that profit functions have good properties.

---

1. The reader should be alerted to the fact that these writings use the term "monopolistic competition" in a much broader sense than the one I define in chapter 10.

### 8.1.1    The Firms' Objectives

In competitive equilibrium a firm's shareholders are unanimous in asking for profit maximization. Assume in effect a consumer $i$ with initial resources $\omega_i$ who possesses a fraction $\theta_i$ of the firm. If he is faced with prices $p$, his indirect utility will be

$$V_i(p, p \cdot \omega_i + \theta_i \pi)$$

when the firm makes a profit $\pi$. This expression is of course increasing in $\pi$; in other respects, the firm, like its stockholders, takes prices as givens by definition. It is therefore clear that all the stockholders desire the firm to maximize its profits.

   Things are more complicated when the firm has market power. Then its profit $\pi(p)$ is a function of a variable that it can choose (the price that it tariffs, e.g., $p_1$). Say, the firm takes the prices of other goods as givens. It will then be necessary for it to maximize in $p_1$ in order to please consumer $i$,

$$V_i[p, p \cdot \omega_i + \theta_i \pi(p)]$$

So clearly this problem is no longer reduced to profit maximization. Rather the maximum is characterized by

$$\frac{\partial V_i}{\partial p_i} + \frac{\partial V_i}{\partial R}\left(\omega_{i1} + \theta_i \frac{\partial \pi}{\partial p_1}\right) = 0$$

Using Roy's identity and denoting the excess demand for good 1 $z_{i1} = x_{i1} - w_{i1}$, the result is

$$\frac{\partial \pi}{\partial p_1} = \frac{z_{i1}}{\theta_i}$$

If $\pi$ is concave in $p_1$ and $z_{i1}$ is positive, that is, if the consumer $i$ consumes a lot of the good 1 that the firm produces, the latter will have to reduce the price $p_1$ below the level that maximizes its profits. Moreover there is no reason for the firm's shareholders to agree on the price that must be fixed. It is therefore impossible to assign the firm a simple objective.

   This theoretical difficulty is not final. Most consumers actually buy a very small quantity of the products of firms in which they are stockholders. It is reasonable, at first approximation, then to think that profit maximization is an acceptable objective. In any case, this chapter rests on this hypothesis.[2]

## 8.1.2 Price Normalization

In competitive equilibrium only the relative prices are important. The price vector can be normalized by fixing any price at 1, for example, without that choice having the least influence on the relative prices or on the allocations of equilibrium. Such is no longer the case in imperfect competition. To see this, it is enough to consider a monopoly that chooses its prices for profit maximization: if its price is fixed at 1, its maximization program does not make any sense.

This difficulty is inherent in all models where agents perceive a relation between prices and quantities: equilibrium depends on the rule of normalization.[3] Subsequently we will implicitly assume the existence of a good (the numéraire) produced and consumed in competitive conditions, and we will normalize its price at 1. However, this solution is not really satisfactory. In fact the definition of the firms' objective and the choice of a price normalization rule are inextricably bound together. Dierker and Grodal (1996) propose solving this double problem by assuming that firms maximize what they call the "real stockholder wealth," but this proposition raises other difficulties.

## 8.1.3 The Quasi-concavity of Profit

The last general difficulty we will address is important, albeit a bit technical. Our objective is to demonstrate the existence of general equilibrium based on Kakutani's fixed-point theorem. The theorem applies to semi-continuous correspondences with convex values. Whatever is the firm's desired strategic variable (its price or its quantity) then that is its best choice correspondence be of convex values. The only simple hypothesis that assumes this property deals with the quasi-concavity of the profit function with respect to the strategic variable.[4]

In partial equilibrium, it is easy to find hypotheses that ensure that the profit function is quasi-concave—concavity of demand, for

---

2. We will see a similar, though more pronounced, difficulty in chapter 13.
3. This discussion is a bit abstract; it will be illustrated by an example in section 8.3.1.
4. Recall that a function $f$ of $IR^n$ in $IR$ is quasi-concave if and only if, for every $y$ of $IR$, the set of $x$ such that $f(x) \geq y$ is convex. The standard example of a function that is not quasi-concave is a multimodal function.

example. Unfortunately, in general equilibrium demand functions themselves proceed from consumer optimization, and they cannot be assumed to be concave a priori. In fact, as Roberts and Sonnenschein (1977) showed, there are instances where the basic economic data satisfy all the usual hypotheses and yet the profit function is not quasi-concave, which brings about the nonexistence of equilibrium.

At the present time there does not exist a satisfactory solution to this problem. All the literature therefore just assumes that profit functions are quasi-concave, as we will do in this chapter.

## 8.2  Subjective Demand Equilibrium

The first contribution of import in this domain is due to Negishi (1961). Negishi's analysis centers on subjective inverse demand functions, in other words, price variations that noncompetitive firms foresee when they modify their production.

Let $s = (p, x, y)$ be an economic state where $p$ represents the price vector, $x$ the consumptions, and $y$ productions. Negishi supposes that the firm $j$ is endowed with a "conjecture" or subjective demand

$$P_j(y_j', s)$$

which represents the price that the firm anticipates for goods for which it has market power when, leaving the state $s$, it modifies its production $y_j$ to $y_j'$. Negishi dictates only that this conjecture be compatible with the state of departure in the sense that

$$P_j(y_j, s) = p_j$$

so that the firm, when it does not deviate from the original state, is not mistaken about the price.

A subjective demand equilibrium is an economic state $s^* = (p^*, x^*, y^*)$ which balances all markets, such that consumers maximize their utility under budgetary constraint and that for each noncompetitive firm $j$ of the production set $Y_j$, $y_j^*$ maximizes its perceived profit

$$P_j(y_j, s^*) \cdot y_j$$

in $y_j \in Y_j$.

We can show that equilibrium exists under the usual hypotheses when perceived profit functions are quasi-concave.[5]

---

5. This is for example, the case where conjectures are linear, as Negishi supposed.

## 8.3   Objective Demand Equilibrium

The disadvantage to subjective demand equilibrium is that it introduces an unknown element (conjectures) into the determination of the equilibrium. There is a risk therefore of the existence of very numerous equilibria when the conjectures vary. Thus competitive equilibrium is obtained when for each noncompetitive firm $j$ and each production plan $y_j$,

$$P_j(y_j, s^*) = p_j^*$$

Moreover certain of these equilibria can rest upon conjectures that are entirely wrong. The polar hypothesis consists of assuming that noncompetitive firms perceive "objective demands," that is, true demand functions. We will see two examples of this, depending on whether firms compete in quantity or in price.

### 8.3.1   Equilibrium in Quantities

Gabszewicz and Vial (1972) integrated Cournot competition in a model of general equilibrium. Suppose that all firms $j = 1, \ldots, m$ are noncompetitive. If they choose production plans $y = (y_1, \ldots, y_m)$, define the "modified resources" of consumers as

$$\omega_i'(y) = \omega_i + \sum_{j=1}^{m} \theta_{ij} y_j$$

which take into account the fact that each consumer is owner, through his shares, of a portion of the firms' production.

Now consider the "modified economy" where there is no firm and where consumers' resources are the modified resources $\omega_i'(y)$. If all goes well (we return later to this point), this economy has a unique equilibrium price vector $P(y)$ that continuously depends on $y$. We can consequently define a "Cournot-Walras equilibrium" by a price vector $p^*$, consumptions $x^*$ which maximize consumers' utility under budgetary constraint, and productions $y^*$ such that

- $p^* = P(y^*)$

- the equilibrium is a Cournot equilibrium, in the sense that for every firm $j$, $y_j^*$ maximizes $P(y_j, y_{-j}^*) \cdot y_j$ in $y_j \in Y_j$

Here again, an equilibrium exists under the usual hypotheses if the profit functions are quasi-concave (recall that this is not in any way guaranteed). Nevertheless, it is not at all obvious that the function $P$ is well defined. It is perfectly possible that $\omega_i'(y)$ is no longer within the consumption set $X_i$ (e.g., because the modified resources have negative components), in which case the modified economy has no equilibrium. If, on the contrary, the economy has several equilibria, it may further be impossible to continuously select only one. We are therefore reduced to assuming that the modified economy has a sole equilibrium, and this is hardly satisfactory.

It is easy to see by this definition why equilibrium depends on the chosen rule for normalizing prices. For example, define the $q$-norm by

$$\|p\|_q = \left( \sum_l p_l^q \right)^{1/q}$$

If one decides to normalize the prices in a modified economy by dividing them by their $q$-norm, then in Cournot equilibrium firm $j$ must maximize in $y_j$ the expression

$$\frac{P(y_j, y_{-j}^*)}{\|P(y_j, y_{-j}^*)\|_q} \cdot y_j$$

But, since the denominator depends on $y_j$, different choices of $q$—which have no effect in perfect competition—will lead to different Cournot equilibria.

Note also that this model is meaningless unless the only inputs are possessed by the consumers. If firm $j$ uses as input a good produced by firm $k$, then when $j$ changes its production, it modifies its demand to $k$ and then cannot reasonably expect the production of $k$ to remain constant, which is the definition of Cournot's equilibrium. Therefore this concept cannot take into account the existence of pure intermediate goods, for which the final consumer demand is nil.

### 8.3.2 Equilibrium in Prices

We can equally integrate price competition in a general equilibrium model. No concept truly prevails here. We will briefly review that of Bénassy (1988), which depends on fixed price equilibrium. By analogy with the Cournot-Walras equilibrium, suppose that the firms have chosen prices $p = (p_1, \ldots, p_m)$. An initial difficulty is that at these prices, there may not be feasible production plans that equalize supply and demand. It may even be optimal for certain firms not to serve all the demand applying to them. For these two reasons Bénassy is interested in fixed price equilibrium when the prices are $p$. Let $y_j^*(p)$ be the production plane of firm $j$ at fixed price equilibrium (assuming here again that it is unique). Then firm $j$ will choose a price $p_j$ that maximizes its profit, given other firms' prices so that

$$\max_{p_j} p_j \cdot y_j^* (p_j, p_{-j})$$

If the profit is quasi-concave, this defines a correspondence $p_j \in \psi_j (p_{-j})$, which has good properties. The general equilibrium of imperfect competition in prices is then the Nash equilibrium in prices $p^*$ given by

$$\forall j = 1, \ldots, m, \quad p_j^* \in \psi_j( p_{-j}^* )$$

The drawback to this concept is of course that it rests on the theory of fixed price equilibrium and is therefore subject to the same criticisms.

## 8.4 Conclusion

What lessons can we extract from this brief overview of general equilibrium in imperfect competition? The one objection we can make is that insofar as we know nothing of firms' conjectures, the equilibrium remains largely indeterminate. We can even show that very many production plans make up subjective demand equilibria when conjectures are varied. The disadvantage to objective demand equilibria is different: each firm is assumed to be capable of calculating the equilibrium of the economy as a whole and to take into account all the effects of general equilibrium in modifying its decisions. This is clearly not realistic.

One way to handle the problem consists in making objective demand equilibria less demanding in terms of information by authorizing firms to neglect certain effects. Thus Laffont-Laroque (1976) assume that the firm neglects its indirect influence on markets where it does not directly intervene. Hart (1985) supposes that the firm neglects the "Ford effect," that is, the impact of its profits on demand aimed at the firm by consumers who may also be its stockholders.

Another solution consists in imposing more restrictions on conjectures in a subjective demand equilibrium. Gary-Bobo (1989) thus shows that if firms cannot be mistaken about the local demand elasticity that applies to them, then the equilibrium coincides with the Cournot-Walras equilibrium. This contribution reconciles to some extent subjective and objective demand equilibria by showing that they can end in the same allocation.

At this stage of research it is very evident that the transposition of the Arrow-Debreu general equilibrium model to an economy where competition is imperfect poses too many problems that have not yet been solved.[6] The literature concentrates, as a result, on the analysis of partial equilibrium situations by using noncooperative game theory; this is the approach we will take in the next five chapters.

## Bibliography

Bénassy, J.-P. 1988. The objective demand curve in general equilibrium with price makers. *Economic Journal* 98: S37–S49.

Bénassy, J.-P. 1991. Monopolistic competition. In K. Arrow and M. Intriligator, eds., *Handbook of Mathematical Economics*, vol. 4. Amsterdam: North-Holland.

Bonanno, G. 1990. General equilibrium theory with imperfect competition. *Journal of Economic Surveys* 4: 297–328.

Dierker, E., and B. Grodal. 1996. The price normalization problem in imperfect competition and the objective of the firm. Working paper 9616. University of Vienna.

Gabszewicz, J.-J., and J.-P. Vial. 1972. Oligopoly "à la Cournot" in General Equilibrium Analysis. *Journal of Economic Theory* 4: 381–400.

Gary-Bobo, R. 1989. Cournot-Walras and locally consistent equilibria. *Journal of Economic Theory* 49: 10–32.

Hart, O. 1982. A model of imperfect competition with Keynesian features. *Quarterly Journal of Economics* 97: 109–38.

Hart, O. 1985. Imperfect competition in general equilibrium: An overview of recent work. In K. Arrow and S. Honkapohja, eds., *Frontiers of Economics*. Oxford: Basil Blackwell.

Laffont, J.-J., and G. Laroque. 1976. Existence d'un équilibre général de concurrence imparfaite: Une introduction. *Econometrica* 44: 283–94.

---

6. These underlying ideas have nevertheless found a fertile field of application in macroeconomics. Following Hart (1982), numerous authors demonstrated that the introduction of imperfect competition can engender Keynesian effects of economic policy measures in a general equilibrium model. Their work is discussed by Silvestre (1993).

Negishi, T. 1961. Monopolistic competition and general equilibrium. *Review of Economic Studies* 28: 196–201.

Roberts, J., and H. Sonnnenschein. 1977. On the foundations of the theory of monopolistic competition. *Econometrica* 45: 101–13.

Silvestre, J. 1993. The market-power foundations of macroeconomic policy. *Journal of Economic Literature* 31: 105–41.

# 9               Prices and Quantities

In this chapter we review the bases of imperfect competition: the theory of monopoly and the theory of oligopoly in prices and in quantities. These theories are often covered in introductory courses, so readers having mastered them can pass over this chapter without considerable loss of continuity.

## 9.1 Monopoly

The usual definition of a monopoly corresponds to the case of a single firm in the market place. If we accept this definition, there exists no economic sector that can be said to have a monopoly. Even firms that manage to create temporary monopolies for themselves, thanks to an invention (e.g., Sony's Walkman), are subject to competition from firms that produce substitutes (e.g., transistor radios). Yet certain firms, for reasons that we will explore below (see chapter 11), effectively succeed in ensuring themselves a monopoly on the market of a good that has no very close substitute. So at first glance, their situation has the semblance of a monopoly.

The distinction between a competitive firm and a monopoly is clear:

• A competitive firm with decreasing returns takes the price $p$ as a given and produces a quantity $q$ such that price and marginal cost are equal: $p = C'(q)$

• A monopoly chooses its price $p$ while considering the effect on the demand $q = D(p)$

A monopoly with cost function $C(q)$ (with marginal costs assumed to be increasing) chooses the price $p$ that maximizes the profit $(pD(p) - C(D(p)))$, or symmetrically, the quantity $q$ that maximizes the profit

$(P(q)q - C(q))$. The first-order condition of this second program is written

$$C'(q^m) = P(q^m) + qP'(q^m)$$

The right-hand member of this equation is, by definition, the *marginal revenue*, $MR(q^m)$, which is lower than the price because $P'(q)$ is negative: the monopoly takes into account the fact that it cannot sell off increased production except by accepting a price cut. We can already deduce from this that a monopoly tariffs above its marginal cost. As for the first program, after some elementary calculations, it gives the formula

$$\frac{p^m - C'(q^m)}{p^m} = \frac{1}{\varepsilon(p^m)}$$

where $\varepsilon(p) = -d\log D(p)/d\log p$ is the elasticity of demand. The left-hand member of this formula is called the *Lerner index* or *markup*. It is a measure of a firm's capacity to exploit its market power in order to tariff above its marginal cost.

We note also that since $p^c = C'(D(p^c))$ while $p^m > C'(D(p^m))$, and since the function $(p - C'(D(p)))$ is increasing,

$$p^m > p^c \quad \text{and} \quad q^m < q^c$$

The monopoly therefore reduces quantities and raises prices. This is sometimes called a *Malthusian behavior*.

Let us point out one last property: it is easy to show that the monopoly price $p^m$ is an increasing function of the costs, as intuition suggests. To see this, let $C_1$ and $C_2$ be two cost functions, and $p_1^m$ and $p_2^m$ be the associated monopoly prices. Since, by hypothesis, $p_i^m$ maximizes the monopoly profit for the costs $C_i$, we get

$$\begin{cases} p_1^m D(p_1^m) - C_1[D(p_1^m)] \geq p_2^m D(p_2^m) - C_1[D(p_2^m)] \\ p_2^m D(p_2^m) - C_2[D(p_2^m)] \geq p_1^m D(p_1^m) - C_2[D(p_1^m)] \end{cases}$$

whence, by adding these two inequalities,

$$C_1[D(p_2^m)] - C_1[D(p_1^m)] \geq C_2 D(p_2^m) - C_2[D(p_1^m)]$$

The last result is rewritten as

$$\int_{D(p_1^m)}^{D(p_2^m)} [C_1'(q) - C_2'(q)] \, dq \geq 0$$

If, for example, $C_1'(q) > C_2'(q)$ for every $q$, then we must get $p_1^m \geq p_2^m$.

In this regard note that even with constant returns, a cost increase can be amplified or, conversely, absorbed in the price, unlike the competitive case where the cost increase is entirely transmitted in the price. Three technical observations can be made about monopolistic behavior:

• The preceding formulations are only valid if the elasticity $\varepsilon$ is greater than 1; in the opposite case, the monopoly sets an infinite price. Then, as quantities become arbitrarily small, the monopoly's returns will tend to infinity.

• The second-order condition of the monopoly program implies $P''$, about which we can deduce very little. In practice, it is always assumed that $P''$ is such that the second-order condition is verified. Moreover it is necessary to suppose that the fixed costs are small enough for the monopoly not to take any losses.

• Monopoly production can be inferior or superior to the efficient scale; everything depends on the demand.

9.1.1   Social Distortion

We saw that a monopoly tariffs above the marginal cost. Considering the results of chapter 7, there is a distortion in relation to the social optimum. Figure 9.1 shows the results of the analysis of surplus in the competitive case (on the left) and in the monopolistic case (on the right). $S$ represents here the consumer surplus and $\pi$ that of the producers (the profit).

Social loss corresponds to the hachured triangle or *Harberger triangle*. Empirical estimates show that it is fairly small.[1] Nevertheless, as stated by John Hicks, "the best of all monopoly profits is a quiet life": a monopoly can be permitted to keep high costs, which entails a social loss often called X-inefficiency and not quantified in figure 9.1. In fact it was the principal objection of classical authors to the monopoly, as shown in this quotation from Adam Smith (*The Wealth of Nations*, bk. I, ch. 11):

Monopoly, besides, is a great enemy to good management, which can never be universally established but in consequence of that free and universal competition which forces every body to have recourse to it for the sake of self-defence.

---

1. Harberger (1954) estimates it at a fraction of a percent of the gross domestic product; more recent estimates converge at a slightly higher scale order.

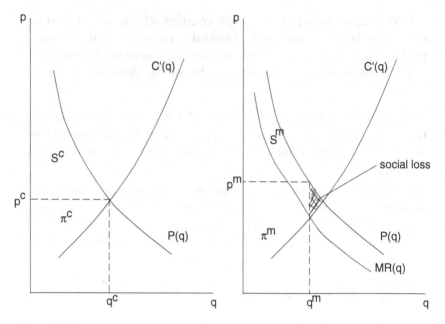

**Figure 9.1**
Competitive and monopolistic surplus

## 9.1.2  How to Avoid Distortions

Now let us see how it is possible to eliminate the social distortion inherent in the monopoly's tarification.

*Two-Part Tariffs*
Assume that in addition to the unit price $p$, the monopoly can demand payment by consumers of a franchise of access $A$. The two-part tariff practiced is thus

$$\begin{cases} A + pq & \text{if } q > 0 \\ 0 & \text{if } q = 0 \end{cases}$$

In the absence of income effect in the utility function of consumers, the franchise does not modify their demand function. The monopoly can therefore choose to tariff $p = p^c$ and

$$A = S^c = \int_{p^c}^{+\infty} D(p)\,dp$$

as in figure 9.2.

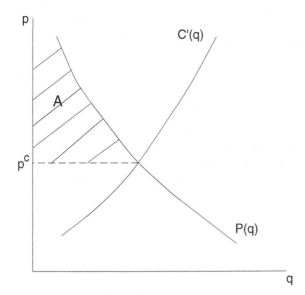

**Figure 9.2**
Two-part tariff and monopoly

All social surplus is then appropriated to the monopoly, which realizes perforce the maximum of its profit, but the social distortion disappears. The obvious disadvantage of such a "solution" is that it entails
a transfer of consumers to monopoly stockholders, which may not be
very redistributive. Moreover, we have implicitly assumed here that all
the consumers are identical. Where this is not the case, the monopoly
could demand a personalized franchise from each consumer, though
the law generally forbids this practice. Such a tarification also assumes
that the monopoly has very detailed consumer preference information
at its disposal.

*Taxation*
We could imagine taxing the monopoly's profit, the product price
remaining $p$ at production but becoming $(p + t)$ at consumption. The
monopoly then seeks to maximize its profit

$$pD(p + t) - C[D(p + t)]$$

whence

$$\{p - C'[D(p+t)]\}D'(p+t) + D(p+t) = 0$$

Social optimality will be re-established if $p + t = p^c = C'(D(p + t))$. However, this brings

$$t = \frac{D(p+t)}{D'(p+t)} = \frac{D(p^c)}{D'(p^c)}$$

which is negative. This says that it is necessary to subsidize the monopoly. This result is in fact logical: since the monopoly tends to restrain production, it is fitting to encourage more production. Here again, the solution is not particularly redistributive, so it is not likely to be popular. Moreover it implies a demand curve and cost information that the government may not have.

*Regulation*
Most governments prefer to regulate monopolies in some way. Researching the optimal regulation mode depends on the methods presented in section 7.3.2.

### 9.1.3   The Case of Durable Goods

The introduction of time in the preceding analysis means that certain themes must be ajusted. Take the monopoly that sells a durable good. It can be thought to compete with itself, since consumers may buy the good at the moment when they think it the least expensive.

To illustrate this phenomenon more fully, consider a model with two periods, $t = 1, 2$, where the demand for services provided by the durable good is given by $D(p) = 1 - p$ in each period. The good is produced at no cost, and the discount rate common to the monopoly and to the consumers is $\delta$.

If the monopoly rents the durable good, at each period it will maximize the profit $p(1 - p)$, whence $p_1 = p_2 = 1/2$ and a discounted profit $(1 + \delta)/4$. When the monopoly decides to sell the durable good, things become a bit more complicated, since the consumers must choose the moment of purchase (if there is a purchase). It is therefore necessary to apply *backward induction*, that is, to reason starting from the second period.

Suppose that the quantity $q_1$ had been sold in the first period. We now find ourselves at the beginning of the second period. The residual demand is $(1 - q_1 - p)$. The monopoly must then choose the quantity it sells, $q_2$, so as to maximize $q_2(1 - q_1 - q_2)$, whence $p_2 = q_2 = (1 - q_1)/2$ and a second period profit $\pi_2 = (1 - q_1)^2/4$.

Let us go back to the beginning of the first period. Since the buyer knows that he can resell the good in the second period at the price $p_2$, he is ready to pay $\delta p_2$ more than the normal price $(1 - q_1)$. We get

$$p_1 = 1 - q_1 + \delta p_2 = (1 - q_1)\left(1 + \frac{\delta}{2}\right)$$

The discounted profit is therefore

$$q_1(1 - q_1)\left(1 + \frac{\delta}{2}\right) + \delta\frac{(1 - q_1)^2}{4}$$

We immediately get $q_1 = 2/(4 + \delta)$ and a discounted profit

$$\pi = \frac{(2 + \delta)^2}{4(4 + \delta)} < \frac{1 + \delta}{4}$$

which shows that the monopoly's profit is smaller when the good is sold than when it is rented. In effect a monopoly that sells the durable good cannot commit itself not to lower the price of that good later; this encourages consumers to wait. As a matter of fact, we can show in our model that $p_1 > p_2$ so that the monopoly effectively lowers its prices in the course of time.

One intuitively senses that the monopoly's profit is smaller because it has more difficulty committing to a price policy. For that matter, Coase has conjectured that if the periods were cut into shorter and shorter subperiods and if correspondingly $\delta$ tends toward 1, then the discounted profit of the monopoly will tend towards 0. In the limit the monopoly's power disappears completely. The validity of this conjecture was demonstrated at the beginning of the 1980s.

To conclude, note that the policy of decreasing prices practiced by the monopoly in our model does correspond to reality. For example, we can cite publishing houses that issue expensive hardbound books and sell them to their strongest customers before issuing more affordable paperbound editions, without the production costs being affected. This is what is meant when one speaks of *skimming* the demand. For this reason we sometimes see a firm commit to compensating its present customers if it ever lowers its prices. This practice does not amount to a gift for consumers; rather, it is simply an incentive for not lowering prices, allowing the firm to protect its profits.

## 9.2  Price Discrimination

We speak of price discrimination when two units of the same good
are sold at different prices without this difference being justified by
differences in cost. We are interested here in price discrimination by a
monopoly.

In 1920 Pigou distinguished three degrees of discrimination:

• First degree: perfect discrimination. The monopoly observes the characteristics of all consumers and appropriates all of their surplus

• Second degree: discrimination. The imperfect observation of consumer characteristics depends on *self-selection* (as in section 7.3.2) or on
nonlinear tariffs, whereby consumers choose different quantities at different prices

• Third degree: discrimination founded on observable signals.
Gender, age, and other distinguishing consumer characteristics come
into play

Note first that discrimination by prices is limited by phenomenons of
arbitrage: if the elderly cannot be kept from letting younger people
travel on their airline ticket, establishing reductions that target the
elderly serves little purpose.

### 9.2.1  First Degree

We have already seen in section 9.1.2 how the monopoly can appropriate consumer surplus as a whole: to this end it is enough for the
monopoly to practice a two-part tariff such that the unitary price is the
competitive one and franchise $A_i$ applied to consumer $i$ is consumer
surplus. Once again, the use of such a tariff of course assumes that
the monopoly perfectly observes the demand functions of all the
consumers. Nor is there much regard for arbitrage problems: it is
often difficult to keep consumers from sending a delegate to buy what
they want.

### 9.2.2  Second Degree

Assume that there are two types of consumers, $i = 1, 2$, and that consumer $i$ has as his utility $\theta_i q_i - p_i$, where $q_i$ is the quantity he consumes,
$p_i$ the sum he pays to the monopoly, and $\theta_i$ a taste parameter. We will

suppose that $\theta_2 > \theta_1$ so that consumer 2 is more eager for the good than consumer 1.

If the monopoly could observe each consumer's type, it would solve for each type

$$\begin{cases} \max_{q_i, p_i} [p_i - C(q_i)] \\ \quad \theta_i q_i - p_i \geq 0 \end{cases}$$

This gives the first-best solution $(q_i^*, p_i^*)$ such that

$$\begin{cases} \theta_i = C'(q_i^*) \\ p_i^* = \theta_i q_i^* \end{cases}$$

In the cases that interest us, each consumer of course knows his type $\theta_i$. In contrast, the monopoly cannot observe a consumer's type but knows only that the proportion of the types 2 in the population is $\mu$. According to chapter 4, the monopoly must therefore offer a direct revealing mechanism: two contracts $(q_1, p_1)$ and $(q_2, p_2)$ such that the type 1 consumer chooses the first and type 2 the second. If the monopoly has production costs $C(q)$, the program it must solve is then

$$\begin{cases} \max_{q_1, p_1, q_2, p_2} \{\mu[p_2 - C(q_2)] + (1 - \mu)[p_1 - C(q_1)]\} \\ \quad \theta_1 q_1 - p_1 \geq \theta_1 q_2 - p_2 \quad (\text{IC}_1) \\ \quad \theta_2 q_2 - p_2 \geq \theta_2 q_1 - p_1 \quad (\text{IC}_2) \\ \quad \theta_1 q_1 - p_1 \geq 0 \quad (\text{IR}_1) \\ \quad \theta_2 q_2 - p_2 \geq 0 \quad (\text{IR}_2) \end{cases}$$

where the $(\text{IC}_i)$ are incentive constraints that express that each type must voluntarily choose the contract meant for him and the $(\text{IR}_i)$ are participation constraints which guarantee to each type a nonnegative utility.

This program is analyzed in detail in Salanié (1997, ch. 2). A preliminary study of the program shows that the only active constraints are $(\text{IR}_1)$ and $(\text{IC}_2)$. It remains therefore to solve

$$\begin{cases} \max_{q_1, p_1, q_2, p_2} \{\mu[p_2 - C(q_2)] + (1 - \mu)[p_1 - C(q_1)]\} \\ \quad p_2 - p_1 = \theta_2(q_2 - q_1) \\ \quad \theta_1 q_1 = p_1 \end{cases}$$

After replacing $p_1$ and $p_2$ by their values, we have

$$\max_{q_1, q_2} \{\mu[\theta_1 q_1 + \theta_2(q_2 - q_1) - C(q_2)] + (1 - \mu)[\theta_1 q_1 - C(q_1)]\}$$

Now we easily get

$$
\begin{cases}
C'(q_2) = \theta_2 \\
C'(q_1) = \theta_1 - \dfrac{\mu}{1-\mu}(\theta_2 - \theta_1)
\end{cases}
$$

This result shows that if $q_2$ is equal to the first-best solution $q_2^*$, $q_1$ is less than $q_1^*$. There is then a loss of efficiency owing to the possibility that consumer 2 understate his type, so the informational rent is measured by $\theta_2 q_2 - p_2$. The intuition of this result is very similar to that noted in section 7.3.2: the monopoly must prevent type 2 from masquerading as type 1 in order to pay the smaller price consigned to type 1's. To succeed in this, the monopoly will sell a smaller quantity to type 1, which makes the lower price less interesting to type 2.

### 9.2.3 Third Degree

Assume that there are $m$ groups of consumers, $i = 1, \dots, m$, distinguishable by observable characteristics: the demand of group $i$ is a function $D_i(p)$ known to the monopoly, and it can therefore tariff distinct prices $p_1, \dots, p_m$ that maximize the total profit

$$
\sum_{i=1}^{m} p_i D_i(p_i) - C\left(\sum_{i=1}^{m} D_i(p_i)\right)
$$

We immediately get the classical formula, but this time good by good:

$$
\forall i = 1, \dots, m, \quad \frac{p_i - C'}{p_i} = \frac{1}{\varepsilon_i}
$$

where $\varepsilon_i$ is the demand elasticity of group $i$. As in the Ramsey-Boiteux formula, it is necessary to make groups with the least elastic demand pay more. These groups of course prefer a tariff that does not distinguish between groups, so the conclusions are ambiguous where surplus is concerned.

### 9.3 Oligopoly

It is said that a market can be called an oligopoly when only a small number of firms can compete in it. This is in fact the case that best represents the majority of economic sectors. In the nineteenth century the oligopoly was the focus of two penetrating analyses whose premises and conclusions were radically opposed.

### 9.3.1 Cournot's Oligopoly

Cournot (1838) studied oligopolistic competition when firms utilize produced quantities as strategic variables. Suppose that there are $n$ firms and that firm $i$ has a cost function $C_i(q_i)$. Let $P(\Sigma_{i=1}^n q_i)$ be the inverse demand function on the market. We look for the Nash equilibrium in quantities, that is, a vector of quantities $(q_1, \ldots, q_n)$ such that producing $q_i$ is optimal for firm $i$ when it takes $q_{-i}$ as given.[2] In solving

$$\max_{q_i}\left[ q_i P\left( \sum_{j=1}^n q_j \right) - C_i(q_i) \right]$$

we easily find the formula that gives the Lerner index for firm $i$:

$$\forall i = 1,\ldots,n, \quad \frac{P - C_i'}{P} = \frac{s_i}{\varepsilon}$$

where $s_i$ is the market share of firm $i$ (which is of course endogenous),

$$s_i = \frac{q_i}{\sum_{j=1}^n q_j}$$

As in the case of the monopoly, we find a price that is superior to the marginal cost (even if the distortion is less, since $s_i \leq 1$): each firm realizes a positive profit, even if it produces at constant returns, $C_i(q_i) = c_i q_i$.

We will note that the average markup of the firms of the sector, weighted by their market shares, is given by

$$\sum_{i=1}^n s_i \frac{P - C_i'}{P} = \frac{H}{10,000\varepsilon}$$

where $H = \Sigma_{i=1}^n (100 s_i)^2$ is the *Herfindahl index*. This index measures the concentration in the studied sector; it is worth 10,000 in the case of a monopoly and $10,000/n$ for an oligopoly of $n$ identical firms. As appears from the formula above, this index is directly linked to the

---

2. We can show that equilibrium exists if $qP'(q)$ is a decreasing function, and that it is then unique if the marginal costs are constant.

average markup; it is for this reason that the index serves as the basis of the mergers and acquisitions control policy in the United States.

Note that if all the firms are identical, then at equilibrium one will have $\forall i = 1, \ldots, n$, $s_i = 1/n$. It is easily seen that in this case there is a convergence toward equality between price and marginal cost when $n$ tends to infinity. Therefore we again find the competitive equilibrium when the firms are very numerous.

### 9.3.2  The Bertrand Equilibrium

The underlying game in the Cournot equilibrium is a bit surprising. Competitors choose their quantities and wait with no further action while the equilibrium price establishes itself on the market, though it would be quite easy for them to modify their prices, which are generally much easier to adjust than quantities. In his famous criticism of Cournot's book, the French mathematician Bertrand (1883) proposed rather that prices be considered the strategic variables. The strength of Bertrand's critique is best shown in the example of two identical firms, $i = 1, 2$, producing at constant returns, $C_i(q_i) = cq_i$. To compute the Nash price equilibrium, we use reductio ad absurdum:

- $p_1 < c$ or $p_2 < c$ is impossible, since the firm in question would take losses

- $c < p_1 < p_2$ is impossible, since 2 sells nothing and gains by reducing its price to just under $p_1$.

- $p_1 = c < p_2$ is impossible, since 1 would gain in slightly raising its price, resulting in $p_1 = p_2 \geq c$

- $p_1 = p_2 > c$ is not an equilibrium, since each firm then has only a part of the market and would gain then by slightly lowering its price, thereby taking control of the whole market

In what must be one of the most concise texts in the history of economic thought, Bertrand concludes (p. 503):

Whatever the common adopted price, if only one of the competitors lowers his price, he attracts, neglecting trivial exceptions, the totality of the sale, and he will double his revenue if his competitor lets him. If Cournot's formulas mask this obvious result it is because by a singular mistake, he introduces with names $D$ and $D'$ the quantities sold by the two competitors and, treating them as independent variables, he assumes that if one happens to change through the will of one of its owners the other can remain constant. In fact, the contrary is obvious.

The conclusion is simple: the only Nash price equilibrium is $p_1 = p_2 = c$, that is, competitive equilibrium, even though there are only two firms on the market. This is called the *Bertrand paradox*. Current observation shows us that firms compete in price (as observed Bertrand) rather than in quantities (Cournot); still the results obtained in a Cournot oligopoly are much more satisfying intuitively than those of the Bertrand equilibrium. The following chapters in large part will be devoted to solving this paradox.

### 9.3.3  Sketches of Resolutions of the Paradox

The overarching question is: How can firms make positive or supranormal profits[3] (confirmed by empirical studies) when they are engaged in a price competition (which better corresponds to the workings of the marketplace)?

We can say, first of all, that if the two firms have constant but different marginal costs, $c_1 < c_2$, then we can distinguish two cases depending on whether the monopoly price $p_1^m$ corresponding to the constant marginal costs $c_1$ is less or more than $c_2$:

- If $c_2 \leq p_1^m$, then at equilibrium firm 1 tariffs at $c_2$ and 2 leaves the market (if it resisted, 1 could slightly lower its price to chase it out)

- If $c_2 > p_1^m$, then at equilibrium firm 2 leaves the market and 1 tariffs at the monopoly price

Firm 1 succeeds in making profits by exploiting its technological superiority. This obvious conclusion does not, however, solve the paradox satisfactorily, since the paradox remains infact when costs are identical.

*Capacity Constraints*
Edgeworth noted in 1897 that in the presence of capacity constraints, firms can avoid throwing themselves into a price war. Assume, for example, that the capacity of firm 1 is $K_1 = D(p)$ with $p > c$. If both firms tariff $p_1 = p_2 = p$, firm 1 will have no interest in unilaterally lowering its price, for it will not be able to serve the whole market anyway.

---

3. I define supranormal profits as profits greater than what can be obtained in a perfectly competitive market.

Clearly, the choice of capacities is endogenous. A firm compares the discounted benefits of an increased capacity and the corresponding investment cost. Here it is important to specify well the *rationing scheme*: if $p_1 < p_2$ and $D(p_1) > K_1$, certain consumers will not be able to buy at the price $p_1$; some of them will pull out of the market and others will apply to firm 2. The rationing scheme defines the demand aimed at firm 2 in these conditions. Kreps-Scheinkman (1983) adopted the so-called efficient rationing scheme[4] where $D_2 = \max[D(p_2) - K_1, 0]$. They analyzed a game in two stages where firms chose their capacities (by incurring a cost proportional to the installed capacity) before fixing their prices. Their result was remarkable in that the subgame-perfect equilibrium was a Cournot equilibrium.[5] Therefore they justified Cournot's analysis in sectors where investments rigidly determine the production capacities.[6] Still this result does not solve the Bertrand paradox if the firms can easily raise their capacities in response to demand.

*Product Differentiation*

Thus far we have assumed that products were homogeneous. In reality two firms rarely produce the same product, though two products can more or less replace each other. It is intuitively clear that this gives the firms then a certain market power. Demand functions continuously depend on two prices, contrary to the case of a homogeneous product. If firm 2 lowers its price below that of firm 1, the latter will lose only a part of its market. If, for example, the demand functions are given by

$$\begin{cases} D_1 = 1 - p_1 + \theta p_2 \\ D_2 = 1 - p_2 + \theta p_1 \end{cases}$$

where $\theta$ is a positive parameter, then the Bertrand equilibrium with constant marginal costs $c$ becomes

---

4. This rationing scheme is called efficient because, while the consumers' propensities to pay differ, it maximizes the total surplus of consumers by having the firm that tariffs the lowest prices serve the consumers who are the most greedy for the good.

5. As shown by Davidson-Deneckere (1986), this result narrowly depends on the choice of the efficient rationing scheme.

6. More generally, it can be shown that competitive equilibrium is no longer a Nash price equilibrium if the cost functions are strictly convex. The analysis of this case is unfortunately fairly technical.

$$p_1 = p_2 = c + \frac{1-(1-\theta)c}{2-\theta}$$

Note that $1 - (1 - \theta)c$ is the common value of demands when $p_1 = p_2 = c$; clearly, it must be positive, so the Bertrand equilibrium prices are superior to the marginal cost.

It remains to give a microeconomic foundation to such demand functions; we will see how to do so in chapter 10.

*Accounting for Dynamic Aspects*

In Bertrand's reasoning, an equilibrium where firms tariff above the marginal cost is not stable because it is in each firm's interest to lower its prices to monopolize the market. However, this supposes that the deviant firm is not "punished" by its competitor. This hypothesis is less solid when the interaction is repeated, since then the two firms run the risk of being thrown into a price war which would be harmful to both. As Fisher (1898) wrote early on:

No business man assumes that either his rival's output or price will remain constant . . . On the contrary, his whole thought is to forecast what move the rival will make in response to his own.

If the game is repeated infinitely, the monopoly price can become an equilibrium. Assume, in effect, that there is an infinite number of periods $t = 0, \ldots, +\infty$, that the discount rate is $\delta$, and that $J$ identical firms of constant marginal cost $c$ interact. Consider the following strategies, where $p^m$ is the monopoly price:

$$\begin{cases} p_t = p^m & \text{if no one has yet tariffed below } p^m \\ p_t = c & \text{in the contrary case} \end{cases}$$

Let $\pi^m$ be the monopoly profit; when the $J$ firms tariff $p^m$, each makes a profit $\pi^m/J$. If one of the $J$ slightly lowers its price, it will make a profit close to $\pi^m$, and the others will have a zero profit. Therefore, if a firm "deviates" on date $t$ in fixing a price that is slightly lower than $p^m$, it will make a profit close to $\pi^m$ on date $t$ and nothing afterward, since the price will then establish itself at the level of marginal cost. The firm will obtain a discounted profit $\pi^m$ as a result. If, on the other hand, the $J$ firms still fix $p^m$, each makes a profit

$$\frac{\pi^m}{J}(1 + \delta + \delta^2 + \ldots) = \frac{\pi^m}{J(1-\delta)}$$

But, if $\delta \geq (J-1)/J$ (so that firms are fairly patient),

$$\frac{\pi^m}{J(1-\delta)} \geq \pi^m$$

and the monopoly price is a Nash equilibrium of the game.

Two observations demand attention. On the one hand, this reasoning applies just as well when replacing $p^m$ by any price superior to the marginal cost. There exist then many other equilibria where $p_1 = \ldots = p_J > c$ if $\delta$ is close enough to 1, so this model is not entirely satisfactory. On the other hand, deviations are not easily observable perforce; each firm observes above all the demand which concerns it, which depends on the price practiced by its competitors but also on numerous other factors. It is not always easy then to determine whether a firm has deviated from the equilibrium. Green and Porter (1984) study a model where the decrease in the demand aimed at a firm can be due to a decrease of the price of a competitor and also to a shock to global demand (a recession). They show that the monopoly price can no longer be sustained with certainty: recessions lead to price wars.

*Illegal Agreements*

The preceding discussion dealt with what is called *tacit collusion* between firms. At times collusion is more explicit. In this regard we should not neglect Adam Smith's cynical remark (*The Wealth of Nations*, I, ch. 10):

> People of the same trade seldom meet together, even for merriment and diversion, but the conversation ends in a conspiracy against the publick, or in some contrivance to raise prices.

Recent history is spotted by numerous instances of such illegal agreements, called cartels. One of the most spectacular concerned electrical appliances makers in the United States in the 1950s. Their cartel system rested on three pillars:

• an agreement on prices for standard appliances

• for large appliances, price books comprising several hundred pages

• a rolling system based on lunar phases that aimed to give the appearance of cut-throat competition and answer supply procurement calls

On the European side, in the 1990s firms of the cement sector found themselves subject to very heavy fines by the European Commission because of their noncompetitive pricing practices.

Certain authors, following Stigler (1950), consider cartels to be intrinsically unstable. The reasoning is simple. A cartel comprises $k$ firms that act as a single firm. In Cournot competition the entire cartel obtains the same profits as any firm situated outside the cartel. A cartel member therefore multiplies its profit by $k$ in leaving it. This reasoning, however, only applies if the competition is strictly that of Cournot, without the cartel having a strategic advantage. Such a hypothesis is in all likelihood not realistic. Stigler's remark stimulated a vast literature on the stability of cartels; as often happens in industrial economics, exact conclusions depend on the type of competition that prevails in the sector under consideration. We will simply note that the concrete examples cited above show fairly well that some sectors can succeed in creating durable cartels.

### 9.3.4   Strategic Substitutes and Complements

The Bertrand paradox finds its source in the very different structures of the two games, of quantities and of prices. First, consider a Cournot duopoly of inverse demand function $P$. If the firm 1 has a cost function $C_1$, its profit is

$$\pi_1 = q_1 P(q_1 + q_2) - C_1(q_1)$$

Fix $q_2$; the best response function of 1 is given by

$$\frac{\partial \pi_1}{\partial q_1}[R_1(q_2), q_2] = 0 \quad \text{and} \quad \frac{\partial^2 \pi_1}{\partial q_1^2}[R_1(q_2), q_2] \leq 0$$

By the implicit function theorem, its derivative is therefore

$$R_1'(q_2) = \frac{\partial^2 \pi_1 / \partial q_1 \partial q_2}{\partial^2 \pi_1 / \partial q_1^2}$$

and has the sign of the crossed derivative

$$\frac{\partial^2 \pi_1}{\partial q_1 \partial q_2} = q_1 P''(q_1 + q_2) + P'(q_1 + q_2)$$

If $P''$ is not too positive, then the crossed derivative is negative, and the best response function $R_1$ is decreasing: in Cournot competition a firm tends to produce less when its competitors produce more. It is then said that quantities are *strategic substitutes* (Bulow, Geanakoplos, and Klemperer 1985).

What about price competition? In the case examined by Bertrand, profit functions are discontinuous, which makes the application of these notions difficult. If, however, there is product differentiation as in the example of section 9.3.3, then we easily see that the crossed derivative

$$\frac{\partial^2 \pi_1}{\partial p_1 \partial p_2} = \theta$$

is positive. The prices are therefore *strategic complements*. A firm reacts to its competitors' price decrease by lowering its own, which is quite natural.

The strategic complements and substitutes games are very different. It may be obvious that competitors' attitudes are more aggressive in a game of strategic complements and more peaceful in a strategic substitute game. This helps explain why profits are higher in competition by quantities than they are in competition by prices.

## Bibliography

Bertrand, J. 1883. Théorie des richesses. *Journal des Savants*, pp. 499–508. Published in English in A. Daughety, ed. *Cournot Oligopoly: Characterization and Applications*. Cambridge: Cambridge University Press (1988).

Bulow, J., J. Geanakoplos, and P. Klemperer. 1985. Multimarket oligopoly: Strategic substitutes and complements. *Journal of Political Economy* 93: 488–511.

Chamberlin, E. 1933. *The Theory of Monopolistic Competition*. Cambridge: Harvard University Press.

Cournot, A. 1838. *Recherches sur les principes mathématiques de la théorie des richesses*. Published in English as *Mathematical Principles of the Theory of Wealth*. San Diego, CA: James and Gordon (1995).

Davidson, C., and R. Deneckere. 1986. Long-run competition in capacity, short-run competition in price, and the Cournot model. *Rand Journal of Economics* 17: 404–15.

Fisher, I. 1898. Cournot and mathematical economics. *Quarterly Journal of Economics* 12: 119–38.

Green, E., and R. Porter. 1984. Noncooperative collusion under imperfect price information. *Econometrica* 52: 87–100.

Harberger, A. 1954. Monopoly and resource allocation. *American Economic Review* 44: 77–87.

Hotelling, H. 1929. Stability in competition. *Economic Journal* 39: 41–57.

Kreps, D., and J. Scheinkman. 1983. Quantity precommitment and Bertrand competition yield Cournot outcomes. *Bell Journal of Economics* 14: 326–37.

Salanié, B. 1997. *The Economics of Contracts: A Primer*. Cambridge: MIT Press.

Stigler, G. 1950. Monopoly and oligopoly by merger. *American Economic Review* 40: 23–34.

# 10            Product Choice

As we saw in the previous chapter, product differentiation is one way to escape the Bertrand paradox. In perfect competition, firms price at marginal cost whether the products are differentiated or not. In this chapter we will see that when competition is imperfect, an oligopoly engaged in price competition will obtain supranormal profits (superior to competitive profits). That is to say, if products are no longer homogeneous, each competitor can raise its prices above the marginal cost without abruptly losing all of its clients.

## 10.1   Definitions

Classically two distinctions are made regarding product differentiation:

• *Vertical differentiation.* All consumers agree to regard products in the same way (e.g., because different products correspond to different qualities of the same product).

• *Horizontal differentiation.* Consumers show differences in subjective tastes.

These two consumer choice models are clearly opposed if all differentiated products are sold at the same price. Then in the model of vertical differentiation, we can assume that there is a blitz of demand upon a single product, whereas in the model of horizontal differentiation demand is spread over several products.

Here are two classic examples we can look at right away.

### 10.1.1   A Model of Vertical Differentiation

Consider a good for which there exist two qualities indexed by a parameter $s$: $s_1$ and $s_2$, with $s_1 < s_2$. The price of the best quality is of course higher, $p_1 < p_2$. The consumers can have at most one unit of the product; their utility function is $U = \theta s - p$, where $\theta$ is a quality preference parameter. The consumers must therefore compare utilities $\theta s_1 - p_1$ (purchase of quality 1), $\theta s_2 - p_2$ (purchase of quality 2), and 0 (no purchase). Accordingly they are classed in terms of how much they appreciate quality. Those who value quality most will of course buy the highest quality.

### 10.1.2   A Model of Horizontal Differentiation

Hotelling (1929) proposed the first horizontal differentiation model. It is still the most used model today.

Imagine a linear city as segment [0, 1]. There are two stores each located at an extremity of the city; their tariff prices are $p_0$ and $p_1$. The consumers are uniformly spread throughout the city. Consumers face a transport cost $t$ per unit of distance covered. There are two possible models:

• of travel costs incurred by consumers in order to reach each store

• of transport costs incurred by the stores in delivering products to consumers.

The second situation is appropriate for certain industrial sectors. The first relates more to retail shoppers: think of two supermarkets. In an abstract interpretation of the model that is less geographical, the product could present itself in numerous varieties indexed by a parameter of [0, 1]. Company 0 chooses to sell variety 0 and firm 1 variety 1. The consumer situated in $x$ prefers variety $x$ and must discharge a cost (in utility) $t \, | x - x' |$ if he buys variety $x'$.

The consumer located in $x$ perceives therefore a generalized price, $p_0 + tx$, for the store situated in 0, and thus $p_1 + t(1 - x)$ for the store situated in 1. If $P$ is the subjective value of the good for each consumer, the demand aimed at store 0 is given by the smallest $x$ such that

$$\begin{cases} p_0 + tx \le p_1 + t(1 - x) \\ p_0 + tx \le P \end{cases}$$

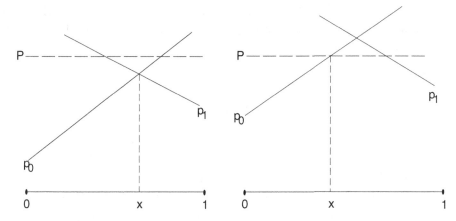

**Figure 10.1**
Generalized prices in the Hotelling model

It is then

$$
\begin{cases}
\dfrac{p_1 + t - p_0}{2t} & \text{if } \dfrac{p_1 + t + p_0}{2} \le P \\[2ex]
\dfrac{P - p_0}{t} & \text{if } \dfrac{p_1 + t + p_0}{2} < P \text{ and } p_0 \le P \\[2ex]
0 & \text{if } p_0 > P
\end{cases}
$$

In figure 10.1 the panel on the left represents the first case and the panel on the right the second case.[1]

## 10.2 Differentiation and Monopoly

Before studying differentiation in oligopolistic competition, we need to examine some novel distortions that can intervene when a monopoly sells differentiated products.

### 10.2.1 Optimal Quality Choice

Take now a vertically differentiated good of quality index $s$. Suppose that the inverse demand function of the consumers is $P(q, s)$, which increases in $s$ since the price that they are prepared to pay increases

---

1. The market is covered in the first case only.

with quality. The production cost of the good $C(q, s)$ also rises with the quality. The monopoly chooses the quantity and the quality that maximize its profit:

$$\max_{q,s}[qP(q, s) - C(q, s)]$$

The first-order condition in $s$ is written

$$q\frac{\partial P}{\partial s}(q, s) = \frac{\partial C}{\partial s}(q, s)$$

Therefore the monopoly decides on its quality in considering the marginal consumer: the consumer who buys the last unit of the good. What should a planner do in maximizing the social surplus? First, the planner computes

$$\int_0^q P(x, s)dx - C(q, s)$$

whence the first-order condition in $s$ is

$$\int_0^q \frac{\partial P}{\partial s}(x, s)dx = \frac{\partial C}{\partial s}(q, s)$$

The planner has to consider next the average consumer. Clearly, *at a given quantity*, the monopoly does not generally choose the socially optimal quality.

Take another example where the consumers have a utility $U = \theta s - p$ and $\theta$ is uniformly distributed on $[0, 1]$. The demand is $D(p, s) = 1 - p/s$, and its inverse is $P(q, s) = s(1 - q)$. We deduce from this that the cross-derivative $\partial^2 P/\partial q \partial s$ is negative. So

$$\int_0^q \frac{\partial P}{\partial s}(x, s)dx > q\frac{\partial P}{\partial s}(q, s)$$

In the reasonable case where $C$ is convex in $s$, it is easily seen that the monopoly will furnish suboptimal quality for any given quantity.

This result of suboptimality is not general, however. One must not forget that the monopoly can reduce the quantity sold (in relation to the social optimum). Barring miracles, it remains that a monopoly normally does not choose the socially optimal quality.

## 10.2.2  Nonobservable Quality

Now let us look more realistically at a situation where only the seller knows the quality $s$ of his product. The buyer knows only that $s$ is uniformly distributed on $[0, 1]$ a priori. The seller's utility is $p - \theta_1 s$, and that of the single buyer is $\theta_2 s - p$, where $\theta_1$ and $\theta_2$ are two publicly known parameters such that $\theta_1 < \theta_2$; hence it is socially optimal for the buyer to acquire any quality from the seller. Still we will see that the unobservability of quality can cause a market breakdown.

First, we must keep in mind that when a good's quality is unobservable, all qualities can be sold at the same price. If buyers anticipate an increasing relationship between price and quality, then it is always in the sellers' interest to tariff the highest price. Clearly, this fact contradicts the buyers' expectations. When a seller proposes a price $p$, the buyer could reason as follows:

· If the seller can sell at the price $p$, it is that $p \geq \theta_1 s$. There are two possibilities:

1. $p \geq \theta_1$. In this case I learn nothing of the quality by observing the price. So I must evaluate the average quality of goods for sale at $1/2$, and the average utility that I can have in purchasing is therefore $\theta_2/2 - p$. If $\theta_2 < 2\theta_1$, this utility is then negative, so I will not buy.

2. $p < \theta_1$. The average quality that I can expect is $p/2\theta_1$, which gives me an average utility $p\theta_2/2\theta_1 - p$. This utility is still negative if $\theta_2 < 2\theta_1$.

· Whatever the price proposed by the seller, it is not in my best interest to buy if $\theta_2 < 2\theta_1$.

The conclusion is immediate: if $\theta_1 < \theta_2 < 2\theta_1$, no quality of the good can be sold, even though a sale would be socially optimal. This situation is often called the *lemon problem* after a famous example of Akerlof (1970).[2]

The *lemon problem* is fortunately not irremediable; it can be solved by introducing a signal of quality for a good. For example, if the product's quality coincides with its reliability, introducing guarantees can establish a more satisfying (albeit second-best) equilibrium: only the sellers of good cars will offer a guarantee, since it would be costly

---

2. In the United States, a new car that has continual mechanical problems is called a *lemon*.

for sellers of bad cars to include guarantees. The offer of guarantee then signals a good car and allows pertinent information to be revealed in equilibrium.

### 10.2.3   Choice of Number of Products to Introduce

Now, in a horizontal differentiation model, would a monopoly introduce too many or too few products with relation to the social optimum? There are two opposing arguments to begin with:

• A monopoly can restrain the variety of its products. In the absence of first-degree discrimination, a monopoly's profit $\pi$ is less than the social surplus $S$, which also comprises consumer surplus. A monopoly will not introduce a new product if its fixed cost $f$ is between $\pi$ and $S$, though the product is socially desirable.[3]

• Monopoly prices above the marginal cost on a product can make other varieties of the product more interesting for consumers. The monopoly can therefore gain by introducing new varieties even if not socially optimal.

Since the second argument is less direct than the first, let us examine it more closely using Hotelling's linear city example. In this model the social surplus maximization reverts to minimizing the sum of the transport costs and firms' production costs (the prices paid are merely transfers between consumers and firms). Suppose that the marginal costs are zero but that opening a store costs $f$. If there is only one store, situated at 0, the total transport costs are given by $\int_0^1 txdx = t/2$; if the monopoly opens a new store at 1, the transport costs become $2\int_0^{1/2} txdx = t/4$. If the cost of creating a new store $f$ is superior to $t/4$, it is therefore socially preferable to open only one store.

What about a monopoly? Suppose that the subjective value of the good $P$ is high so that the whole market is covered. Then the monopoly will tariff so as to leave a zero surplus to the most distant consumer: $p = P - t$ if there is only one store, and $p = P - t/2$ if there are two. The opening of a new store reduces the transport costs of consumers and thereby allows the monopoly to raise its prices. Since the monopoly's

---

3. This is a common argument, but it depends as much on nonconvexities (the cost $f$ of creating a new product) as in imperfect competition: when $f$ is not zero, it is equally possible that a competitive sector will not create a new product, though it may be socially optimal.

profit (outside of opening costs) is simply $\pi = p$, it will prefer opening two stores provided that $f < t/2$.

Where $t/4 < f < t/2$, the monopoly will indeed open one more store than a social planner.

## 10.3   Differentiation and Oligopoly

When there are several firms, one must take into account their differentiation strategies. This is what we will do within the framework of Hotelling's model. We can then study the optimality of the entry process of the firms, which permits us to present the monopolistic competition model of Chamberlin and his more recent descendants.

### 10.3.1   The Maximal Differentiation Principle

Let us return to the horizontal differentiation model of Hotelling for two firms, by way of three new hypotheses:

- $P$ is very high, and consumers then always buy.
- The marginal production costs are constant and equal to $c$.
- The transport costs are quadratic.

The last hypothesis is a technical one that enables us to avoid problems owing to the discontinuity of demand functions when transport costs are linear. Consider in effect that situation represented in figure 10.2, where the firms are localized in $a$ and $1 - b$ and the lines represent the generalized prices when the transport costs are linear. Then firm $a$'s market is (approximately) $[0, 1 - b]$ and that of firm $1 - b$ is $[1 - b, 1]$. Now, if firm $a$ lowers its price a little, it will monopolize the entire segment since its generalized price will be everywhere inferior to that of $(1 - b)$.

It is easy to see that if the prices are fixed in the quadratic costs model, the firms will gain by drawing nearer the center of the segment: it is the *minimal differentiation principle* stated by Hotelling (1929):

- Buyers are confronted everywhere with an excessive sameness.

To see this, assume that the prices practiced by the two firms are equal (to $p$), that one firm is localized in $a$, and the other firm in $(1 - b)$, with $a \le 1/2 \le 1 - b$. So the limit of markets is given by

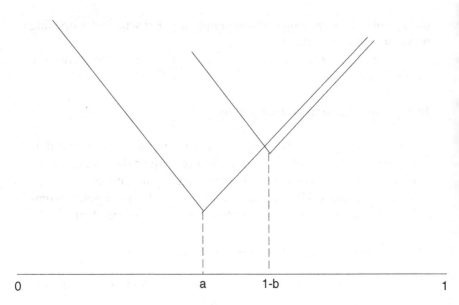

**Figure 10.2**
Discontinuity with linear transport costs

$$(x-a)^2 = (1-b-x)^2$$

being $x = (a + 1 - b)/2$. The first firm's profit is $px$, and the profit increases in $a$. So its dominant strategy is to be established in $1/2$. The same reasoning also brings the second firm to set up in $1/2$. We have indeed a matter of "excessive sameness," since the social optimum is to minimize the total transport costs[4]

$$\int_0^{(a+1-b)/2}(x-a)^2\,dx + \int_{(a+1-b)/2}^1(1-b-x)^2\,dx = \frac{(1-b-a)^3}{3} + \frac{a^3}{3} + \frac{b^3}{3}$$

From the expression above we easily see that the costs are minima for $a = b = 1/4$.

We will find, however, that this principle must be inverted when the prices are freely chosen by the firms (d'Aspremont, Gabszewicz, and Thisse 1979). In a first stage the two firms are free to localize themselves wherever they wish on the segment $[0, 1]$. So we can consider this as a two-stage game:

---

4. The production costs do not come into play since the market is supposedly covered.

1. The firms choose their localizations $a$ and $(1 - b)$.
2. They subsequently choose their prices $p_0$ and $p_1$.

We want to characterize the perfect equilibrium of this game and to demonstrate that $a = b = 0$ at equilibrium, that is, that the firms seek to differentiate themselves to the maximum.

As usual, we start at the game's end, after the firms have settled in their localizations. If they tariff $p_0$ and $p_1$, the coordinate $x$ that delimits their territories is given by

$$p_0 + t(x - a)^2 = p_1 + t(1 - b - x)^2$$

The demand applying to 0 is therefore

$$D_0(p_0, p_1, a, b) = a + \frac{1 - b - a}{2} + \frac{p_1 - p_0}{2t(1 - b - a)}$$

It comprises three terms. The first is the territory situated to the left of firm 0, the second corresponds to the equal distribution of the territory situated between the two firms, and the last is the effect due to the difference in price. Naturally the demand aimed at 1 is simply

$$D_1(p_0, p_1, a, b) = 1 - D_0(p_0, p_1, a, b)$$

If each firm has a constant marginal cost $c$, the Nash price equilibrium is given by the maximization of $(p_0 - c)D_0$ in $p_0$ and of $(p_1 - c)D_1$ in $p_1$. Simple calculations give

$$p_0(a, b) = c + t(1 - b - a)\left(1 + \frac{a - b}{3}\right)$$

and a similar formula for $p_1(a, b)$.

Now we can go to the first stage. The firm 0 will choose $a$ to maximize

$$\pi_0 = (p_0(a, b) - c)D_0(p_0(a, b), p_1(a, b), a, b)$$

In differentiating, it gets

$$\frac{\partial \pi_0}{\partial a} = \frac{\partial \pi_0}{\partial p_0}\frac{\partial p_0}{\partial a} + (p_0(a, b) - c)\frac{\partial D_0}{\partial p_1}\frac{\partial p_1}{\partial a} + (p_0(a, b) - c)\frac{\partial D_0}{\partial a}$$

The first term is zero by the envelope theorem, since $p_0$ makes $\pi_0$ maximal. The second term is the strategic effect: as $\partial D_0/\partial p_1 > 0$ and $\partial p_1/\partial a < 0$, to reduce $a$ (to distance itself from 1) permits 0 to incite 1 to raise its price, and therefore 0 acquires more clients. The last term simply expresses (as $\partial D_0 / \partial a > 0$) that being near downtown permits 0 to take clients from 1.

After some calculations of little interest, we can show that the strategic effect carries it away and that one therefore gets $\partial \pi_0 / \partial a < 0$, so at equilibrium, 0 is positioned in $a = 0$. Identical reasoning bearing on 1 would show that one gets $b = 0$, so the two firms choose to position themselves at the two extremities of the segment. This is the *maximal differentiation principle*. It calls for several remarks:

• This principle is not very general. For example, it is false if the transport costs are in $x^{3/2}$, which is no less reasonable than quadratic costs.

• Various considerations are missing from the model. For example, consumers' prospecting costs would militate rather in favor of a minimal differentiation principle, which is effectively observed at work in many of our cities.

• The maximal differentiation principle induces too much differentiation. We saw earlier than $a = b = 1/4$ at the social optimum.

### 10.3.2   Entry and Number of Products

The previous model did not include fixed costs of entering the market and did not therefore permit us to examine entry decisions. To this end, consider another model by Salop (1979). This model's theme is that there are too many products at equilibrium in relation to the social optimum. A firm that enters the market does not take into account the decrease of profits of already installed firms induced by its own entry: this is *business stealing*. What is concerned therefore is a pecuniary externality, which can create an inefficiency here only because the competition is imperfect.

Consider then a circular city upon which consumers and $n$ firms are uniformly arranged.[5] The transport costs are supposed linear (in $tx$). Here again the value of the good for each consumer is assumed to be very high, so the whole market will be covered at equilibrium. Each firm has a fixed cost $f$ and constant marginal costs $c$.

---

5. Readers desiring another concrete illustration can think of the positioning of London–New York flight schedules on a clock.

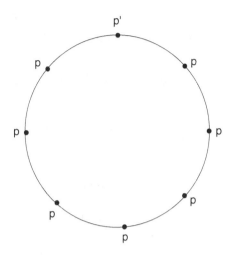

**Figure 10.3**
The Salop model

At symmetrical equilibrium, all firms tariff the same price $p$. A firm that chooses a different price $p'$, as in figure 10.3, can ensure itself a market of size $x$ to both sides of itself, where $x$ is given by

$$p' + tx = p + t\left(\frac{1}{n} - x\right)$$

The firm would then get a demand $(1/n + (p - p')/t)$ and a profit

$$\pi = (p' - c)\left(\frac{1}{n} + \frac{p - p'}{t}\right) - f$$

which is maximal in $p' = (p + t/n + c)/2$. The condition $p' = p$ gives the equilibrium

$$p = c + \frac{t}{n}, \quad \pi = \frac{t}{n^2} - f$$

At free-entry equilibrium, this profit is zero and there are therefore (to the nearest round number) $\sqrt{t/f}$ firms.

The social optimum minimizes the sum of fixed costs $nf$ and of transport costs $2n\int_0^{1/2n} txdx = t/4n$, which this time gives $n = \frac{1}{2}\sqrt{t/f}$. Clearly, there are too many firms at free-entry equilibrium, because of *business stealing*: a firm that decides to enter the market takes into account only its own profit and not the decrease of profits of firms already there.

The conclusion of this model recalls that of the classical analysis of monopolistic competition of Chamberlin (1933). Chamberlin considers a sector producing differentiated products where

1. the demand that applies to every firm decreases when the firm raises its price

2. every firm makes zero profits

3. when a firm changes its price, the effect on other firms' demands is negligible

The third hypothesis is of course crucial: since no firm has an impact on the others, each one can neglect reactions to its price policy and have no further reason to carry a strategic policy. In fact all strategic considerations are abandoned, and this greatly simplifies the analysis.

So one can characterize equilibrium quite simply. Let $D(p_i \mid p_{-i})$ be the demand function[6] of the firm $i$. By hypothesis, it decreases in $p_i$ (and increases by $p_{-i}$). Since the firm can neglect its competitors' reactions, it maximizes

$$p_i D(p_i | p_{-i}) - C_i[D(p_i | p_{-i})]$$

by taking $p_i$ as given. Assume (which is the only interesting case) that the average cost curve engendered by $C_i$ is U-shaped. Since the firm must make zero profit, it must tariff on a point where the demand curve cuts the average cost curve; the demand curve must even be tangential to the average cost curve from below: failing this, the firm could make positive profits by modifying its price. We then get the "tangency solution" represented in figure 10.4. Note that at such a point, each firm's production is inferior to the efficient scale $q^*$. It is generally said that the sector has an excess capacity.[7]

The solution Chamberlin proposed has since lost much of its attraction. It was quickly realized that there were very few industries to which hypotheses 1 to 3 could be applied. It is generally hypothesis 3 that poses a problem; in retail trade, for example, it is without a doubt true that the price policy of a small retailer little affects the demand of a sufficiently distant competitor, but it is from current experience that a supermarket's installation has important effects on neighborhood

---

6. Note that the demand function depends on prices tariffed by the firm $i$ and by its competitors, and therefore implicitly on the number of firms in the industry.
7. There could be several points of tangency, but each point would correspond to an excess capacity.

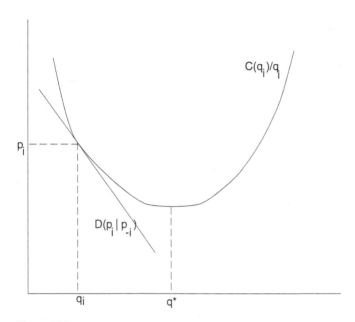

$C(q_i)/q_i$

$p_i$

$D(p_i | p_{-i})$

$q_i$          $q^*$

**Figure 10.4**
The tangency solution

retailers. Then, as in many comparable cases, the situation is best modeled as an oligopoly (here, local).

What interests us in Chamberlin's and Salop's analyses converges upon an important point: at equilibrium firms price too high, sell too little, and are too numerous. This analogy is actually less strong than it appears. On the one hand, Salop's model is not a true monopolistic competition model, since it violates hypothesis 3: a firm's price policy affects its neighbors in a non-negligible way. On the other hand, Chamberlin's approach completely neglects the positive effect due to the entry of a new firm, which increases the variety of available products (this is manifested by decrease of transport costs in Salop's model). It is therefore not obvious that there are always too many firms at equilibrium. In effect, if the *business-stealing* phenomenon presented by Salop leads to too many firms, the fact that the entering firms cannot appropriate all of the social surplus implies that there may be too few at equilibrium.

Dixit-Stiglitz (1977) proposed a monopolistic competition model that verifies hypotheses 1 to 3 and allows for the study of trade-offs between these two pecuniary externalities. It is assumed that there exists in the economy a nondiversified good $x_0$ and diversified goods $(x_i)_{i=1,\ldots,\infty}$. Each diversified good is produced by a firm of fixed cost $f$ and of constant marginal cost $c$.

The economy's demand side can be summarized by a representative consumer with a utility function

$$U = x_0^{1-\gamma}\left[\sum_i v(x_i)\right]^\gamma$$

where $0 < \gamma < 1$ and $v$ is a concave increasing function. All things being equal in other respects, the introduction of a new variety therefore raises the consumer's utility: it is said that the consumer has a taste for variety.

The consumer's budgetary constraint is written (the good $x_0$ being the numéraire)[8]

$$x_0 + \sum_i p_i x_i \leq R$$

The consumer's demands are obtained by maximizing

$$\left(R - \sum_i p_i x_i\right)^{1-\gamma}\left[\sum_i v(x_i)\right]^\gamma$$

whence

$$\frac{(1-\gamma)p_i}{R - \sum_i p_i x_i} = \frac{\gamma v'(x_i)}{\sum_i v(x_i)}$$

Now suppose that there are very many firms (and therefore products). Then the terms $\sum_i p_i x_i$ and $\sum_i v(x_i)$ are practically independent of $p_i$, so hypothesis 3 is valid asymptotically: firm $i$ approximately perceives a demand given by $p_i = Kv'(x_i)$, whose elasticity is

$$\varepsilon_i = -\frac{v'(x_i)}{x_i v''(x_i)}$$

the symmetrical equilibrium is characterized by a price $p_e$ and a production $x_e$ for every firm and a number of firms $n_e$. Every firm tariffs like a monopoly, so

---

$$p_e = \frac{c}{1 - (1/\varepsilon_e)} = \frac{c}{1 + [v'(x_e)/x_e v''(x_e)]} \tag{1}$$

Since the profits are zero, we get

$$(p_e - c)x_e = f$$

so

$$\frac{cx_e + f}{f} = -\frac{v'(x_e)}{x_e v''(x_e)} \tag{2}$$

We lack only one equation. We know that at equilibrium the consumer determines $x_e$ by maximizing in $x$

$$(R - n_e p_e x)^{1-\gamma} [n_e v(x)]^{\gamma}$$

We now define two auxiliary functions

$$\rho(x) = \frac{xv'(x)}{v(x)} \quad \text{and} \quad w(x) = \frac{\gamma\rho(x)}{\gamma\rho(x) + 1 - \gamma}$$

The function $\rho(x)$ plays an important role in what follows. As $p$ and $v'(x)$ are proportional, $\rho(x)$ is proportional to the ratio of $px$ (the firm's revenue) to $v(x)$, the gross social surplus brought in by its production. The firm's capacity to appropriate surplus engendered by its production $x$ is therefore measured. Elementary calculations show that the consumer demand is given by

$$x_e = \frac{R\omega(x_e)}{n_e p_e}$$

so, utilizing the zero profit condition, we obtain

$$n_e = \frac{\omega(x_e)}{f + cx_e} \tag{3}$$

Under reasonable hypotheses, equilibrium is well defined by these three equations: (2) gives $x_e$, then (1) gives $p_e$, and (3) gives $n_e$.

What about the social optimum? In the face of the facts, the planner must make firms tariff at the marginal cost $p = c$ and subsidize their fixed costs by levying $nf$ of the consumer. The consumer then determines his demand, from which

$$V(n) = \max_x (R - npx)^{1-\gamma} [nv(x)]^{\gamma}$$

and the planner permits the entry of a number of firms equal to $n^* = \arg \max_n V(n)$. Simple calculations show that we get

$$\rho(x^*) = \frac{cx^*}{f + cx^*} \quad \text{and} \quad n^* = \frac{\gamma}{f + cx^*}$$

Dixit and Stiglitz demonstrate the following theorem:

THEOREM 10.1

1. $x_e > x^* \Leftrightarrow \rho(x)$ increases in $x$.
2. If $\rho(x)$ increases in $x$, then $n_e < n^*$.

To better see this, return to the zero-profit condition

$$\frac{cx_e + f}{f} = -\frac{v'(x_e)}{x_e v''(x_e)}$$

Noting that

$$1 + \frac{xv''(x)}{v'(x)} = \rho(x) + \frac{x\rho'(x)}{\rho(x)}$$

this condition can be rewritten in the form

$$\frac{cx_e}{cx_e + f} = \rho(x_e) + \frac{x_e \rho'(x_e)}{\rho(x_e)}$$

Comparing it with the social optimum condition

$$\rho(x^*) = \frac{cx^*}{f + cx^*}$$

we easily get conclusion 1 of the theorem. Conclusion 2 is demonstrated by noting that the function $\omega(x)$ is always smaller than $\gamma$, whence

$$n_e < \frac{\gamma}{a + cx_e}$$

But, if $\rho(x)$ increases by $x$, then $x_e > x^*$, and therefore

$$n_e < \frac{\gamma}{a + cx_e} < \frac{\gamma}{a + cx^*} = n^*$$

There is then excess capacity at equilibrium (as with Chamberlin's model) if and only if a firm that raises its production sees its portion of the social surplus diminish. In the opposite case, there will be too few firms and they will be too large. It therefore seems that many configurations are possible a priori. Dixit and Stiglitz cite a simple example where $v(x) = x^\rho$, with $0 < \rho < 1$. Then $\rho(x)$ is constant and the scale of the firms at equilibrium is socially optimal, contrary to the analyses of Chamberlin and Salop[9]. This particular case of the Dixit-Stiglitz model is often used today in international trade theory and in spatial economics.

## Bibliography

Akerlof, G. 1970. The market for "lemons": Qualitative uncertainty and the market mechanism. *Quarterly Journal of Economics* 84: 488–500.

d'Aspremont, C., J.-J. Gabszewicz, and J.-F. Thisse. 1979. On Hotelling's "stability in competition." *Econometrica* 47:1145–50.

Chamberlin, E. 1933. *The Theory of Monopolistic Competition*. Cambridge: Harvard University Press.

Dixit, A., and J. Stiglitz. 1977. Monopolistic competition and optimum product diversity. *American Economic Review*, 67: 297–308.

Hart, O. 1985a. Monopolistic competition in the spirit of Chamberlin: A general model. *Review of Economic Studies* 52: 529–46.

Hart, O. 1985b. Monopolistic competition in the spirit of Chamberlin: Special results. *Economic Journal* 95: 889–908.

Hotelling, H. 1929. Stability in competition. *Economic Journal* 39: 41–57.

Salop, S. 1979. Monopolistic competition with outside goods. *Bell Journal of Economics* 10: 141–56.

---

9. Hart (1985a, b) criticized the behavior of the utility function used by Dixit and Stiglitz in the case where $n$ becomes very large. In a more vigorous model, very similar results to those of Dixit-Stiglitz are obtained, albeit less easily interpretable ones.

# 11    Long-Term Entry and Competition

Among the factors that can explain how firms that compete against each other by price can sustain supranormal profits, barriers to entry hold an important place. Several different types of barriers to entry can exist:

• Legal barriers. In certain countries the law restricts the number of operators in certain professions. Other industries are ruled by permit systems or by claim to financial guarantees[1] (e.g., financial institutions).

• Scale economies. The presence of fixed costs or of subadditive cost functions can constitute effective barriers to entry.

• Strategic barriers. We will see that these can also exist.

• Technological barriers. A firm with technological advantages at its disposal (e.g., an accumulation of research and development) can make entry difficult for competitors.

## 11.1  Sustainability and Contestability

Baumol, Panzar, and Willig (1982) (hereafter BPW) showed that the force of potential competition (the existence of potential entrants) could be sufficient to compel even a natural monopoly to behave in a (nearly) socially optimal manner. To this end they considered *perfectly contestable* markets where, by definition, entry and exit are executed at no cost. This definition particularly excludes unrecoverable expenses (*sunk costs*) that a firm can be induced to incur upon entrance to the market.

---

1. Moreover some countries practice, or have practiced, a policy of promoting "national champions" which favors the existence of very large conglomerates.

Consider therefore a market where all firms are identical, with costs $C(q)$. Let $D(p)$ be demand and $P(q)$ its inverse function. BPW propose focusing on *sustainable configurations*, defined as follows: A configuration of $m$ firms $(p, q_1, \ldots, q_m)$ is sustainable if and only if

• supply and demand are equal,

$$\sum_{i=1}^{m} q_i = D(p)$$

• none of the $m$ firms takes any losses,

$$\forall i = 1, \ldots, m, \quad C(q_i) \le pq_i$$

• no entrant firm can propose a lower price and still make positive profits, $\nexists(p', q')$ such that

$$\begin{cases} p' < p \\ q' \le D(p') \\ C(q') < p'q' \end{cases}$$

Note first of all that in a sustainable configuration, all firms make zero profits. Suppose otherwise, and let $i$ be a firm whose profits are strictly positive:

$$pq_i > C(q_i)$$

Then an entrant firm can tariff $p - \varepsilon$, sell $q_i$, and obtain a profit that is smaller but always strictly positive.

Moreover no firm can tariff below its marginal cost. If one had $p < C'(q_i)$, then an entrant could tariff at the same price $p$, sell a quantity $(q_i - \varepsilon)$, and make a profit:

$$p(q_i - \varepsilon) - C(q_i - \varepsilon) \approx [pq_i - C(q_i)] + \varepsilon[C'(q_i) - p] > 0$$

Now assume that there exists a sustainable configuration of several firms $(p, q_1, \ldots, q_n)$ where firm 1 prices above marginal cost: $p > C'(q_1)$. If an entrant tariffs $p - \varepsilon^2$, it will be able to sell all or part of $D(p - \varepsilon^2)$. But this new demand is larger than

$$D(p) = q_1 + \ldots + q_n$$

The entrant firm can then choose to sell $q_1 + \varepsilon$ if $\varepsilon$ is fairly small. It will thus obtain a profit

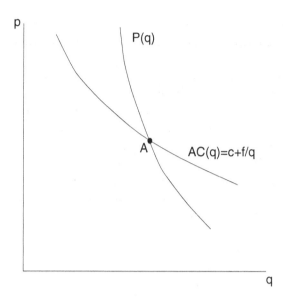

**Figure 11.1**
Sustainable configuration

$$(p - \varepsilon^2)(q_1 + \varepsilon) - C(q_1 + \varepsilon) \simeq [pq_1 - C(q_1)] + [p - C'(q_1)]\varepsilon > 0$$

Such a sustainable configuration therefore cannot exist.

We know then that in a sustainable configuration of several firms, the price must be at once equal to both average and marginal costs; that is, each firm must produce at its efficient scale. But this is only possible if the demand at minimum average cost is an exact multiple of the efficient scale, which could only result from a miraculous coincidence. The theory of contestable markets therefore faces serious difficulties in accounting for an equilibrium where several firms coexist.

BPW then apply their demonstration to the following example:[2] Suppose that $C(q) = f + cq$ so that the market is in a state of natural monopoly. Then, by the preceding discussion, there can only exist one sustainable configuration: it is point $A$ in figure 11.1, situated at the intersection of the inverse demand and average cost curves. It is easy to verify that this configuration is indeed sustainable.

This configuration is remarkable for several reasons. First of all, a single firm produces, which is indeed desirable since the sector is a

---

2. Contestable market theory is more complex than it appears in my treatment here. The question of multi-product firms, in particular, holds an important position in the theory. I will be content to refer the reader to the book by BPW or to Baumol (1982).

natural monopoly. Moreover the monopoly has zero profits, which seems to contradict all the normal intuitions: the danger of entry alone is enough to force it to lower its price. Finally, this configuration is a constrained social optimum (in the absence of compensatory transfers, which would allow the monopoly to price at marginal cost).

Unfortunately, or perhaps fortunately for our intuition, the attention given to sustainable configurations by BPW is excessive. First of all, no sustainable configuration can exist, as shown in figure 11.2, where the average cost curve is U-shaped and intersects the inverse demand curve to the right of the minimum of average cost. Only point $B$ in the figure could be sustainable, but it is destabilized by a point such as point $C$, where the entrant rations demand.

BPW make strong claims for their theory, emphasizing that like Chamberlin's monopolistic competition theory, it allows very strong results to be obtained without burdening oneself with strategic considerations. Still we would like to have at our disposal a description of the firm's strategic behavior which could justify the sustainable configurations. In fact such a game does exist, and it has two stages. In the first, firms choose their prices; then they decide whether or not to enter, and they fix their production level. Such a game is open to

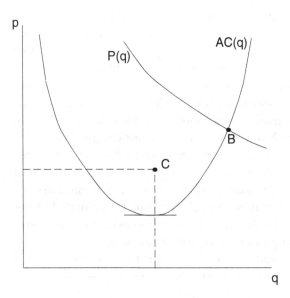

**Figure 11.2**
Absence of Sustainable Configuration

criticism, for price decisions are habitually more flexible than those of entry and production. The behavior credited to firms by BPW particularly assumes that established firms do not modify their prices when an entrant presents itself, which is somewhat hazardous practice.

Finally, no doubt the hypothesis of the absence of unrecoverable expenses is very strong, and it can describe realistically only a limited number of markets. The case of airline companies is interesting insofar as their deregulation in the United States in the 1980s was considered a propaganda success of the contestable market theory.[3] It seems a priori that the air transportation market is close to contestability, inasmuch as airplanes can be rented or resold fairly easily. In a first period one effectively observed a massive entry in this industry, where the number of firms tripled. But in a second phase, a consolidation of supply was witnessed: the number of airline companies is even smaller than before regulation, and the Herfindahl index of the industry has fallen to its original level. The barriers to entry were probably underestimated: the scarcity of airport slots, the role of electronic reservation systems, and so on. More fundamentally, potential competition seems to be an imperfect substitute for the real thing, and the reactions of established firms have certainly been underestimated.

In conclusion, it does not seem that the concepts elaborated by BPW overturn classical analysis. They succeed nonetheless in attracting out attention to the influence of the existence of potential entrant firms on the behavior of those already established on a market.

## 11.2  Preemption

Under the rubric of preemption are regrouped strategies that consist, for a firm established on a market (an *incumbent*), in accumulating capital to dissuade entry. Here the term "capital" has acceptance in a much larger sense than that of physical or production means; it can also refer to experience accumulated in a learning situation (*learning-by-doing*), to goodwill acquired in the course of time, or again to a stock of patents resulting from previous R&D.

The intuition of the fact that accumulating capital can dissuade entry dates back to Stackelberg in 1934, and it was later developed by Spence (1977) and Dixit (1980). Consider therefore an established

---

3. I refer the reader to the article of McGowan and Seabright (1989) for details.

firm and a potential entrant. We assume that the *timing* of the game is as follows:

• The established firm decides to carry its capital to $K_1$.

• Then the potential entrant carries its capital to $K_2$ (one can have $K_2 = 0$, in which case there is no entry).

• Finally, the two firms compete in prices.

To simplify, we do not specify the conditions of the price competition. We simply suppose that at the given capitals $K_1$ and $K_2$, it leads to reduced profit functions $\pi_1(K_1, K_2)$ and $\pi_2(K_1, K_2)$ which verify the following properties:

• $\pi_1$ is concave in $K_1$.

• $\partial \pi_1 / \partial K_1$ is a decreasing function of $K_2$.

• $\pi_2$ possess two symmetrical properties.

Numerous forms of price competition in fact lead to reduced profit functions which verify these properties. To fix ideas, we will give the following analytical form to reduced profit functions:

$$\forall i = 1, 2, \quad \pi_i(K_1, K_2) = K_i(1 - K_1 - K_2)$$

If the capacities game was simultaneous (the established firm and the potential entrant firm choose their $K_i$ at the same time), then the equilibrium would of course be symmetrical, and it is easily calculated that $K_1 = K_2 = 1/3$ and $\pi_1 = \pi_2 = 1/9$. This equilibrium of the simultaneous game will serve us as a reference.

The game that interests us is a Stackelberg game, with a *leader* that is the established firm and one *follower* that is the potential entrant. It is easily seen that the reaction function of the entrant (i.e., the $K_2$ which maximizes $\pi_2$ to given $K_1$) is

$$K_2 = R_2(K_1) = \frac{1 - K_1}{2}$$

As for the established firm, it will choose $K_1$ to maximize $\pi_1[K_1, R_2(K_1)]$, which at equilibrium finally gives

$$K_1 = \frac{1}{2}, \quad K_2 = \frac{1}{8}, \quad \pi_1 = \frac{1}{8}, \quad \pi_2 = \frac{1}{16}$$

The established firm therefore overinvests and thus succeeds in limiting entry (since $K_2$ is smaller than in the simultaneous game). It guarantees itself a higher profit than that of the entrant firm.

Note that the hypothesis that the established firm can commit on the value of $K_1$ is very important: if it updates the value of $K_1$ after having observed $K_2$, it will choose $K_1 = R_1(K_2) = 3/8$ and not $K_1 = 1/2$. Therefore the investment must have an irreversible character.

Thus far we have assumed that the entry costs are zero, which is unrealistic. Now suppose that every entrant must discharge a fixed cost $f$ that is still inferior to the equilibrium profit $\pi_2 = 1/16$, so entry remains viable a priori. The reaction curve of the entrant then becomes discontinuous. In effect we let the capital level be $K_1^b$ which verifies

$$\max_{K_2}\left[K_2\left(1 - K_1^b - K_2\right) - f\right] = 0$$

If $K_1 > K_1^b$, the potential entrant has no interest in entering, since its profits do not allow for the recovery of the entry cost. We therefore get $R_2(K_1) = 0$. If $K_1 < K_1^b$, we again see the reaction function $R_2(K_1) = (1 - K_1)/2$. Figure 11.3 shows the reaction function $R_2$.

The established firm must always maximize $\pi_1[K_1, R_2(K_1)]$, which is now discontinuous. Two cases must therefore be distinguished:

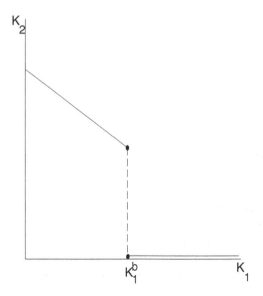

**Figure 11.3**
Reaction function in the Dixit-Spence model

• If $K_1 < K_1^b$, the entrant firm participates in the market; since $f < 1/16$, we find that $K_1^b > 1/2$. The optimum is therefore always $K_1 = 1/2$, which gives a profit $\pi_1 = 1/8$

• If $K_1 \geq K_1^b$, the potential entrant remains outside the market. The maximum profit is reached when $K_1 = K_1^b$ (so that the entrant is just dissuaded from entering), and it is worth $\pi_1 = 2\sqrt{f}(1 - 2\sqrt{f})$.

Take $f$ close to $1/16$. Then $2\sqrt{f}(1 - 2\sqrt{f})$ is close to $1/4$, and therefore the established firm's optimum is to invest up to $K_1^b$ to completely dissuade entry, which permits the firm to double its profits in relation to the Stackelberg equilibrium without entry costs.

## 11.3   Limit Price and Predation

In this section we consider the potential reasons for an established firm to practice an aggressive low-price policy.

### 11.3.1   Limit Price

We speak of limit price when the incumbent firm practices a price that is less than the monopoly price to make entry less profitable. The underlying idea is that the entrant knows it will have to practice even lower prices in order to win a market share, so the game is not worth the candle.

This classical intuition, however, is not very satisfactory: it assumes a none too credible engagement in prices, since they are an easily changeable strategic variable. If the potential rival firm effectively enters the market, then the best response of the established firm is to maximize its profits in this new situation, and not to maintain an artificially low price. Moreover it is essential for the established firm to persuade the entrant of its readiness to fight. Sacrificing its present profits to this end may not be optimal.

Milgrom and Roberts (1982) propose a more modern analysis of limit pricing that rests on the asymmetry of information between the entrant firm and the established firm. Actually it is reasonable to suppose that the established firm is better informed of its costs than is the entrant. In fixing a low price, it signals to the entrants that its costs are low and that it can therefore easily sustain a price war. Such a game is one of signals and, as such, comprises large numbers of perfect Bayesian equilibria. Nonetheless, the most reasonable among them (the only one that is stable in a certain sense) indeed possesses the property that the firms having a low cost tariff below the monopoly price.

Analysis of the limit price in terms of social surplus is ambiguous. The established firm succeeds in dissuading entry when its costs are low, which tends to reduce social surplus, but it tariffs below the monopoly price, which in compensation is desirable. The regulation policy that the state must adopt in the situation must then be examined in terms of a specific situation.

## 11.3.2   Predation

Predation, For an established firm that has just seen an entrant firm take a share of its market, consists in launching into a price war to oblige the entrant to exit the market.[4] This behavior is fairly common. It can reach a high degree of savagery, as in the case of the Cola wars between Coca-Cola and Pepsi-Cola in the 1970s: at times the prices for these beverages were barely sufficient to cover the cost of the aluminum cans containing them.

Any explanation of predation assumes that the established firm has an advantage over the entrant, which permits it to win a price war. This advantage can of course be due to a lower production cost. Cabral and Riordan (1994) invoke learning effects that result in the established firm's seeing its costs decrease according to past production. Things can become more complex if the two firms are identical. Then one can appeal to imperfections of the capital markets. A common explanation is that the entrant firm's bank fears that a price war will raise its probability of failure and thus refuse to continue to finance the firm if it jumps into an aggressive policy of low prices.

The asymmetry of information is another possible explanation. It is based on "reputation effects": if the entrant firm thinks there is more than a slight possibility that the established firm will fight entry even when it is not in the latter's interest to do so, and the game can be prolonged for a fairly long period of time, then the potential entrant will not enter the market. It is therefore desirable for the established firm to create a reputation of aggressiveness in order to dissuade entry.

---

4. Strictly speaking, there is predation only when the price is so low that both firms take losses.

## 11.4   Research and Development

As shown by the *growth accounting* literature, research and development is responsible for a fair portion of economic growth. This alone suffices in justifying that industrial organization is interested in the impact of market organization on R&D. Its place in this chapter is primarily due to the advantage that a firm can draw from its stock of R&D, thanks to the patent system which confers upon it de facto a temporary monopoly.

As early as 1942 Schumpeter[5] expressed the idea that monopolies are a necessary evil for the development of R&D inasmuch as

1. being larger, it is easier for monopolies to invest and benefit from increasing returns tied to R&D activity

2. being more diversified, monopolies are better prepared to absorb the inherent risks of R&D

3. having monopoly power makes innovation more profitable for them.

We will interest ourselves, above all, with the last reason. We will see that we must slightly temper Schumpeter's enthusiasm for monopolies.

We should first note that effectively the patent system is a compromise. After an innovation occurs, the socially optimal decision would be to make it public. However, this would leave no incentive for firms to innovate, and for this reason all countries protect innovations for a limited duration. For our purposes, we will nevertheless take the patent system as given.

We will depend on Arrow's (1962) article, where he considers a process innovation[6] that reduces the (constant) marginal production cost of a good from $\bar{c}$ to $\underline{c} < \bar{c}$. This innovation is protected by a patent that, to simplify, we assume has an unlimited life span. Let $r$ be the interest rate, so that the discounted value (in continuous time) of a constant flux of 1 is $\int_0^{+\infty} e^{-rt} dt = 1/r$.

---

5. See Schumpeter (1942). This book is reputed to have predicted an inescapable convergence of capitalism and socialism, a vision that seemed reasonable until the 1980s but has fallen out of fashion since.

6. A process innovation reduces the production cost of an existing good, in opposition to a product innovation, which creates a new good.

First, we compute the social value of this innovation. If the demand function for the good is $D(p)$, the discounted social surplus when the production cost is $c$ is

$$\frac{1}{r}\int_c^{+\infty} D(x)dx$$

since at the social optimum firms must price at marginal cost. The social value of innovation is therefore

$$V^s = \frac{1}{r}\int_{\underline{c}}^{+\infty} D(c)dc - \frac{1}{r}\int_{\bar{c}}^{+\infty} D(c)dc = \frac{1}{r}\int_{\underline{c}}^{\bar{c}} D(c)dc$$

What about different market organizations? Suppose, first of all, that innovation is realized by a monopoly. Let $p^m(c)$ be the monopoly price when the cost is $c$ and $\pi^m(c)$ the corresponding profit:

$$\pi^m(c) = \max_p (p - c)D(p)$$

By the envelope theorem we get

$$\frac{\partial \pi^m}{\partial c} = -D[p^m(c)]$$

Therefore the value of innovation for the monopoly is due to the increase of its profits when its costs go down:

$$V^m = \pi^m(\underline{c}) - \pi^m(\bar{c}) = \frac{1}{r}\int_{\underline{c}}^{\bar{c}} D[p^m(c)]\,dc$$

Right away we note that since the monopoly prices above marginal cost, we get $D(p^m(c)) < D(c)$ and therefore $V^m < V^s$: the value of innovation for the monopoly is less than its social value. This was foreseeable, insofar as cost reduction operates on a smaller production because the monopoly restricts its production.

Now assume that the starting situation is competitive, with several firms all pricing at the marginal cost $\bar{c}$. If the innovator continues to conduct itself in a competitive manner, its profits will remain zero, and the encouragement to innovate is therefore nonexistent. Yet this hypothesis is obviously unrealistic. So we must distinguish two cases, depending on whether the new monopoly price $p^m(\underline{c})$ is superior or inferior to $\bar{c}$:

• If $p^m(\underline{c}) \geq \bar{c}$ (*nondrastic* innovation), the innovator is interested in tariffing a slightly inferior price to $\bar{c}$ in order to monopolize the market. Then it realizes a discounted profit

$$V^c = \frac{1}{r}(\bar{c} - \underline{c})D(\underline{c})$$

which is easily shown to lie between $V^m$ and $V^s$

• If $p^m(\underline{c}) < \bar{c}$ (*drastic* innovation), the innovator is interested in tariffing the monopoly price $p^m(\underline{c})$. In this case it will still monopolize the market and realize a discounted profit

$$V^c = \frac{1}{r}(p^m(\underline{c}) - \underline{c})D(p^m(\underline{c}))$$

Here again, it is easily shown that $V^c$ lies between $V^m$ and $V^s$.

Therefore in all cases we get the conclusion $V^m < V^c < V^s$. Schumpeter's perception is likely wrong: a monopoly gains less than a competitive firm by innovating (and is consequently less encouraged to do so).[7] This is the *replacement effect*: through innovation the monopoly replaces itself, and if it earns new profits, it loses old ones.

Still it would not be right to conclude from this analysis that an innovation always has more value for a potential entrant than for an established monopoly. It all depends on the conditions of innovation. If innovation has been achieved by a firm outside the market looking to sell to the monopoly or to the entrant, we can show that under reasonable conditions, the monopoly will be prepared to pay more than the entrant for innovation. This is due to the monopoly's fear of seeing itself in competition with the entrant and to the *efficiency effect*, which implies that competition reduces total industry profits. This result explains, for example, why Xerox remained for a long time a monopoly on the photocopier market; it got in the habit of buying back all the patents registered in this domain and of leaving them "dormant," at least until forbidden this practice by antitrust authorities.

In this chapter we sidelined many interesting subjects. There are more dynamic aspects of R&D, in particular, the "patent races" that dissipate at least a part of the monopoly rents potentially brought in ex ante by an innovation.

---

7. Neither type of firm receives all of the social advantages of innovation, since the consumers benefit as well.

# Bibliography

Arrow, K. 1962. Economic welfare and the allocation of resources for inventions. In R. Nelson ed., *The Rate and Direction of Inventive Activity*. Princeton: Princeton University Press.

Baumol, W. 1982. Contestable markets: An uprising in the theory of industry structure. *American Economic Review* 72: 1–15.

Baumol, W., J. Panzar, and R. Willig. 1982. *Contestable Markets and the Theory of Industry Structure*. New York: Harcourt Brace Jovanovic.

Cabral, L., and M. Riordan. 1994. The learning curve, market dominance, and predatory pricing. *Econometrica* 62: 1115–40.

Dixit, A. 1980. The role of investment in entry deterrence. *Economic Journal* 90: 95–106.

McGowan, F., and P. Seabright. 1989. Deregulating European airlines. *Economic Policy* 9: 284–344.

Milgrom, P., and J. Roberts. 1982. Limit pricing and entry under incomplete information: An equilibrium analysis. *Econometrica* 50: 443–60.

Schumpeter, J. 1942. *Capitalism, Socialism and Democracy*. New York: Harper and Brothers.

Spence, M. 1977. Entry, capacity, investment and oligopolistic pricing. *Bell Journal of Economics* 8: 534–44.

# 12         Vertical Relations

Until now we have considered producers who were selling their products directly to consumers. In reality such a configuration is very rare. There are generally one or several intermediary participants. In this chapter we will concern ourselves with what are called *vertical relations*, which link a producer (often a monopoly in this chapter) and its distributors. The central question deals with the control that the producer would like to exercise over the distributors' activities. The producer could have recourse to a contract that specifies a nonlinear tariff. However, in practice, the producer usually cannot observe the sales of each of its distributors, so a nonlinear tariff is diverted from its objectives by arbitrage between distributors.[1] The producer is then only able to utilize linear prices, possibly with a franchise, if he can observe whether the retailer actually sells his product. Historically these instruments of control have seemed insufficient to producers, who have compensated with a whole panoply of *vertical restrictions* (or *constraints*):

• Exclusive territories. In this system the producer grants a local monopoly on his product to each distributor. By way of example, we can cite franchise stores or insurance agents. Note that the term "local monopoly" is not necessarily a purely geographical one. The producer could, for instance, grant to each distributor a monopoly on a variety of his product.

• Exclusive dealing. The producer prohibits the distributor from selling a brand that rivals his product. Examples are European automobile dealers and, again, insurance agents.

---

1. At least this is the point of view we will take in this chapter. Note, however, that in the retail sector, certain participants practice a complex system of rebates that actually has much in common with a nonlinear tariff.

• Tied sales. The producer assumes that the distributor will transform the product by combining it with products of others. Then the producer could insist that the distributor buy all of his products from him.

• Resale price maintenance. The producer directly fixes the retailer's selling price (or at least a minimal price). This practice is common in the European book business (where several EU states fix minimum prices) and perfumery.

• Buying quota. The producer imposes on the retailer a minimal amount of sales.

These restrictions are the subject of still quite animated legal and economic debates that center upon the comparison of the economic efficiency and the anticompetitive distortions that restrictions can bring on. The Chicago school, which was very influential in the United States in the 1980s, has insisted upon the efficiency contribution of vertical relations and has praised laissez-faire in this regard. American jurisprudence therefore fluctuated over that period of time. In Europe the dominant attitude is much more skeptical; the accepted wisdom is more restrictive legislation.

A vertical relation could be analyzed, from a technical point of view, as a *hierarchy*, that is, as a Principal-Agent problem where the Principal is generally the upstream firm and the Agent the downstream one. However, the difficulty is dealing with the fact that in the most interesting cases there are actually several Principals in competition and several Agents also in competition. This type of model is at the limit of what economists currently know how to solve, and we only skim the surface of its complexity.

## 12.1  Double Marginalization

We will start by examining a classic model due to Spengler (1950). This model gave rise to the dictum that "the only thing worse than a monopoly is a chain monopoly."

Consider first the producer in this monopoly situation. He produces with a constant marginal cost $c$; he sells the good at a price $w$ to a retailer, himself in a situation of monopoly, who distributes the good at a price $p$ without incurring costs. The final demand is given by $D(p)$ $= d - p$, where $d$ is supposed to be larger than $c$ (in order for production to be profitable). This situation is summarized by figure 12.1.

Now consider the retailer's program. For a given upstream price $w$, he must choose the downstream price $p$ to maximize his profit

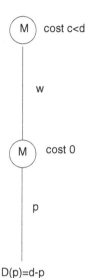

D(p)=d-p

**Figure 12.1**
Chain monopoly

$$\pi_d = (d - p)(p - w)$$

We can deduce from this that

$$p = \frac{w+d}{2}, \quad \pi_d = \frac{(d-w)^2}{4}, \quad x = \frac{d-w}{2}$$

where $x$ is the quantity sold. As for the producer, he must choose $w$ to maximize his profit which, since $x = (d - w)/2$, is written $\pi = (w - c)(d - w)/2$. So we get

$$w = \frac{c+d}{2}, \quad \pi = \frac{(d-c)^2}{8}$$

where finally for prices

$$c < w = \frac{c+d}{2} < p = \frac{c+3d}{4}$$

This double inequality is called "double marginalization"; it refers to the fact that each of the links of the chain, being a monopoly, prices above its marginal cost.

For the profits of the producer, the distributor, and the vertical structure, we find that

$$\pi = \frac{(d-c)^2}{8}, \quad \pi_d = \frac{(d-c)^2}{16}, \quad \pi_t = \frac{3(d-c)^2}{16}$$

Interestingly, in comparing these results with those of the "integrated structure," we see that if the producer and the retailer had merged into a single firm, this structure would tariff a price $q$ that maximizes $\pi_i = (d-q)(q-c)$, whence

$$q = \frac{c+d}{2}, \quad \pi_i = \frac{(d-c)^2}{4}$$

The profit of the integrated structure is therefore higher than the total profit of the nonintegrated chain.[2] Moreover the downstream price $q$ is inferior to the price $p$, and therefore the consumers' surplus increases. From this result we can deduce that vertical integration of a chain monopoly leads to that fairly rare thing in economics, an improvement in the Pareto sense. In effect there exists in this vertical relation an externality exerted by the retailer upon the producer: when the retailer lowers $p$, $x$ increases, and as $w > c$, the producer's profit increases. The inefficiency of the chain monopoly is in part due to the fact that the retailer does not take this effect into account; vertical integration internalizes the externality.

Could we arrive at the same result without making the simple but radical decision to integrate the two firms? With perfect information, the response is yes. The producer could in effect adopt three vertical restrictions that are perfectly equivalent:

• Price at marginal cost $w = c$. The retailer would then tariff $p = q$, and the producer could recuperate his profits by making him pay into a franchise $A = \pi_i$.

• Impose onto the retailer the selling price $p = q$ (or simply impose $p \le q$). The optimal downstream price is then $w = q$.

• Impose onto the retailer a sales quota $x \ge D(q)$.

With asymmetric information, things become more complicated. For example, if the retailer is better informed on the state of demand than is the producer, it will be necessary to consider optimal

---

2. To see this more directly, note that by definition,

$$\pi_i = \max_q (d-q)(q-c) > (d-p)(p-w) + (d-p)(w-c) = \pi_d + \pi = \pi_t$$

risk-sharing and a good decentralization of decisions, as we will see section 12.3.

## 12.2   Justifications of Vertical Constraints

Let us start by examining the arguments that could justify (from either a private or a social optimum point of view) the use of a certain vertical constraint.

### 12.2.1   Retailer Effort Incentive

We can designate as retailer effort all services that permit the retailer to increase sales. Grouped under retailer effort are advice to clients, local publicity, after-sales service, among other such business promoting sales. The retailer effort has two external effects:

• Toward other retailers. Certain consumers seek advice from one retailer and end up buying from another retailer the same product at a lower price. Thus a discount audio store can benefit from its proximity to a more traditional store by "diverting" its clients. This type of external effect leads to a suboptimal effort

• Toward the producer. Anything that increases the sales of the retailer likewise increases the sales of the producer. Here again, the retailer's effort risks being inferior to that of an integrated structure.

Clearly, it is advisable for the producer to encourage the retailer to make the effort to provide sales enhancement services. One of the tools used most often to this end is resale price maintenance. By assuring a margin to the retailer, such effort is validated, and he is encourage to continue his services in behalf of the producer. The retailer incentive argument dates back to Telser's (1960) classical article. Moreover, if this practice is imposed on all distributors, client diversion to discount stores will be avoided,[3] allowing retailers to fully harvest the fruits of their labor. Laws on book pricing have been motivated in various European countries by such consideration.[4]

---

3. Discount stores actually practice *free-riding* on the public good which comes from the effort of other retailers.
4. The more commonly accepted justification of resale price maintenance has had more to do with the influence of the *Fair Trade Movement* in the United States which sought to preserve small traditional stores. This movement was quite powerful between the 1930s and the first oil crisis in 1973.

### 12.2.2  Price Discrimination

Assume the existence of several submarkets which have different demand elasticities. Then the producer will want to appropriate as much as possible the consumer surplus by causing more to be paid on submarkets with less elasticity. For example, a publisher will sell hardbound books to libraries (whose demand is generally inelastic) and paperback books to individual consumers.

The producer will be able to achieve his ends by granting exclusive territories to his retailers, each "territory" here being a submarket. He may then resort to a two-part tariff to recover the maximum profit.

### 12.2.3  Tied Sales

Consider the situation represented on figure 12.2. The retailer buys an input $x$ at the price $w$ from a monopoly, producing it at constant marginal cost $c$, and another input $x'$ from a competitive sector, which prices $x'$ at the marginal cost $w' = c'$. Under these conditions $w/w' > c/c'$, since $w > c$. So the input $x$ will be underused by the retailer, which will not do for the monopoly concerned. The monopoly could solve this problem by dictating that the retailer also procure the input $x'$ from them, and by pricing it at a price $w'$ such that $w/w' = c/c'$: this is the practice of tied sales. Note that in this very simple case, tied sales have a social utility, for they bring the retailer to the production optimum.

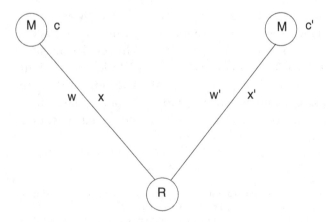

**Figure 12.2**
Tied Sales

### 12.2.4   Reduction of Price Competition

The effect of certain vertical constraints can be to reduce the downstream competition. This is the case with exclusive territories, since each retailer becomes a local monopoly. Rey and Stiglitz (1995) show that when producers of differentiated products sell to consumers via retailers, the establishment of exclusive territories permits them to reduce price competition not only downstream but also upstream and therefore to come closer to a cooperative optimum; producers can then recuperate retailers' excess profits by a franchise. Naturally, such a strategy is detrimental to consumers and to social welfare.

## 12.3   Comparison of Different Practices

In most cases the retailer is better informed of the state of demand than is the producer. Any comparison of different vertical restrictions must take this factor into account. Following Rey and Tirole (1986), we assume in this section that the final demand $D(p) = d - p$ contains a parameter $d$ that is known to the distributor but not to the producer. It is a matter then of the producer's solving a self-selection problem, with two new imperatives:

• assure a good decentralization of decision making. This implies that the downstream price $p$ must vary with the intensity of the demand $d$.

• Achieve good risk-sharing with the retailer. The producer presumably intervenes in numerous independent markets and can therefore by supposed to be risk-neutral; the retailer presumably finds it more difficult to diversify away his risk. The producer must therefore partially insure the retailer.

We will compare three possible strategies for the producer from the perspective of these two new imperatives introduced by the asymmetry of information:

• Exclusive territories. Each retailer is a local monopoly.

• Resale price maintenance. The imposed price is supposed to be the same for each retailer.

• Competition among retailers. The producer can simply let competition take place among retailers.

First of all, where the decentralization of decisions is concerned,

• in resale price maintenance, the downstream price is set by the producer, who does not know $d$; the price cannot then vary with $d$

• the retailer who discharges an exclusive territory is a local monopoly and will therefore make $p$ vary with $d$

• in perfect competition between retailers, the retailers price at (supposedly constant) marginal cost, which does not depend on $d$, so the downstream price is independent of $d$

In view of this criterion, exclusive territories appear to be preferable to competition and to resale price maintenance.

Let us move on to the second criterion: insurance of retailers against profit variations.

• with resale price maintenance, the retailer's profit is an increasing function of the risky parameter $d$

• this is also the case with exclusive territories

• by contrast, in competition, the retailers' profit is zero and therefore independent of $d$

This time competition clearly dominates exclusive territories and resale price maintenance.

From this analysis we can conclude that resale price maintenance is dominated according to our two criteria.[5] The comparison between exclusive territories and competition depends on the retailer's aversion to risk. If the retailer is very adverse to risk, the imperative of insurance will prevail and competition will be the best of systems; if his aversion to risk is weaker, exclusive territories will be preferable to competition.

The comparison that we just executed used the perspective of the economic efficiency of the vertical relationship. If we place ourselves now at the social point of view, we must further take into account consumer surplus, which is a decreasing function of the downstream price $p$. Competition, which assures the lowest downstream price, is of course the consumers' preferred system. It can even be shown that whatever the retailer's aversion to risk, competition maximizes the

---

5. Deneckere, Marvel, and Peck (1997) show, however, that if retailers supply themselves from the producers before observing demand, then resale price maintenance can raise the profits of the producer and even consumer surplus.

social surplus, which is hardly surprising. This conclusion could change if we consider the necessity of providing effort incentive to retailers or the existence of specific investments, or even if we consider the impact of vertical restrictions on interbrand competition.

## 12.4   Elements of Law

To conclude this chapter, I would like to provide the reader with some notion of the legislation and jurisprudence in the domain of vertical restrictions. At issue is one of the essential elements of what the Americans call *antitrust policy* and the Europeans prefer to call *competition policy*. In the United States, antitrust policy has its origins in the Sherman Act of 1890 and the Clayton Act of 1914. But these texts are fairly vague, and the jurisprudence has been altered in the course of time (see Scherer and Ross 1990). The European laws are more recent. The 1957 Treaty of Rome, which created the Common Market, played a driving role,[6] particularly through Article 85 which forbids agreements that thwart competition without improving productive efficiency (see Korah 1994). It has been completed since that time by several "common regulations."

There have long been debates in the law and economics literature with the objective of finding out if one should decree the systematic legality or illegality *per se* of different vertical constraints, or if their effect on social welfare should be examined on a case by case basis (by applying what is called the *rule of reason*). In the United States, the Chicago school thus lobbied for the legalization, as such, of most vertical constraints. In practice, jurisprudence generally depends on the rule of reason rather than on per se decisions. For example, it evaluates the degree of interbrand competition in order to justify its decisions: vertical restrictions are judged less severely where interbrand competition is brisk. Still there are major exceptions. For instance, the practice of resale price maintenance is illegal per se in Europe.[7] It has also been illegal in the United States since the oil crisis, after a much more permissive period which, in numerous states, even imposed upon retailers to respect the minimum prices decreed by producers. The practice of tied sales, as such, is also considered illegal. On the other

---

6. Like all international treaties, the Treaty of Rome has a higher value than the national laws of its signing countries.
7. Even if minimum prices for books are authorized, for reasons that are more political than economic.

hand, exclusive territories and exclusive dealing are usually judged according to the rule of reason. European authorities even issued an *exemption rule* which authorized the automobile retail sector to conserve its own particular practices.

## Bibliography

Deneckere, R., H. Marvel, and J. Peck. 1997. Demand uncertainty and price maintenance: Markdowns as destructive competition. *American Economic Review* 87: 619–41.

Korah, V. 1994. *EC Competition Law and Practice*. London: Sweet and Maxwell.

Rey, P., and J. Stiglitz. 1995. The role of exclusive territories in producers' competition. *Rand Journal of Economics* 26: 431–51.

Rey, P., and J. Tirole. 1986. The Logic of Vertical Restraints. *American Economic Review* 76: 921–39.

Scherer, F., and Ross, D. 1990. *Industrial Market Structure and Economic Performance.* Boston: Houghton Mifflin.

Spengler, J. 1950. Vertical integration and antitrust policy. *Journal of Political Economy* 58: 347–52.

Telser, L. 1960. Why should manufacturers want fair trade? *Journal of Law and Economics* 3: 86–105.

# IV                    Incomplete Markets

The theory of general equilibrium proceeded in the 1960s on the hypothesis that all markets necessary to the successful working of the economy could be opened. It escaped no one that this hypothesis was a bit heroic, that its negation would generally destroy the optimality of the equilibrium, but the technical tools that would permit one to treat the incompleteness of markets did not yet exist. The technical tools did not become available until the beginning of the 1970s. The theory of incomplete markets has rapidly developed since then, to the point where it seems possible to me today to give a summary without becoming mired in overly technical considerations. This is what I will endeavor to do in this last chapter. The general theme will be that when markets are incomplete, equilibrium can be efficient only in very exceptional cases, which clears the way (in theory at least) for a new genre of governmental interventions.

# 13

# Elements of the Theory of Incomplete Markets

The first section in this chapter shows how the theory of general equilibrium in incomplete markets naturally ensues from the generalization of the model of general equilibrium to situations of uncertainty. The next two sections study the question of the existence of equilibrium, which poses delicate problems, and that of its inefficiency. These three sections are located within the framework of an exchange economy; I will subsequently expose the difficulties presented by the introduction of production.

These four sections are fairly theoretical, as is, unfortunately, the bulk of the literature on the subject. In order to refute the impression that incomplete market theory is but a gadget for specialists, I devote the last section of this chapter to one of its applications.

The experienced reader will note that I am only interested here in real assets. Indeed, I consider that this is the most natural framework in which to present market incompleteness. Nevertheless, in the appendix, I give some elements of the theory's development when the available assets are nominal.

## 13.1 General Framework

As the reader knows, the model of competitive general equilibrium was extended by Arrow (1953) to account for uncertainty. This extension consists simply of assigning to each good *at each date and in every state of the world* a market and a price. To simplify the account, for the bulk of this chapter we will place ourselves in a two-period exchange economy where uncertainty is symmetrical and bears on the state of the world at the second date.[1] We will assume that there exist $L$ goods,

---

1. This choice of modelization is not necessary for treating the case of complete markets, but it will become very useful when we approach the question of incomplete markets.

$l = 1, \ldots, L$, available on each date and in every state of the world and $n$ consumers, $i = 1, \ldots, n$. At date 0, the consumers do not know what the state of the world will be at date 1; they simply know that it can be $s = 1, \ldots, S$. A consumption plan for a consumer $i$ is therefore a vector $(x_0, x_1, \ldots, x_S)$, where $x_0 \in \mathbb{R}^L$ is his consumption vector on date 0, and for $s \geq 1$, $x_s \in \mathbb{R}^L$ is his consumption vector at date 1 in state $s$. His utility is written then $U_i(x_0, x_1, \ldots, x_S)$. We will denote $(\omega_0^i, \omega_1^i, \ldots, \omega_S^i) \in \mathbb{R}^{L(S+1)}$ the resources of the consumer $i$ on date 0 and in every state of the world on date 1.

Arrow's original idea consists of introducing contracts of contingent delivery, one for every good in every state of the world. It is then said that the markets are *complete*. Thus a consumer, for example, could buy at date 0 three units of good $l$ which are deliverable only if the state $s$ is realized and at a unit price which we will denote $p_{ls}$. A consumer who wants to have a delivery of good $l$ whatever the realized state then will have to pay $\Sigma_{s=1}^S p_{ls}$ for each unit. If $p_0$ is the price vector for available goods at date 0 and $p_s$ the price vector for available goods at date 1 in state $s$, the consumer's budgetary constraint $i$ is then written

$$p_0 \cdot x_0^i + \sum_{s=1}^S p_s \cdot x_s^i \leq p_0 \cdot \omega_0^i + \sum_{s=1}^S p_s \cdot \omega_s^i$$

The conditions of equilibrium are

$$\sum_{i=1}^n x_0^i = \sum_{i=1}^n \omega_0^i$$

at date 0 and

$$\sum_{i=1}^n x_s^i = \sum_{i=1}^n \omega_s^i$$

in state $s$ at date 1.

Under the usual hypotheses (in particular, that of the convexity of preferences[2]), equilibrium exists and the two fundamental theorems of welfare apply: the equilibrium is Pareto-optimal and any Pareto optimum can be decentralized. We will denote $p_0^*$, $(p_s^*)_{s=1, \ldots, S}$, $x_0^*$ and $(x_s^*)_{s=1, \ldots, S}$ the prices and allocations of equilibrium.

The introduction of complete contingent markets therefore apparently permits the accounting of uncertainty with a large economy of

---

2. Recall that in the expected utility framework, preferences are convex if and only if the agents are averse to risk.

means.[3] This extension of the general equilibrium model is nonetheless open to criticism in at least two ways:

• Even in a simple two-date model, a very static vision of the world is proposed: all markets are open on date 0, and there is no need to reopen them on date 1, for all contingent transactions have been already decided.

• A very high number of markets is required: $L(S + 1)$.

We will see below that incomplete market theory partially responds to the first criticism with a more sequential vision of exchange. Arrow also proposed a sequential implementation of the equilibrium that requires only $(2L + S)$ markets, as we will now see.

Suppose that the consumers can exchange assets so as to transfer buying power between date 0 and the different states of the world on date 1. For $s = 1, \ldots, S$, asset $a_s$ entitles to a unit of the good 1 (taken arbitrarily as numéraire so that $p_{1s} = 1$ for all $s$) in state $s$ and to nothing at all in the other states: such an asset is called an Arrow-Debreu asset. The total supply of each asset $a_s$ is zero. At date 0, consumers exchange goods consumed on that date and assets: $(L + S)$ markets are therefore open.[4] If state $s$ is realized on date 1, consumers use their goods endowments and their asset stocks $a_s$ to finance their consumptions. Let $q_s$ be the asset price $s$ on date 0 and $\theta_s^i$ the quantity of assets bought by consumer $i$; the budgetary constraints of this consumer are written

$$p_0 \cdot x_0^i + \sum_{s=1}^{S} \theta_s^i q_s \leq p_0 \cdot \omega_0^i$$

at date 0 and

$$p_s \cdot x_s^i \leq \theta_s^i + p_s \cdot \omega_s^i$$

in state $s$ at date 1.

In this chapter (as in all these writings) we will use the rational expectations hypothesis: each consumer anticipates without error at date 0 the prices $p_s$ that will prevail on each "spot" market at date 1. We multiply then the second constraint by $q_s$, sum on $s$, and add the result to the first constraint, so we get

---

3. This explains the subject's occupying only four pages in Debreu (1959, ch. 7).
4. It will be noted that consumers cannot gauge their asset purchases by future resources.

$$p_0 \cdot x_0^i + \sum_{s=1}^{S} q_s p_s \cdot x_s^i \le p_0 \cdot \omega_0^i + \sum_{s=1}^{S} q_s p_s \cdot \omega_s^i$$

The expression above is exactly equivalent to the consumer's budgetary constraint in the complete contingent markets equilibrium, as we see by posing $p_0 = p_0^*$ and $p_s^* = q_s p_s$. The equilibrium of this new model is therefore identical to that of the first. Agent $i$ buys $\theta_s^{*i} = p_s^* \cdot (x_s^{*i} - \omega_s^i)$ units of asset $a_s$ to finance his consumptions in state $s$, so there is equilibrium on each asset market:[5]

$$\sum_{i=1}^{n} \theta_s^{*i} = p_s^* \cdot \left( \sum_{i=1}^{n} x_s^{*i} - \sum_{i=1}^{n} \omega_s^i \right) = 0$$

However spectacular it may seem, the fall in the number of markets necessary for implementing an equilibrium has a slightly abstract character: in a real world, $S$ is an enormous number (perhaps infinity), and it is improbable that markets exist for all Arrow assets. Nevertheless, the Arrow construction is important because it introduces the basic concepts of incomplete market theory, such as was created by Radner (1972).

Radner generalized Arrow's idea in two directions:

• The asset market includes only $J \le S$ assets $a_j$, $j = 1, \ldots, J$.

• Each asset entitles the consumer to a basket of different goods in every state of the world. Thus $a_j$ entitles to $a_j^{ls}$ units of good $l$ in state $s$. In this way each asset is represented by a matrix $(L, S)$.

We will maintain the hypothesis that the total supply of each asset $a_j$ is zero, so that we have $\sum_{i=1}^{n} \theta_j^i = 0$ in equilibrium,[6] where $\theta_j^i$ is the demand for asset $j$ of consumer $i$. The budgetary constraints of the consumer $i$ are now written

$$p_0 \cdot x_0^i + \sum_{j=1}^{J} \theta_j^i q_j \le p_0 \cdot \omega_0^i$$

at date 0 and

$$p_s \cdot x_s^i \le p_s \cdot \sum_{j=1}^{J} \theta_j^i a_j^s + p_s \cdot \omega_s^i$$

---

5. We will note that Arrow's asset prices are indeterminate at equilibrium: we can change $q_s$ to $\lambda_s q_s$ on the sole condition of modifying $p_s$ to $p_s / \lambda_s$ so as to maintain the equality $p_s^* = q_s p_s$. Such a transformation affects asset purchases but not consumptions.
6. If the asset $a_j$ is an action of firm $j$ in a model with production, we would actually have $\sum_{i=1}^{n} \theta_j^i = 1$. This would not fundamentally change the analysis.

in state $s$ at date 1, where $a_j^s \in \mathbb{R}^L$ denotes the basket of goods to which asset $j$ entitles in state $s$ and $q_j$ is the price of asset $j$ at date 0.

It is necessary to introduce some notation. If $s$ is a state of the world and $j$ an asset, we can denote by $p_s \cdot a_j^s$ the value in state $s$ of the basket of goods to which $a_j$ entitles the consumer:

$$p_s \cdot a_j^s = \sum_{l=1}^{l} p_{ls} a_j^{ls}$$

Let $p \,\square\, a_j$ be the vector of $\mathbb{R}^S$ that represents the value of the asset $a_j$ in different states of the world:

$$p \,\square\, a_j = \begin{pmatrix} p_1 \cdot a_j^1 \\ \vdots \\ ps \cdot a_j^S \end{pmatrix}$$

Finally, let $p \,\square\, a$ be the matrix $(S, J)$ whose column $j$ is $p \,\square\, a_j$. With this notation, the budgetary constraints on date 1 can be written in a condensed format:

$$p \,\square\, (x^i - \omega^i) \le \theta^i \cdot (p \,\square\, a)$$

If the utility functions are strictly increasing so that the budgetary constraints are active at equilibrium, this constraint is at equality and therefore implies that

$$p \,\square\, (x^i - \omega^i) \in sp\,(p \,\square\, a)$$

where sp($M$) is the image (*span*) of matrix $M$, that is, the subspace of $\mathbb{R}^S$ engendered by the columns of $M$. Note that the weights of the different columns of $p \,\square\, a$ in $p \,\square\, (x^i - \omega^i)$ are simply the portfolios $\theta_j^i$.

The vector $p \,\square\, (x^i - \omega^i)$ of $\mathbb{R}^S$ formed by the values of excess demand in different states is therefore constrained to evolve within the span of $p \,\square\, a$. All of this will seem less abstract if we return to the Arrow-Debreu assets. Then $J = S$, and the matrix $p \,\square\, a$ is simply the identity matrix $(S, S)$, since (good 1 being the numéraire) $p_s \cdot a_j = \delta_{sj}$ where $\delta$ is the Kronecker symbol.[7] The image of $p \,\square\, a$ is therefore $\mathbb{R}^S$, which translates as the fact that when markets are complete, the consumer can transfer buying power among states as he wishes.

The interesting case is of course that where sp($p \,\square\, a$) $\neq \mathbb{R}^S$, which is necessarily true if $J < S$. Now the consumer's capacity for transferring buying power among states is limited by the lack of assets: markets are

---

7. Recall that $\delta_{sj}$ is worth 1 when $s = j$ and 0 if not.

said to be incomplete. Let $V_s^i$ be the value of excess demand of consumer $i$ in state $s$ at Arrow-Debreu equilibrium:

$$V_s^i = p_s^* \cdot (x_s^{*i} - \omega_s^i)$$

If we wanted to implement this equilibrium with assets $a_1, \ldots, a_J$, it would be necessary to solve in $\theta_1^i, \ldots, \theta_J^i$ the $S$ equations

$$V_s^i = \sum_{j=1}^{J} \theta_j^i p_s^* \cdot a_j^s$$

But there are $S$ equations in $J$ unknowns, which is clearly impossible to solve once $J < S$.[8] For example, if there is only one asset and it entitles one unit of good 1 in every state of the world, then the consumer can only equalize the value of his demand excess in every state of the world, which represents an overly strong constraint on consumption plans.

## 13.2   Existence of Equilibrium

One might think that the existence of equilibrium in incomplete markets naturally ensues from that of complete market equilibrium. Unfortunately, the problem is much more complex. This is a fairly technical subject, but I will nonetheless devote some paragraphs to it in order to give the reader a sense of the difficulties.

For example, assume that there are two goods (of which the first is always taken as numéraire), two states and two assets. The first asset brings a unit of good 1 into every state of the world and the second a unit of good 2 into every state. So the matrix $p \, \square \, a$ is simply

$$p \, \square \, a = \begin{pmatrix} 1 & p_{21} \\ 1 & p_{22} \end{pmatrix}$$

If $p_{21} \neq p_{22}$, this matrix is of full rank: $\mathrm{sp}(p \, \square \, a) = \mathrm{I\!R}^2$. We see that the demand functions for the goods coincide with those of the Arrow-Debreu model. If, on the other hand, $p_{21} = p_{22}$, then $\mathrm{sp}(p \, \square \, a)$ is unidimensional, and the consumer is constrained in his capacity for transferring purchasing power between the two states because the two assets have become linearly dependent. This phenomenon, called *drop in rank* and evidenced by Hart (1975), introduces a discontinuity in the

---

8. It is an equally impossible computation when $J = S$, when one of the assets is a linear combination of the others.

budgetary constraints, and therefore a fortiori in demand functions. It is easy to see that when $p_{22}$ tends toward $p_{21}$, the asset demands tend toward infinity. Radner (1972) avoided this difficulty by imposing a constraint of the form $\theta_j^i \geq -C$ on asset short sales, but this "solution" is artificial, since the equilibrium can then depend on the arbitrary constant $C$.

Still we have hope that the nonexistence of equilibrium caused by a demand function discontinuity accompanying a drop in rank is an exceptional phenomenon. This is what Duffie and Shafer (1985) effectively showed. Since the difficulty stems from dimensional changes of $\text{sp}(p \,\square\, a)$, Duffie and Shafer defined a pseudoequilibrium by writing the budgetary constraint

$$p \,\square\, \left(x^i - \omega^i\right) \in L$$

where $L$ is a given subspace of $\mathbb{R}^S$. From this it was easy to see that a pseudoequilibrium could exist under usual conditions. Duffie and Shafer proceeded to show, using fairly sophisticated tools of differential topology, that the demand functions are almost always continuous in pseudoequilibrium. But then the space $\text{sp}(p \,\square\, a)$ is locally independent of $p$, and as a result it can be substituted for $L$ in the definition of pseudoequilibrium. The latter now becomes a true equilibrium. Duffie and Shafer actually obtained a result of *generic* existence: the set of specifications of utility functions, of initial resources, and of assets such that equilibrium does not exist is of (Lebesgue) measure zero in the set of possible specifications. In other words, if we take "at random" one specification of economy among all the possibilities, equilibrium exists with a probability of one.

### 13.3   Inefficiency of Equilibrium

When it exists, equilibrium is of course not Pareto optimal when $J < S$. Indeed, we saw in section 13.1 that the Arrow-Debreu equilibrium cannot generally be implemented in incomplete markets. But since all Pareto optima are decentralizable by an Arrow-Debreu equilibrium, it follows that incomplete market equilibrium is suboptimal.

This result is not all that interesting. If the government wanted to intervene to restore the optimality of equilibrium, it would be necessary for it to proceed with transfers of purchasing power inaccessible to agents, that is, in order to complete the markets. This is a lot to ask of government: if there are profound reasons (as we will see in the conclusion of this chapter) for markets' being incomplete, these reasons are generally imposed both on the government and on consumers.[9]

We must therefore define a less demanding concept of optimality that takes market structure as a given. For this we turn to constrained Pareto optimality as defined by Diamond (1967).[10] We assume that the only possible reallocations must take place on the market for goods and that for assets at date 0. A planner can only intervene in redistributing the assets and consumptions on that date; the planner must subsequently let the equilibrium be established on date 1. A constrained Pareto-optimal allocation is therefore such that there exists no reallocation of goods and of assets at date 0 that raises the utility of all consumers.

Diamond demonstrated that when there is only one good ($L = 1$), equilibrium is always constrained Pareto optimal. Hart (1975) exhibited an example in a two-good model where one equilibrium dominates another, which shows that Diamond's result cannot be extended to $L \geq 2$. Stiglitz (1982) showed in a fairly general model (with production) that constrained optimality was only obtained in very specific cases. Finally Geanakoplos-Polemarchakis (1986) confirmed this result by demonstrating that if there are at least two goods and two agents, a planner who can redistribute asset portfolios and consumptions on date 0 and possibly proceed to interagent transfers can improve the equilibrium in the sense of constrained optimality, and at that for a generic set of economies. It will be noted that most of the incomplete market models used in macroeconomics rely on the representative agent hypothesis ($n = 1$), which guarantees constrained optimality of equilibrium.

The proof of these inefficiency results is not simple, but we will attempt at some intuition. When the government redistributes at date 0, it changes consumer wealth in all states (direct effect). This results further in modification of the equilibrium prices on date 1 (indirect effect). While the government can at once take into account the direct

9. There are important exceptions. The equilibrium's inefficiency in the presence of externalities can be analyzed as a phenomenon of market incompleteness, since, for example, the market for the pollution imposed on consumers by a firm does not exist. The creation by the government of a market for pollution rights reverts then to completing the structure of markets.

10. Grossman (1977) invoked a concept of "Nash social optimality" that permits the two fundamental welfare theorems to be obtained: any equilibrium is a Nash social optimum and any Nash social optimum is decentralizable in equilibrium. Still this optimality concept is very weak, as shown in Hart's example cited below.

and indirect effects, the consumers only integrate the direct effect in their calculations, since their price expectations are independent of the portfolios they hold. It is this superiority of government that leads to constrained inefficiency of equilibrium.

At always in such cases, we must ask ourselves the question of how much information is necessary for the government in order to proceed to such interventions. It can be shown that the government must in fact know demand functions of goods and assets in terms of current *and* expected prices, which sounds of course fairly presumptuous. Moreover it would be dangerous to believe that opening a new market when several markets are missing necessarily improves welfare; Hart (1975) gave a famous counterexample.

## 13.4   Equilibria with Production

The introduction of production in the model of incomplete markets comes up against serious obstacles that stem from the difficulty in assigning to firms an objective on which their shareholders are unanimous. When markets are complete, all shareholders agree that the firm should maximize its market value. Indeed, imagine a firm whose input on date 0 is a vector $y_0 \in \mathbb{R}^L$ and output on date 1 is a vector $y_s \in \mathbb{R}^L$ in state $s = 1, \ldots, S$. In the Arrow-Debreu model, a consumer who possesses a nonzero share $\theta^i$ of this firm will have as budgetary constraint

$$p_0 \cdot x_0^i + \sum_{s=1}^{S} p_s \cdot x_s^i \le p_0 \cdot \omega_0^i + \sum_{s=1}^{S} p_s \cdot \omega_s^i + \theta^i \left( \sum_{s=1}^{S} p_s \cdot y_s - p_0 \cdot y_0 \right)$$

Clearly, in order to relax this constraint as much as possible, each shareholder will want the firm to maximize its profit

$$\sum_{s=1}^{S} p_s \cdot y_s - p_0 \cdot y_0$$

Things are not so simple when markets are incomplete. Considering the obstacles that keep consumers from transferring their buying power between states ad libitum, the production vector $(p_1 \cdot y_1, \ldots, p_s \cdot y_s)$ can no longer be evaluated in a way that enables unanimity between shareholders. To give an example, a shareholder who fears finding himself unemployed in state $s$ and who has difficulty transferring a sizable purchasing power there because of market incompleteness will want the firm to emphasize the term $p_s \cdot y_s$. The other shareholders, however, will not agree if the same state is not unfavorable to them.

More precisely, let $q_s^i$ be the marginal rate of substitution of consumer $i$ between the numéraire at date 0 and the numéraire at date 1 in state $s$. It is easy to see that if $\pi_s$ is the firm's profit in state $s$, the consumer $i$ would want the firm to maximize $\Sigma_{s=1}^S q_s^i \pi_s$. But since this expression depends on $i$, the consumers will not generally agree between them.[11] As noted by Drèze (1974), the firm's profit takes on the character of a public good for which consumer evaluations are divergent, and we know from chapter 5 all the difficulties created by this situation.[12]

A natural solution consists of constructing an objective for the firm by weighting that which the shareholder $i$ would like to assign the firm by his share $\theta^i$. The firm should then maximize.

$$\sum_{i=1}^{n} \theta^i \sum_{s=1}^{S} q_s^i \pi_s.$$

This solution, due to Drèze and to Grossman and Hart (1979), possesses certain properties of optimality (see Laffont 1989). Still it is not universally accepted. The reason is that the "state prices" $q_s^i$ are unobserved; they depend on subjective probabilities of states for consumers, on their resources, and on their utility functions. It is therefore difficult to imagine that a firm's director can easily maximize such an objective. Moreover any change of stockholder composition should, according to this formula, modify the firm's objectives (so that a long-term decision becomes inverted after some operations on the stock exchange!). Finally there is the risk that managers will follow the majority shareholders' directives and neglect the desires of minority shareholders. It is clear that to this day there does not exist a fully satisfactory way to integrate production into the incomplete markets model, except in very special cases.

To end this section, I would like to point out that if the Drèze–Grossman-Hart solution to the problem of shareholders' nonunanim-

---

11. This difficulty does not arise in complete markets, since then the consumers can equalize the marginal rate of substitution rate and the price. Therefore we get $q_s^i = p_{1s}^*$ for each consumer $i$, where $p_{1s}^*$ is the Arrow-Debreu numéraire price in state $s$. Since this price obviously does not depend on $i$, there will be unanimity on the firm's objective.
12. The problem of defining the firm's objectives recalls one that we saw in chapter 8. But here there is no good reason to consider it negligible.

ity is adopted so that firms have well-defined objectives, then constrained Pareto optimality could be examined for the production equilibrium. The reader will not be surprised to learn that to exchange inefficiencies are added those of production, so equilibrium is even less often optimal under this constraint than in an exchange economy.

## 13.5 Application to International Trade

Accounting for market incompleteness may transform certain results that seem to be the best established. Thus the majority of economists consider that under certain reasonable hypotheses, free trade improves social welfare without ambiguity. Newbery and Stiglitz (1984) show, however, that the optimality of free trade may not hold when markets are incomplete.

To see this, suppose that American and Australian farmers can produce wine and wheat at zero cost. Wheat production is independent of climactic hazards, while wine production is very strongly affected. It is not possible to insure farmers against these risks (it is here that market incompleteness comes into play). Australia is very far from the United States. As is well known the weather down under is perfectly anticorrelated with American weather: when it is sunny in the United States, it rains in Australia, and vice versa. In addition consumers' demand functions have a unitary price elasticity, so agricultural profit does not depend on the price of wine. In autarky, price variations therefore perfectly insure farmers against climactic hazards. Now, if we let open the borders, the price of wine becomes perfectly stable, and the agricultural profit from wine in each country becomes variable. This then raises the perceived risk of each country's farmers and reduces their welfare.

What about the consumers? In autarky, they withstand the entire risk. The opening of the borders has a beneficial effect for them in this sense. On the other hand, profit variability introduced by free trade pushes the farmers to produce less wine, and the price increases, thereby reducing consumer surplus. It is conceivable that by choosing the parameters of the model well, this second effect can dominate the first. Free trade therefore hurts both agricultural producers and consumers, contrary to the gospel taught by generations of economists.

## 13.6   Conclusion

The theory of incomplete markets promises to furnish new bases for finance, for the study of the effect of bankruptcies, but also for macroeconomics (especially by providing more solid arguments for the theory of money). It is also a means by which to analyze precisely the reasons why markets are incomplete, and to characterize in an endogenous way the market structures that are the most likely to arise. Until recent years, justifications of market incompleteness relied above all on the existence of transaction costs (a market will only be open if the surplus to which it gives access is superior to private costs incurred in creating it) and asymmetries of information (which make markets less liquid, particularly in the domain of credit and insurance).[13] One approach can be to fix the number of assets and to find out which combination of assets is the most efficient (Demange and Laroque 1995).

The reader who wants to explore the theory of general equilibrium in incomplete markets, more than I have completed here, can refer to the reviews of Duffie (1992), who is particularly interested in financial markets, Geanakoplos (1990), and Magill and Shafer (1991) or to the book by Magill and Quinzii (1996) if he is feeling particularly ambitious. I must, however, point out that these references are fairly technical.

## 13.7   Appendix: Nominal Assets

The assets with which we were interested in this chapter were *real*; that is, they procure a basket of goods in each state of the world. Their return was therefore linear in relation to prices. Indeed, this hypothesis corresponds to future contracts on goods or, as we have seen, to firms' actions. It could also take into account derivative assets, like options, provided that we accept returns that are nonlinear in relation to prices.

Cass (1984) and Werner (1985) proposed considering *nominal* assets,[14] whose return does not depend on prices. To see this, suppose that con-

---

13. There are different reasons for market incompleteness, even in the absence of uncertainty. In the presence of externalities, for example, the reasons relate to the inexistence of markets for personalized goods, like "consumption by consumer $i$ of a pollutant produced by firm $j$".

14. These are also often called financial assets, which can create confusion, real assets having just as much right to that name.

trary to the rest of this chapter, there exists in the economy a good that does not enter into agents' utility function. This good is therefore only used for transferring purchasing power between dates. Since a price can be normalized to one on all dates and in all states of the world, we choose to do so with this particular good. It is then an accounting unit sometimes called "money," even though, as we will see, it does not possess all the properties of money. A nominal asset is then a asset whose return is expressed in money.

To take a more precise example, a one-dollar bond that bears an interest rate $r$ can be represented by a nominal asset that brings $1 + r$ in each state of the world. Money itself can be represented by a bond with zero interest rate. More generally, a structure of $J$ nominal assets will be a matrix $(J, S)$ of which the element $(j, s)$ represents the return of asset $j$ in state $s$, measured in money.

The primary advantage of considering nominal assets is that the existence of equilibrium holds under the usual hypotheses: the analogue of "drop in rank" cannot happen here because the returns no longer depend on prices. This was actually the primary motivation of the introduction of nominal assets.

The indetermination of equilibrium is also a property that differentiates nominal assets from real ones. In the real asset model, it can be shown that equilibrium is usually locally unique: for nearly all possible specifications, there is a finite number of equilibria, as in the Arrow-Debreu model. Geanakoplos and Mas Colell (1989), on the contrary, showed that if markets are incomplete ($J < S$) in the nominal asset model and if there are at least ($J + 1$) consumers,[15] the set of equilibrium allocations is generically ($S - 1$)-dimensional. It is in fact easy to see that in this model, inflation rate variations between different states are indeterminate; this is what engenders the ($S - 1$) dimensions of the space of equilibrium allocations. We may note moreover that the result of equilibrium indetermination implies a fortiori that equilibrium is generally not constrained Pareto optimal.

In my opinion, the nominal assets model suffers several lacunae. The first is that assets' returns are postulated as exogenous variables, even though it would be desirable that they be determined in an endogenous manner: thus the interest rate of a bond is in principle an equilibrium price. The second is how "money" is introduced in this model. In effect it can be shown that money can only have a positive

---

15. Here again, this assumption excludes the representative agent models.

price if its stock is zero, so certain agents can detain a negative quantity of money and stand counterpart for those who detain a positive quantity. The result is what is called inside money, by opposition to outside money, which is created by the Central Bank and whose stock is positive. Moreover, while this so-called money fulfills its functions as a unit of account and a means for liquidity in this model, its essential role for facilitating transactions is left aside. Finally the indeterminacy result leaves the impression that the model is not completely specified.

## Bibliography

Arrow, K. 1953. Le rôle des valeurs boursières pour la répartition la meilleure des risques. In *Econométrie*, CNRS, 41–48; reprinted in English as "The role of securities in the optimal allocation of risk bearing," *Review of Economic Studies* (1963), 31: 91–6.

Cass, D. 1984. Competitive equilibria in incomplete financial markets. CARESS Working Paper, University of Pennsylvania.

Debreu, G. 1959. *Theory of Value*. New York: Wiley.

Demange, G., and G. Laroque. 1995. Optimality of incomplete markets. *Journal of Economic Theory* 65: 218–32.

Diamond, P. 1967. The role of a stock market in a general equilibrium model with technological uncertainty. *American Economic Review* 57: 759–76.

Drèze, J. 1974. Investment under private ownership: Optimality, Equilibrium and Stability. In J. Drèze, ed., *Allocation under Uncertainty*. London: Macmillan.

Duffie, D. 1992. The nature of incomplete security markets. In J.-J. Laffont, ed., *Advances in Economic Theory*, vol. 2. Cambridge: Cambridge University Press.

Duffie, D., and W. Shafer. 1985. Equilibrium in incomplete markets, I: A basic model of generic existence. *Journal of Mathematical Economics* 14: 285–300.

Geanakoplos, J. 1990. An introduction to general equilibrium with incomplete asset markets. *Journal of Mathematical Economics* 19: 1–38.

Geanakoplos, J., and A. Mas Colell. 1989. Real indeterminacy with financial assets. *Journal of Economic Theory* 47: 22–38.

Geanakoplos, J., and H. Polemarchakis. 1986. Existence, regularity, and constrained suboptimality of competitive allocations when markets are incomplete. In W. Heller, R. Starr, and D. Starrett, eds., *Essays in Honor of Kenneth Arrow*, vol. 3. Cambridge: Cambridge University Press.

Grossman, S. 1997. A characterization of the optimality of equilibrium in incomplete markets. *Journal of Economic Theory* 15: 1–15.

Grossman, S., and O. Hart. 1979. A theory of competitive equilibrium in stock market economies. *Econometrica* 47: 293–330.

Hart, O. 1975. On the optimality of equilibrium when the market structure is incomplete. *Journal of Economic Theory* 11: 418–43.

Laffont, J.-J. 1989. *The Economics of Uncertainty and Information.* Cambridge: MIT Press.

Magill, M., and M. Quinzii. 1996. *Theory of Incomplete Markets,* vol. 1. Cambridge: MIT Press.

Magill, M., and W. Shafer. 1991. Incomplete markets. In K. Arrow and M. Intriligator, eds., *Handbook of Mathematical Economics,* vol. 4. Amsterdam: North-Holland.

Newbery, D., and J. Stiglitz. 1984. Pareto inferior trade. *Review of Economic Studies* 51: 1–12.

Radner, R. 1972. Existence of equilibrium of plans, prices, and price expectations in a sequence of markets. *Econometrica* 40: 289–303.

Stiglitz, J. 1982. The inefficiency of the stock market equilibrium. *Review of Economic Studies* 49: 241–61.

Werner, J. 1985. Equilibrium in economies with incomplete financial markets. *Journal of Economic Theory* 36: 110–19.

# Index